Opera Cinema

Opera Cinema

A New Cultural Experience

Joseph Attard

BLOOMSBURY ACADEMIC
NEW YORK · LONDON · OXFORD · NEW DELHI · SYDNEY

BLOOMSBURY ACADEMIC
Bloomsbury Publishing Inc
1385 Broadway, New York, NY 10018, USA
50 Bedford Square, London, WC1B 3DP, UK
29 Earlsfort Terrace, Dublin 2, Ireland

BLOOMSBURY, BLOOMSBURY ACADEMIC and the Diana logo are trademarks of
Bloomsbury Publishing Plc

First published in the United States of America 2022
Paperback edition published 2024

Copyright © Joseph Attard, 2022

For legal purposes the Acknowledgements on p. xii constitute an extension
of this copyright page.

Cover design: Eleanor Rose
Cover image: still from *Lucia Di Lammermoor* performed by The Royal Opera
© Photo by Robbie Jack / Corbis via Getty Images

All rights reserved. No part of this publication may be reproduced or transmitted in
any form or by any means, electronic or mechanical, including photocopying,
recording, or any information storage or retrieval system, without prior permission in
writing from the publishers.

Bloomsbury Publishing Inc does not have any control over, or responsibility for,
any third-party websites referred to or in this book. All internet addresses given in this
book were correct at the time of going to press. The author and publisher regret any
inconvenience caused if addresses have changed or sites have ceased to exist,
but can accept no responsibility for any such changes.

Library of Congress Cataloging-in-Publication Data
Names: Attard, Joseph, author.
Title: Opera cinema : a new cultural experience / Joseph Attard.
Description: New York : Bloomsbury Academic, 2022. |
Includes bibliographical references and index.
Identifiers: LCCN 2021060124 (print) | LCCN 2021060125 (ebook) |
ISBN 9781501370373 (hardback) | ISBN 9781501370359 (epub) |
ISBN 9781501370342 (pdf) | ISBN 9781501370335
Subjects: LCSH: Simulcasting of opera. | Opera–Social aspects–History–21st century.
Classification: LCC ML3918.O64 A77 2022 (print) | LCC ML3918.O64 (ebook) |
DDC 782.109–dc23/eng/20220405
LC record available at https://lccn.loc.gov/2021060124
LC ebook record available at https://lccn.loc.gov/2021060125

ISBN: HB: 978-1-5013-7037-3
PB: 978-1-5013-7036-6
ePDF: 978-1-5013-7034-2
eBook: 978-1-5013-7035-9

Typeset by Newgen KnowledgeWorks Pvt. Ltd., Chennai, India

To find out more about our authors and books visit www.bloomsbury.com
and sign up for our newsletters.

Fred, you would love the music.
Joyce, you would love the drama.
And Aimee – you would love arguing about every sentence that I have written.

CONTENTS

Preface: The new normal viii
Acknowledgements xii
About the author xiii

1. What is opera cinema? 1
2. The history of opera cinema 47
3. What makes it opera cinema? 81
4. The opera virgins project 131
5. A night at the opera cinema? 187

Bibliography 207
Index 225

PREFACE: THE NEW NORMAL

When I first began my PhD thesis on live cinema broadcasts of opera in 2014, I was certain digital remediation would figure heavily in opera's destiny, but the extent and acceptance of this was a point of conjecture. Suspicion still lingered over the intrusive eye of the camera penetrating the auditorium. Longstanding prejudices led some critics, academics and audiences to equate opera cinema with an attempt to 'dumb down' the medium in the name of continued relevance – and to chase an elusive, youthful, mass audience. There was also some concern about further damage to the fragile operatic ecology should the big houses monopolize even more attention from global audiences than in the past.

Then, six years later, as I set about writing this book, a worldwide pandemic triggered a long-threatened economic collapse, and social distancing measures to control the spread of a novel form of coronavirus (Covid-19) turned society on its head. Theatres of all kinds across the globe were emptied for months to avoid becoming centres of contagion. This grievous blow to the arts was initially met with a shrug by the Conservative administration in Britain. A damning report by the Digital, Culture, Media and Sport in 2020 found that the government's sluggish response to this unprecedented crisis placed the entire culture sector at existential risk, after it lost more than £630 million in income during the first twelve weeks of lockdown.[1] This only got worse when an entirely avoidable new wave of infections in the winter of 2020 denied the hospitality sector the crucial holiday season footfall.

The main arts funders eventually threw money at the wall to prevent a total collapse, coupled with the government-funded furlough scheme that provided financial support to arts workers driven out of employment. Nevertheless, a 2021 report by the Centre for Cultural Value estimates that the number of jobs in music, performing and visual arts fell by 55,000 in 2020, or around 30 per cent.[2] Across the creative industries more generally (encompassing 'non-creative roles' like hospitality and support staff), 110,000 jobs were lost. These figures were inflated by the freelancers and precariously employed staff who make up a large portion of the sector, and who were not necessarily eligible for the government's furlough scheme.

This lack of state support resulted in private charitable initiatives like the Theatre Arts Fund, set up by stage and screen director Sam Mendes, the Society of London Theatre (SOLT) and UK Theatre, stepping in to provide some emergency relief to artists. But this was not nearly sufficient to stem the flow of job losses. The cinema industry was also badly hit, with tent pole releases like the latest entry in the James Bond franchise (*No Time to Die*) delayed by over a year due to the pandemic, and overall attendances across the industry in 2020 down 75 per cent in Britain compared to the previous year.[3]

Tragically, none of this was inevitable. As confirmed by a detailed World Health Organization (WHO) report in 2021, the global capitalist system and its callous, incompetent public representatives turned a public health emergency into a catastrophe. This has translated into a death toll unheard of outside of a world war, and a nightmare for countless industries, with culture and hospitality being one of the biggest casualties. Despite much talk of the 'resilience' of British theatre, the truth is that decades of over-centralization of funding and cuts to state subsidies across the board have left the sector vulnerable to economic dislocation (see *Bringing Down the House: The Crisis in Britain's Regional Theatres* by Olivia Turnbull and 'Funding, Philanthropy, Structural Inequality and Decline in England's Theatre Ecology', by Jen Harvie). The fact that a pandemic triggered this calamity was incidental: the dire state of the arts today meant this was an accident waiting to happen.

At the time of writing, theatres and cinemas are just about to open their doors following a six-month lockdown to contain the winter 2020 infections surge, which the government refused to do anything about before the National Health Service was already overrun. A queasy sense of uncertainly undercuts any sense of optimism at this fresh start, with highly transmissible new variants of the coronavirus lurking throughout the UK that threaten to set everything back to square one. Hopefully, by the time you read this, some semblance of normalcy has returned. With any luck, the cultural pursuits we took for granted in the past are once again available to us. Maybe not. But in either case, the arts will never truly return to normal. Notably, none of the main opera houses scheduled any new live cinema transmissions for most of 2021. After a sixteen-month hiatus, they are about to resume from the Royal Opera House in December 2021. I had hoped to include impressions from an additional opera cinema show to comment on the aesthetic growth of the experience. I hope you will forgive this absence, given the exceptional circumstances. My solidarity goes out to the thousands of artists, technicians and other staff who have suffered loss of work or income because of this disaster. And to my fellow audience members, I share your sense of loss at having gone so long without being able to enjoy the escape and enrichment that comes from a good show. Here's to better days ahead.

It is appropriate (though certainly not fortunate) that the coronavirus crisis brought many of the issues I sought to address in this book to the centre stage. Digital remediation served as opera's understudy during the pandemic: stepping up to ensure that the show could go on in some form. Denied a traditional live audience, the large opera houses turned to a virtual one. At the beginning of the pandemic, my former research partners at the Royal Opera House launched a months-long programme of pre-recorded content for free via their YouTube channel: 'Our House to Your House', with the Met and Bolshoi taking similar initiatives. These included short recitals and master classes, in addition to full operas. Later, the Royal Opera House drew on established forms of public theatre, reviving the 'big screen' public shows it has previously run with great success, as well as facilitating drive-through screenings of crowd-pleasers like *La Boheme*. They have experimented with other digital experiences as well, including an immersive VR show, planned for the new year of 2021 and sadly cancelled due to a new lockdown. Other theatre companies have similarly expanded their digital repertoire, taking the opportunity to explore novel ways of remediating their performances.

While opera cinema shows have stalled, digital live streaming to home screens is still going strong. It is a pity that my research did not encompass this experience, on which I have limited data beyond anecdote and personal impressions. I would love to perform some fieldwork on live-streaming audiences to see what sort of behaviours they engage in. What sort of viewing conditions do they establish? How do these compare with other forms of home viewing, like television and film? Do home opera audiences snack on fizzy drinks and junk food, or sip flutes of champagne? Is there general consistency across households or are behaviours variable? All these questions must be left to future researchers. As will the impact of the coronavirus on the relationship between opera, its audiences and digital technology, though I will of course pass comment on these issues where appropriate.

Happily, the philosophical enquiries of my research on opera cinema retain their pertinence, and I humbly suggest have acquired new significance given recent events. For example: *what constitutes a 'live' performance?* Peggy Phelan's notion of 'live theatre' exclusively consisting of a co-present audience, sitting down to watch a show, has surely been dismantled if the Royal Opera's primary mode of exhibition is currently 'live' streams of years-old performances to smart TVs and laptops. Clearly, the experience of lockdown will have altered millions of people's preconceptions about the role of technology in operatic exhibition, and about live experiences of all kinds. In an age where physical exhibition is one small part of a large and more complex whole, it is all the more important to deepen our understanding of media ontology. Rather than retreat to postmodern solipsism, we need to do the work: keep following the trends, analysing cultural experiences and asking the audiences what it means to spend a night at the opera in the twenty-first century.

I hope this book contributes to the fuller objective of understanding of opera in this new normal.

Notes

1 'Impact of COVID-19 on DCMS Sectors: First Report', Culture and the Creative Industries, last modified 13 July 2020, accessed 13 June 2021, https://publications.parliament.uk/pa/cm5801/cmselect/cmcumeds/291/29102.htm.
2 'The Impact of Covid-19 on Jobs in the Cultural Sector – Part 3', Centre for Cultural Value, last modified March 2021, accessed 13 June 2021, https://www.culturehive.co.uk/CVIresources/the-impact-of-covid-19-on-jobs-in-the-cultural-sector-part-3/.
3 'UK Cinema Attendances Dropped by 75 Per Cent Last Year', *Time Out*, 4 February 2021, accessed 4 February 2021, https://www.timeout.com/london/news/uk-cinema-attendances-dropped-by-75-percent-last-year-020421.

ACKNOWLEDGEMENTS

This work spent several years in rehearsal, and too many individuals have contributed to the final production to credit in full here.

I would like to thank Professor Chris Berry for his invaluable support, expertize and guidance as an academic supervisor, advocate and colleague. From putting me in a room with representatives of the Royal Opera House all the way back in 2013; to countless hours of feedback, discussion and pouring over chapter drafts; to stumping up for last-minute emergency opera cinema tickets to rescue an ailing bit of fieldwork, you have been the only constant over the course of this entire fascinating journey.

I would also like to thank the Royal Opera House for a close working relationship over the years. While conducting research for this book, I had the unique privilege of speaking with many of the artists, technicians and administrators responsible for bringing the Royal Opera and Ballet to life. Each exhibited true dedication and passion for these remarkable art forms, and were always gracious and eager to assist in my work. To preserve your privacy, you are not named here, but you know who you are. *Grazie mille!*

To my research subjects: should any of you read this, I hope you stuck with opera after losing your virginity. Please tell people that I am the one who put you onto it!

Many thanks as well to Hannah Joshua, for her stellar work editing my academic thesis, on which this book is based.

Thanks as well to Bloomsbury for helping to bring this work about.

It would be remiss of me not to note the fact that the writing of this book coincided with a terrible public health crisis, which has claimed millions of lives and hit cinema and the performing arts especially severely. A deep thank you, from the bottom of my heart, goes out to the many thousands of performers, workers, venues and donors who have done their utmost to prevent the magic of culture from being extinguished in the long night of Covid-19.

And finally, thanks to friends and family for all the generosity and kindness, without which no book could be written.

ABOUT THE AUTHOR

Joseph Attard completed his PhD in Film Studies at King's College London, UK, in 2018 and is now an academic author and political journalist. His research focuses on the intersection between media technology, social science and politics, all from a Marxist perspective. He has written several articles and contributed book chapters about opera cinema, and in 2018 co-edited and wrote for a special edition of *Opera Quarterly* themed around the subject.

1

What is opera cinema?

I arrive half an hour before curtain up. It would be wrong to say that I have donned my full regalia, but I have certainly made an effort; more so than for, say, the latest instalment of the Marvel Cinematic Universe. The small crowd surrounding the snacks bar is undeniably on the mature side, though interspersed with a few younger faces. The spectrum of attire runs from formal eveningwear to t-shirts and jeans. The only thing everyone seems to have in common is a shared enthusiasm that has broken the terribly British embargo on spontaneous dialogue – people are *talking* to one another – *at the cinema!* I hear someone discussing the show. 'This Katie Mitchell version is already very cinematic,' someone says. 'Plenty of sex and bloodshed.' As it happens, despite the salacious impression given by the promotional material (showing Lucia in a bathtub, her eyes wide with anguish), the actual performance is pretty modest on both counts.

We are ushered into the auditorium. A member of staff hands each of us a programme titled, *Lucia di Lammermoor: Live from the Royal Opera House*. On the screen, there is a graphic of a clock, its hands ticking down to the beginning of the show. The countdown elapses, the lights come down and the murmur of a live audience together with the strident tones of the players tuning up issues over the sound system. The camera pans across the cavernous Covent Garden auditorium, showing attendees at the physical performance filing in. I cannot banish the sound of hands rummaging in Minstrel packets, and nor does the compressed, digital simulacrum of the sounds of the Royal Opera quite transport me to Covent Garden. This is still cinema, and yet more than cinema. It is less than opera, yet more than opera. As tweets pour onto the screen from viewers in Portugal, France, Russia and the United States, I feel the presence of the Royal Opera House's global network of admirers. For tonight, we are a single, virtual community. This is opera cinema. The camera comes to rest on a celebrity talking head, beaming out of the screen and addressing us directly: 'We are coming to you live from the Royal Opera House, in Covent Garden, London.'

Lights, camera, curtain up!

Live, international satellite transmissions of opera to cinemas were debuted by New York's Metropolitan Opera in 2006. They were presented as the modern successor to the company's famous television broadcasts, launched in 1977 – which were themselves preceded by *Live from the Metropolitan Opera* radio transmissions, beginning in 1931. The cinema broadcasts have gone on to acquire an audience of millions; they have been replicated by opera companies worldwide, topped the weekend box office multiple times and drawn their fair share of both accolades and scepticism. Yet despite their remarkable rise (to borrow a phrase from Martin Barker),[1] these events remain poorly understood by both the academic and popular arts community. This is a shame, as they represent a miniature cultural revolution for performance media.

Over the last several years, I have been trying to get a firmer handle on what this experience really is, for whom it caters and what it portends for the future of opera. Starting from first principles – what do we call it? Names are important – especially when we are talking about a hybrid entity. The choice of nomenclature implies the essence of the experience. The early industry designation, 'Digital Broadcast Cinema', emphasized cinema over performance, reflecting the origin of these events as part of the analogue-to-digital cinema changeover of the mid-2000s.[2] A later term, 'live relay', evoked the familiar, established tradition of TV relays of live opera performances.[3] Another designation, 'livecasting', underlined the unique selling point of instantaneous transmission to the movie house. With the establishment of the Event Cinema Association in 2012, there was a concerted effort to achieve brand recognition for the term 'event cinema'.[4] Sarah Atkinson distinguishes this from the related term 'live cinema', which she attributes to a swathe of successful events like Secret Cinema, Rooftop Cinema and 4D cinema, which augment a conventional, recorded film by introducing 'live and theatrical experiences within the cinema auditorium'.[5] Meanwhile, event cinema consists of live performances relayed digitally, via satellite, to cinemas.

For the sake of clarifying language, I employ these terms throughout the book. However, they are still not quite precise enough on their own. The experience of watching opera is distinct from watching simulcast dramatic theatre, live concert performances or sporting events at the movies. Opera has also taken a unique route to the cinema, has its own dedicated audience and involves its own unique ritual behaviours and social practices. As such, with my own coinage, I want to distil the defining experiential elements of these events – in which the rich, unique, idiosyncratic operatic medium is blended with cinematic exhibition practices. Thus, I have settled on something rather plain, but hopefully properly descriptive: *opera cinema*.

The purpose of this book is to define it.

Opera cinema is a (fairly) new cultural experience. In 2015, only 19 per cent of British consumers had even seen live content in the cinema, with the opera cinema audience constituting a minority within this minority.[6] Half a decade later, audiences are still familiarizing themselves with opera cinema, and developing a strategy for engaging with it (what to wear, how to behave, whether to clap and so on). This is a maturation process through which all cultural phenomena must pass. And in part because it is new, opera cinema is subject to suspicion. For some, it is merely a parasitical shadow of 'true' opera, which cheapens the medium and seeks to lure fickle audiences away from the stage. Such scepticism is evident in musicologist James Steichen's professed discomfort while attending simulcasts, which he likens to 'cheating on opera'.[7] He also explicitly voices concern that technological remediation will replace the real thing, cautioning that, 'in our zeal to rediscover opera through the easy access of the digital cloud, we should also take care to tend opera on the ground … [S]tars such as Stephanie Blythe are not going to be discovered and nurtured by viral YouTube clips or Facebook campaigns'.[8] Opera critic Alexandra Coghlan goes further still, excoriating opera cinema as being to opera what 'Walt Disney's original fantasy of Epcot was to America; everything might be visually tidier, more convenient, more heightened in close-up, but it's also hollow – a cartoonish reality'.[9] Moreover, she fears that the influence of cinema will diminish the integrity of stage productions:

> What happens when digital audiences routinely outnumber live ones? What happens when cinema screenings subsidize performances, as they are beginning to do? Surely the temptation will be to start catering to this new format, designing productions around what works best in the new medium, casting according to Hollywood's standards rather than musical ones.[10]

A few points of information: firstly, opera cinema does not tend to subsidize stage performance directly - it is very seldom profitable.[11] The main institutional objectives behind simulcasting are brand promotion and audience outreach.[12] Also, opera cinema has already exerted a discernible effect on stage opera design and direction. For instance, at a conference I hosted in 2017, soprano Corinne Winters discussed how make-up and performances are made more 'naturalistic' on the night of the simulcast, for the benefit of audiences watching close-ups on the big screen.[13] These points aside, Coghlan and Steichen's anxiety expresses something more fundamental: the idea that the influence of cinema and digital media will somehow contaminate and weaken stage opera. But in fact, opera has always interacted with other media and adapted under pressure from competing cultural experiences. From the incorporation of ballet sequences in the eighteenth century,[14] to distributing Enrico Caruso compilations on phonograph records,[15] to playing abbreviated English-language productions on television in the 1940s,[16] media hybridity has figured prominently in opera's past, and will continue to do so in its future.

As mentioned, opera cinema is poorly understood by the musicological and media academe. The former is often dismissive of opera cinema, and opera on screen more generally. For instance, opera scholar Sam Abel accuses screen adaptations of stripping the medium of 'the most concrete appeal of live performance – the erotic interest of the spectator in the physically present body of the star'.[17] Similarly, Linda and Michael Hutcheon condemn opera on screen for 'erasing' the living human body that gives opera performance its vitality, resulting in something vapid and bloodless. In sum, as Steichen puts it, this is simply 'not the way opera is supposed to be'.[18] Meanwhile, media scholars raised on screens, who attempt to tackle this phenomenon, in many cases simply do not understand opera. Part of the problem, according to Marcia Citron (an author with a foot in both the musicological and media camps), is that the term 'operatic' can mean many different things:

> Operatic can refer to a range of elements, such as genre, structure, expression, style, music, or tone. Operatic can pertain to the comic antics of opera buffa or the grandeur of serious opera. Operatic can imply a theatrical approach, one that recalls the stage techniques of live opera. It can describe expressive content that displays opera's exaggeration, whether emotional, aesthetic, thematic, or structural. It can imply similarities with certain operas or their cultural context. Operatic can suggest a certain formal organization found in opera, be it a division into set numbers, tableaux, or larger units, or a characteristic pacing or texture. Of course, the ways in which music is used in a film can be operatic, in structure, function, tone, affect, or style. The possibilities are many.[19]

The two main stumbling blocks for media scholars, based on my experience, are that they can get their heads around neither the medium's histrionic melodrama (that Lesley Stern calls 'operality'),[20] nor the very particular culture surrounding it, embodied by highly knowledgeable and intensely devoted audiences.[21] Many a production has fallen afoul of opera aficionados dissatisfied with subpar performances or perceived excessive meddling. For example, conductor Riccardo Muti once fatefully instructed a tenor to omit some high Cs from the end of Manrico's aria 'Di quella pira' in a 2000 production of Verdi's *Il trovatore* (1853). As historians Carolyn Abbate, Roger Parker relate in *A History of Opera: The Last 400 Years*:

> The tenor trembled and obeyed. The *loggionistii*, opera fans who haunt the upper reaches of the theatre and who know every recording intimately, went mad with rage, cries of 'Vergogna' (shame) rained down on the stage.[22]

These worshipful audiences bring their exacting standards to opera cinema as well. In a 2014 survey of opera cinemagoers, when asked about their broader film preferences, 'Screenings of theatre performances' were the most popular category, with 73 per cent having attended another event cinema show, in the prior twelve months.[23] It is notable that, given the relatively small proportion of box office revenue provided by event cinema, most of these respondents spend most of their time at the cinema watching live theatre rather than traditional films. In another piece of research, over 30 per cent of respondents opened their answers to interview questions with unprompted declarations of devotion to the medium ('I/we love opera ... I'm an opera fan/nut ... We are passionate about opera').[24] This deep, enduring love was evident in the backlash faced by Barbara Willis Sweete's experiments with a mosaic image during a 2008 simulcast of *Tristan and Isolde*. Her attempt at stylistic innovation was met with uproar, and demands that Sweete never again be allowed to direct an opera simulcast.[25]

In my opinion, no other performance medium commands this level of fervent devotion. For this reason (among others), opera cinema cannot be lumped in with other forms of live broadcast performance. The opera cinema audience strongly dictates the level of artistic freedom that directors are afforded to reinterpret the subject matter. The high cost of staging opera forces companies into an awkward balancing act between private donations, state support and box office receipts, which in turn necessitates reaching out for reliable income by targeting experienced audiences via simulcasting. Audiences' exacting demands thus impede simulcasting from taking creative risks, to a certain extent.

Another problem with existing literature on opera cinema is that some media researchers, investigating event cinema in its early years, displayed a certain utopianism, claiming that opera cinema was a brand-new medium, or would introduce this esoteric art form to a new generation. Early interventions focused their attention on the democratizing potential of simulcasting. For instance, audience researcher Paul Heyer's 2008 work on *Live from the Met* lauded simulcasting for 'bridging the divide between high culture and mass entertainment'.[26] I confess to being affected by this impression, as evidenced by an article published in Sarah Atkinson's 2017 edited collection on live and event cinema, in which I define opera cinema as a new, hybrid medium.[27] Among wider operaphiles, however, this kind of enthusiasm was short lived. When opera cinema's limitations as an ambassador became apparent in the early 2010s, more critical analyses began to emerge: particularly from musicologists. As Steichen points out, not unfairly, 'anyone who has attended an HD broadcast and has talked at any length with fellow audience members has quickly discovered that most people there are indeed not opera newcomers but rather the already initiated'.[28] He goes on to argue that the real innovation of opera cinema is not to promote or restage opera per se, but to promote opera companies. He explains this through the concept of 'institutional dramaturgy':

> Institutional dramaturgy consists of the practices through which an arts institution structures its patrons' experiences in the service of advancing its goals or articulating its identity ... It is concerned with managing the public profile of the presenting institution and lending that extra bit of star power to the artistic product ... The Met's broadcasts invite and enable the audience to inhabit imaginatively the status-imbued space of the Metropolitan Opera House, the corporate headquarters of the initiative.[29]

In short, the goal of the Met's simulcasts is to sell a virtual ticket to the auditorium rather than creatively reinterpret the text itself.[30] Putting it uncharitably, this makes opera cinema little more than an elaborate advertisement for a night at the opera. Despite Steichen's professed traditionalism, there is a bit of truth to this. But the reasons for this are more complicated than he lets on and have more to do with the need to hold onto a shrinking pool of aging opera attendees than a lack of imagination on the side of opera cinema directors, or any innate conservatism imposed by the technology involved.

Social scientist and media researcher Martin Barker produced by far the most comprehensive and nuanced work on opera cinema. His monograph *Live to Your Local Cinema: The Remarkable Rise of Livecasting*, published in 2012, provides a detailed, historical account of the institutional imperatives that drove the emergence of livecasting, and combines it with demographic and audience data.[31] Throughout the monograph, Barker places a great deal of emphasis on livecasting's appeal to the cinema industry, noting that: '[livecasts] are attracting back to cinemas audiences who had largely deserted them. They command a higher ticket price [than recorded film] ... And they are, in the main, sell-out successes.'[32] Barker rigorously profiles event cinema audiences with industry data and original fieldwork. He describes a 'very particular kind of audience' for livecasting, made up of individuals that are 'overwhelmingly not traditional cinema audiences'.[33] These audiences are 'mature, self-aware, knowledgeable ... They are also literate, self-confident, assertive and sure in their judgements of the world.'[34] He notes a substantial dip in his subjects' expressed enjoyment of opera cinema between their first and second show, which suggests that a cross-section 'tried the experience once and gave it the benefit of the doubt, tried it once more less enthusiastically ... and then may select themselves out'.[35] These would be people who like opera but were turned off by the cinema. However, he found that respondents' enjoyment sharply increased by their third, fourth, fifth and sixth performance, which suggests that those who remain with opera cinema have 'fallen in love with this mode of encountering theatre and opera because of its differences'.[36] However, Barker is a little unclear on what these differences are – a gap I will endeavour to fill with this book.

On the aesthetic front, Barker argues that the composition of simulcasts is driven by 'the limits and compromises imposed by the need to protect the source-event and the experience of the physically present [house] audience'.[37] These include the requirement that camera placement in the auditorium be unobtrusive, which has consequences for shot options. For example, dialogue tends to be shown by two shots, while camera locations often produce a combination of low-angle shots ('as from the sides of the auditorium or the orchestra pit') and eye-level shots ('as from the sides of the stage'), with some high angles.[38] Sound capture is typically achieved by head or throat mics. Apparently, microphone positioning used to cause *Singin' in the Rain*-esque mishaps when performers turn their heads to face 'dead' areas, though I have never witnessed this myself. Stage lighting results in non-naturalistic depth for the camera, with the consequence that characters can seem to be pooled by light, meaning that the stage and sets drop out of sight.[39] Finally, 'there is a predominance of un-cleaned sound, so that any non-diegetic music or sound carries the timbre of its whole–theatre source'.[40] Overall, Barker characterizes the aesthetic principles of livecasting as cautious: 'the cinematic capture almost consciously avoids adding much.'[41] Having attended many simulcasts during the years since Barker published his research, I can confirm that their formal conventions have not changed substantially (I devote a chapter to this later on). Barker is non-committal about whether opera cinema is a distinct medium, other than to urge caution over 'exaggerated claims about the benefits or implications of livecasting', which he deems 'a relatively cheap way for people to get to see things otherwise denied to them'.[42]

While Barker's work is very important, with this statement he articulates a major problem with understanding opera cinema: it is too often reduced to a next-best-thing to 'proper' opera – that is to say, stage opera. This is the single-biggest preconception affecting research into this phenomenon. But even if this is an opinion shared by a big cross section of its audience, if we want to understand opera cinema beyond a superficial, surface level, we must ask the question of what it changes, what it keeps the same and what it innovates about the experience of watching opera. That cannot be done by looking at existing data or abstract philosophising alone: it necessitates going to real audiences and asking them the right questions.

'Who really goes to these things?' Profiling opera cinema audiences

While opera cinema is very much a global phenomenon (in normal times, the Royal Opera House transmits its performances to more than forty territories),[43] for the purposes of this research, I am focusing on UK audiences. The important but ambitious task of dealing with opera cinema's international reception remains for the future. Prior research suffers from the following limitations:

1. Existing data have tended to be London-centric, with scant investigation into the experiences and preferences of regional audiences. This is counter-intuitive, given that a key advantage of opera cinema includes its capacity to extend the opera audience beyond the physical confines of the opera house and the geographical limits of metropolitan centres.
2. It assumes that opera cinema is the next best thing to the stage. This presumption affects the way that researchers approach opera cinema, which is almost always compared with staged opera, rather than being analysed on its own merits. This tells us only what is obvious from the outset: opera cinema is more convenient, cheaper and more accessible than the auditorium, which presents a 'special' experience that cannot be replicated by a simulcast. It tells us nothing about what is unique about opera cinema per se.
3. Researchers are preoccupied with mollifying the concern that opera cinema pulls a substantial cross section of operagoers away from auditoria, despite the fact there is still no hard evidence of this.

These contentions aside, what sort of attendees do we see from the data? According to Phil Clapp, chief executive of the Cinema Exhibitors' Association, event cinema has become an 'increasingly important strand of income for cinemas at a time when they are very keen to broaden their reach and get a different audience to the traditional cinemagoer'.[44] The 'traditional' cinemagoer is, of course, a vexed term, and one that I shall not tackle here. However, even a surface-level comparison between the profiles of the general UK cinema audience and audiences for opera cinema reveals striking differences. For instance, the general UK cinema audience is heavily weighted towards young people, with just 36 per cent of seats occupied by individuals over the age of thirty-five.[45] By contrast, internal audience research conducted by the Royal Opera House during a twelve-month period ending in September 2014 found that 53 per cent of its cinema audience was over the age of sixty-five.[46] These data also suggest opera cinema audiences are distinct from auditorium attendees, being 'older … and less ethnically diverse than Royal Opera House ticket buyers [and] therefore less representative of the UK population.'[47] Furthermore, 43 per cent of the Royal Opera House cinema audience attended staged opera 'more than once a year' and 47 per cent had seen at least one other opera simulcast in the year prior to taking part in the survey, compared with just

13 per cent of ticket buyers in the 2013/14 season.[48] As Barker correctly pointed out, these veterans mostly go to the movies for opera – and they have a very clear idea about what opera is supposed to be.

The issue of cannibalization (the idea that simulcasting draws opera fans away from the stage) is frequently addressed in sector research. It is connected to a broader question about the health of the cultural ecology, which has in the past decade been hampered by an austerity-induced funding shortage that has concentrated arts subsidies in metropolitan centres.[49] This was of course exacerbated by the coronavirus pandemic, which effectively halted live theatre for over a year. But this is only the culmination of a longer trend. Since the Second World War, the history of arts policy in Britain has seen a continual struggle for breathing space between regional and metropolitan institutions, with the Arts Council generally favouring increased centralization of support under the principle of 'few, but roses' (concentrated in London).[50] Competition has only intensified under the recent period of crisis, stagnation and austerity, and opera cinema has been identified as one way that large opera companies can justify their (ever-diminishing) subsidies – by proving their commitment to technological innovation.

In this context, the capacity for large, globally visible, state-subsidized institutions like the Royal Opera House, Royal Shakespeare Company and National Theatre to extend their reach digitally is an understandable source of chagrin for the rest of the sector. Simulcasting is simply too expensive for smaller companies without government support, as evident by the fact that 53 per cent of Arts Council England National Portfolio Organizations (NPOs) have digitally transmitted their work, compared with 19 per cent of non-NPO respondents.[51] However, research into the cannibalization effect of opera cinema is inconclusive at best. For instance, based on a sample of 228 participants, John Holmes examined the demographics, motivations and experiences of opera attendees in cinemas and theatres outside London - a rare example of such work. Holmes identifies some risk of cannibalization, because his respondents claimed to be more likely to attend opera simulcasts than travel to the physical opera house, 'due in large part to practical concerns, including comfort, convenience, and value for money'.[52] However, he cites no actual evidence of this happening. The best information available suggests simulcasting has little impact on auditorium attendance one way or the other. A recent paper published by Arts Council England noted an ambiguous 'range of positive effects' from the uptake of cinema simulcasts and streaming, including 're-energised audiences' and a 'halo effect' of increased interest in live repertoire.[53] Of course, it is in the Arts Council's interests to prove that public money has been well spent, so these figures should be taken with a pinch of salt. It does not provide any data to back up its claims other than the fact that 74 per cent of suppliers surveyed stated that their digital initiatives had a positive or neutral effect on their organization, whereas only 13 per cent reported a negative effect (the rest non-responding).[54] These positives included audience acquisition, new business and creative partnerships and building a stronger brand.[55] However, all these effects are nebulous and difficult to quantify.

A related question to cannibalization is that of audience democratization, on which industry data is more conclusive. As mentioned, early research was optimistic about opera cinema's democratizing potential. One of the first notable pieces of independent research into event cinema was carried out in 2010 by the non-profit National Endowment for Science, Technology and the Arts (NESTA). The paper presents digital broadcasting as a way of meeting the 'aspirations of consumers who want the freedom to access content anywhere, anytime', citing the early successes of *Live from the Met* and *Royal Opera House Live*, and advocating the development of 'novel platforms and strategies to reach audiences and generate revenues' in British cultural industries.[56]

But the reality did not meet these lofty ambitions. Far from being new audiences, opera cinema attendees tend to be even older and more experienced than auditorium audiences. Simulcasting's disappointing performance as an audience acquisition tool invited a backlash. In 2012, the English National Opera's (ENO) director, John Berry, attacked the Royal Opera House's 'obsession about putting work out into the cinema' for distracting 'from making amazing quality work' – although the ENO eventually capitulated and launched its own, albeit short-lived event cinema initiative.[57] Research conducted by Karen Wise on behalf of the English Touring Opera company intensified the hostility. Aside from asserting that opera cinema does not draw new people to opera, Wise's equivocal comment that 'attending cinema relays is more likely to inspire further attendance at a cinema rather than encourage people to transition to a theatre experience'[58] was adopted by the press, in an exaggerated fashion, as validation of the cannibalization thesis.[59] The controversy forced a retreat by the Royal Opera House, whose chief executive Alex Beard was quoted in the *Financial Times* as subscribing to 'democratising access' but not 'democratising art'.[60] The article did not clarify what he meant by this ambiguous statement, but the clear implication was that opera was not being deliberately 'dumbed down' in the pursuit of a bigger audience.

In fact, opera cinema has had little effect on diversifying audiences for opera, in terms of age, race or socio-economic status. The research by the Royal Opera House,[61] the English Touring Opera,[62] NESTA[63] and indeed virtually every piece of audience research ever carried out on arts audiences has drawn a variation on the conclusion that they are 'white and well-heeled'.[64] Among other factors, this reflects the tendency of mainstream arts institutions to make grabs for the low-hanging fruit. As Richard Schechter comments: 'Every theatre wants to pinpoint that "two percent" of the population who will pay to go to the theatre. The inescapable result is a middle-class audience.'[65] Consequently, Susan Bennett suggests that existing demographic data offer 'limited value beyond establishing the particular cultural construction of mainstream audiences'.[66] The evidence unambiguously shows that working-class and minority groups are systematically excluded from the so-called high arts, including opera. A combination of high-priced tickets, erosion of leisure time and an escalating cost of living compared to stagnant wages renders theatre inaccessible to millions (at least on a regular basis),[67] in turn denying the familiarity that would compel one to seek it out in the cinema, even when given the opportunity. And let us not forget, event cinema tickets don't come cheap either. This is not to mention the snobbery and elitism (real and perceived) that undeniably presents a barrier to entry where classical music is concerned. It would be unreasonable to expect opera cinema to level a cultural playing field so heavily stratified according to background and social class. However, this book does ask why opera cinema has failed to meaningfully capture the attention of budding operaphiles of *any* background. I also speculate about whether it ever could.

A big part of answering these questions involves speaking to audiences. My audience research design project was partly determined by my relatively limited resources (necessitating a small sample size) and the inductive nature of the research, given the lack of much existing data on simulcasting. One advantage of this is that I can pay more attention to my participants, unlike research using larger data sets, which are of course invaluable for illustrating general trends, but lack the subjective and qualitative depth I needed to get a sense of what opera cinema is really like. I exclusively recruited total opera novices, because I felt that they would be less inclined than the existing simulcasting audience to adjudicate opera cinema through comparison with stage opera, and thus perceive the former on its own merits. Of course, novice subjects are not complete operatic ignoramuses or *tabulae rasae*. This would be inconceivable given opera's profound influence over other mediums: film and television scores, for example, and opera's regular appearance in popular culture - from *Looney Tunes* to *Star Wars*. As such, my subjects offer a fresh perspective on opera cinema, if not a neutral one. Finally, I was curious as to whether any of the unique characteristics of opera cinema might contain intrinsic appeal for newcomers that may be lacking in auditoria, and might explain why traditional opera is currently failing to draw them in.[68]

The key questions for my audience study were as follows:

1. In what way is opera cinema experientially distinct from stage opera and recorded cinema?
2. Is it a new medium?
3. If not, could it ever become one?
4. What are the 'rituals' for viewing opera cinema? Do people applaud? Do they dress up?

5. Have these conventions stabilized into a viewing strategy, or are behavioural codes still malleable?
6. What do these data tell us about contemporary media more generally?

A brief aside on question four. I describe the behavioural codes of opera and cinema engagement as rituals throughout the book – a term that requires some unpacking. In *Ritual Theory, Ritual Practice*, Catherine Bell describes ritualism as repetitive, contextual action distinguished from the typical flow of everyday life: 'the type of authority formulated by ritualization tends to make ritual activities effective in grounding and displaying a sense of community without overriding the autonomy of individuals or subgroups.'[69] While Bell focuses on religious activities, ritualized behaviour is also evident in secular contexts, including cultural events. As Kevin Corbett demonstrates for cinema,[70] Roger Silverstone for television[71] and Daniel Snowman for opera,[72] the practices and etiquette associated with cultural experiences must be inculcated into audiences by cultural institutions over time. And these rituals can change: it was not always taken as given that people would arrive on time or sit in silence either for cinema or opera performances, for example. But once adopted, these media rituals demonstrate remarkable inertia.

The media philosopher Lisa Gitelman explains how ritual acts become established protocols for engagement. These protocols can follow media into new exhibition contexts; for example, whenever domestic viewers switch the lights off and buy popcorn for home movie nights. The transmission of operatic ritual behaviour to the cinema is evident in the case of opera cinema, whose exhibition practices hybridize conventions from the cinema and the auditorium. Critical to Gitelman's thesis is the idea that media constitute not only technologies, but the experiential and social protocols surrounding them. Moreover, she emphasizes that media are 'complicated historical subjects', whose specificity must be understood in historical terms:

> Specificity is key. Rather than static, blunt and unchanging technology, every medium involves a 'sequence of displacements and obsolescences, part of the delirious operations of modernization' … Consider again how fast digital media are changing today. Media, it should be clear, are very particular sites for very particular, importantly social as well as historically and culturally specific experiences of meaning.[73]

Fully understanding any media phenomenon means illustrating concretely how it is situated in everyday life, and how its protocols are learned, enacted and negotiated. As media and audience researcher Barbara Klinger neatly summarizes: 'a more fulsome definition of media means addressing the role played by affiliated forms in a specific medium's experience while studying applicable ritual protocols that characterize it within an historical era or nation.'[74] Furthermore, I argue that opera cinema's protocols have yet to settle precisely because it is new, and its identity as is still very much in flux. Once a set of stable protocols cohere into a proper viewing strategy for opera cinema, it will demonstrate the phenomenon reaching a new point of maturity.

One limitation of my audience research is that my few dozen subjects provide insufficient data to make generalizable claims about people's engagement with opera cinema. I have only captured a snapshot. But my objective was not to make bold claims about opera cinema audiences in general. I will leave that to the Royal Opera House's market research teams. Rather, I sought to better understand opera cinema as an entity and experience. For this purpose, a more qualitative approach seemed appropriate.

What does it mean to be a medium?

The main enquiry for this book is basically ontological. What exactly is opera cinema? Is it a new medium? Just a way of seeing opera? Something entirely new? Debates on media ontology stem from two central questions: how are representations of the world changed by the intervention of technology, and what is the relationship between these media technologies and wider society?

In media studies, Marshall McLuhan and Raymond Williams established the main competing perspectives on this matter – respectively, the idea that technologies determine society and that society determines technology. McLuhan succinctly outlines his technological determinist position with the aphorism: 'the medium is the message'.[75] He argues that 'the personal and social consequences of any medium – that is, of any extension of ourselves – result from the new scale that is introduced into our affairs by each extension of ourselves, or by any new technology'.[76] McLuhan argues that new technologies extend the capacity of the human body to move and communicate, and in so doing, determine the nature of human life in new ways – as such, we are determined by technology. Williams admonished McLuhan for overlooking the fact that technologies emerge in a pre-existing social context. Using the example of television, Williams pointed out that an audio-visual broadcast technology was developed in a society that already had need of it - given the rapid, global expansion of capitalism in the first half of the twentieth century. This economic context made television 'a by-product of a social process that is otherwise determined. [It] only acquires effective status when it is used for purposes which are already contained in this known social process.'[77] In sum, we make the technology, it does not make us. I think Williams is basically right about this, but he is also rather mechanical in his outlook. The idea of digitally transmitting operas to the cinema did not spring, fully formed, from somebody's mind one day. But simply asserting this doesn't tell us very much. There was not a perfect niche awaiting opera cinema to fill it. Instead, it emerged via complex process of development, with many false starts and dead ends.

Later historiographical interventions have sought to investigate the evolutionary process by which media emerge and develop under a multitude of social, political and economic pressures. Through this kind of analysis, we see that media do not exist on parallel lines of development. There is much interplay and crossover between them. As historian Paolo Cherchi Usai writes: 'The history of cinema did not begin with a "big bang" … Rather there is a continuum which begins with early experiments and devices aimed at presenting images in sequence … Magic lantern, film, and television, therefore, do not constitute three separate universes (and fields of study), but belong together as part of a single process of evolution.'[78] The ontology of opera cinema similarly exists on a continuum, drawing many different media phenomena into a shared evolutionary process.

But acknowledging this continuum does not deny specificity or categorization. Cinema and television have changed a lot in the past century. They have swapped and shared characteristics (digital images, liveness, large and small screens etc.), they can even be viewed on the same device, there might be intermediate forms between them and yet there is still cinema and television. Where do we draw the line? One factor is the technology and delivery systems to which media lend themselves. To use an extreme example: there are always going to be concrete, material differences between watching a piece of cinema and reading a book. That is true whether the film is watched on a smartphone or the silver screen; the book on paper or a Kindle. Of course, things get trickier with intermediate forms, like opera cinema. Social scientist and philosopher Joshua Meyrowitz's provides a useful concept in medium theory, which focuses on the 'particular characteristics of each individual medium or of each particular type of media' and seeks to identify how these characteristics impact on a wider society.[79] While there is a clear McLuhanite influence here, Meyrowtiz does not overlook social forces, arguing that the characteristics of newer media interact with everyday life at both the micro and macro level:

> On the micro level, medium questions ask how the choice of one medium over another affects a particular situation or interaction (calling someone on the phone versus writing them a letter, for example). On the macro level, medium questions address the ways in which the addition of a new medium to an existing matrix of media may alter social interactions and social structure in general.[80]

According to this hypothesis, the characteristics of a medium include its 'relatively fixed features' of communication: for example, whether it favours bi- or unidirectional communication, the number of people who are typically presented with its message and the difficulty of encoding and decoding said message. Meyrowitz stipulates that these characteristics calibrate a medium's social, political and psychological impact. A televised relay of *Don Giovanni* will involve a markedly different experience and engagement strategies from viewing the same performance in the Royal Opera House auditorium, or watching a tape recording at home, for example. Moreover, the capacity for audiences to engage with live opera simultaneously across continental divides fundamentally transforms their relationship to the art form. The very presence of live opera inside cinemas results in entirely new audiences entering this exhibition space and diversifies the functions of the movie house as a site of media use.

We must begin with objective features to understand anything, but (to put it in a very banal way), art is subjective. Media are intended to elicit aesthetic, emotional or intellectual responses. Therefore, for a medium to be a medium, I posit it must create an experience that is different from related media, and be socially acknowledged as such. This requirement is very important today. At the time when many canonical theories of media ontology were written, it was possible to draw relatively clear lines of demarcation between media based on delivery systems alone. This permitted media ontologists such as André Bazin (for cinema) and Antonin Artaud (for theatre) to determine the 'defining essence' of media without recourse to historical context or audience perspectives.[81] However, in the era of digitization, media messages readily move between different platforms. We require means of demarcating media that go beyond technological characteristics, and also incorporate historical development, social context and audience experience. This is not just a matter of expediency: without attention to the way that media are used and integrated into everyday life, they are reduced to static schema, isolating from history and the real world – eternal and unchanging. Counterposed this mechanical materialism, the method of dialectical materialism worked out by Karl Marx and Friedrich Engels (more on this later) put us on much better footing. Though I do not share very many of his conclusions, I think Lucien Goldmann makes the point well in *The Hidden God*:

> I set out from the fundamental principle of dialectical materialism, that the knowledge of empirical facts remains abstract and superficial so long as it is not made concrete by its integration into a whole; and that only this act of integration can enable us to go beyond the incomplete and abstract phenomenon in order to arrive at its concrete essence, and thus, implicitly, at its meaning.[82]

There is an exclusionary aspect to my analysis. Not all media phenomena are true art forms. A whole variety of fancies, distractions and novelties come and go without ever coming out as a medium at the other side. The history of cinema demonstrates this point, and shows that a media phenomenon's maturation into a discrete medium is marked by audience acknowledgement and recognition. Cinema began as a scientific tool, before entering a transitional period where it was a sideshow and saloon attraction that adapted existing media forms like vaudeville, theatre and the novel.[83] As historian Roberta Pearson points out, by the end of its first decade of existence

> [C]inema had established itself as an interesting novelty, one distraction among many ... very much dependent upon pre-existing media for its formal conventions and story-telling devices, upon somewhat outmoded individually-driven production methods, and upon pre-existing exhibition venues such as vaudeville and fairs.[84]

However, by 1917 - the end of cinema's 'transitional' period - films had 'freed themselves from dependence upon other media, and could now tell cinematic stories using cinematic devices; devices which were becoming increasingly codified and conventional'.[85] There was also a 'standardization of production practices, consonant with the operations of other capitalist enterprises, [which] assured the continuing output of a reliable and familiar product, the so-called "feature" film'.[86] Furthermore, the building of elaborate movie palaces 'heralded the medium's new-found social respectability'.[87]

There are things to be learned from the history of film in determining the ontology of opera cinema, although the comparison is not a perfect one. Cinema emerged in markedly different historical conditions than digital simulcasting. However, like cinema after its first decade of existence, opera cinema remains an 'interesting novelty', a distraction 'among many' that is largely dependent on existing media for its formal conventions and exhibition practices. This would imply from the outset that opera cinema cannot be described as a medium. So, what are we dealing with? In *Remediation*, Jay David Bolter and Richard Grusin observe that modern (especially digital) media are 'continually commenting on, reproducing and replacing each other'.[88] Remediation differs from adaptation (defined by Linda Hutcheon as a 'palimpsestic' work that is derived from a source text)[89] in that it aims not to reinterpret but merely represent cultural products through new technologies. Bolter and Grusin contend that remediation lies on a continuum of Western visual representation that strives for transparency, starting with the emergence of linear perspective in the Renaissance.[90] However, they argue that remediation is the defining paradigm of digital media, which almost invariably 'remediate' other forms of representation.[91] If not a medium in its own right, opera cinema is certainly a digital remediation of opera.

Opera cinema accords with other aspects of Bolter and Grusin's thesis as well. For example, they argue that remediation operates on a dual logic of immediacy and hypermediacy. The former refers to the deliberate concealment of the remediation process – such as when a classical portraitist attempts to conceal evidence of their brushstrokes.[92] In the case of opera cinema, the unobtrusive direction of simulcasts aims to seamlessly remediate live opera from stage to screen.[93] Hypermediacy is the aesthetic effect of two or more media interacting in the same frame.[94] This occurs because completely unadulterated translation is impossible – a paradox that Bolter and Grusin acknowledge: '[while] there should be no difference between the experience of seeing a painting in person and on the computer screen ... this is of course never so. The computer always intervenes and makes its presence felt in some way.'[95] Opera cinema is profoundly hypermedial: exhibiting operatic events through the visual language of cinema, in addition to exhibiting some formal influences from television and networked digital communication.

Theoretical ontologies tied to technology alone suffer from many limitations, including their tendency to draw strict lines between media, based on the capabilities of delivery systems. For instance, Jane Feuer contends that 'from a certain technological and perceptual point of view, television is live in a way film can never be'.[96] Klinger attributes the categorical juxtaposition between live television and cinema to the fact that the former was 'the first [medium] to be able to automatically reproduce continuous movement in its duration and space'.[97] There is some truth in this. Opera cinema's aesthetic strategies owe much to live televised relays of opera performances, so that opera cinema carries a prominent televisual streak. However, the analysis is one-sided. Film and cinema have a closer historical relationship than many authors acknowledge. Moreover, live experience has always constituted a part of the cinema experience in one form or another, from the live pianists who used to accompany silent film to the emergence of digital event cinema in the present day.

Here, we should acknowledge the institutional pressures inform and shape the kind of media that is created, and our attitudes towards it. Market trends inform the kinds of art that is funded, created and sold. Certain kinds of art are marketed to specific kinds of people. All of this must be brought to bear on the study of media ontology, as it constitutes the context in which media develop, and affects the form they take. John Ellis argues that any new technology is implemented 'according to the prevailing patterns of use into which it can be fitted, and according to the emerging forms of social organisation with which it can align itself'.[98] He contends that cinema has aligned with public forms of entertainment (vaudeville and music hall), and the television with domesticity.[99] However, these are not essential characteristics. For example, Ellis notes that 'public TV' and 'private cinema' can be respectively observed in open-air TV broadcasts and home projection set-ups.[100] In sum, Ellis proposes that the characteristics of

TV and cinema, as well as their ontological boundaries, are interconnected, socially constructed and malleable – to a point. Additionally, Ellis draws a distinction between film as a text, and cinema as experience: 'cinema marketing sells two rather distinct things: the single film in its uniqueness ... and the experience of cinema itself'.[101] This has clear relevance to event cinema, in which the experience of attending a theatrical exhibition is emphasized as a key selling point.

The study of media ontology also touches on debates about the ways in which media rise, fall and diverge from one another. The term new media is ubiquitous in media studies, but has been criticized by many theorists and historians. Carolyn Marvin and Gitelman both argue that all media experiences and technologies were at one time 'new'. Therefore, we cannot talk uncritically about new media in an epochal sense.[102] However, media trends can exemplify a historical period and its defining communication technologies. Event cinema is one of a host of experiences that have only become feasible through digital means. Perhaps the most salient impact of digitization is a greater fluidity of content, and increased agency of media audiences over their consumption habits, as summarized by historian William Boddy:

> Electronic cinema calls into question the social contexts and meanings of the electronic moving image's proliferating sites of reception, including mobile consumption via handheld devices and the growth of interactive digital signage in public spaces, as well as the theatricalization of the domestic consumption of feature films.[103]

These conditions of digitization upset static media ontologies. Treating even stalwart art forms like cinema as a fixed category is highly suspect given that films can be accessed digitally in a multitude of contexts through many different delivery systems, with sprawling narratives criss-crossing all of these. Some theorists, including Marsha Kinder, Henry Jenkins and Atkinson have adopted the term 'transmedia' to describe instances of 'integrating multiple texts to create a narrative so large that it cannot be contained within a single medium'.[104] Atkinson goes further, coining post-transmedia to describe the current, 'post-platform-specific and platform-agnostic age',[105] in which the boundaries between media forms are profoundly blurred. Event cinema – as a hybridized, networked and theatrical event – is emblematic of some of these new media trends. However, as a social activity, it is not especially 'new'. It is very much like going to the movies as per normal, and indeed adapts rituals and etiquette from even older media, like television and theatre. It also does not show much evidence of the new media effect suggested by cultural theorist Norman Taylor (and others) of levelling boundaries between 'high' and 'low' culture.[106] As explained, current simulcast audiences are generally mature, middle-class and well-versed in staged opera. If anything, it is a bit regressive in this regard. Moreover, live cinema is not a new idea: there were unrealized attempts to deliver electronic images to cinemas as early as the 1920s.[107] In sum, opera cinema straddles the boundary of old and new: digitally expanding access to a centuries-old medium and transferring its traditional exhibition practices to a novel context.

One new media trope that opera cinema clearly exemplifies is hybridity. In the 1980s, media theorist Ithiel de Sola Pool described the tendency of media to combine, cross-pollinate and develop greater complexity over time as 'convergence'.[108] As Henry Jenkins later explained, this process also applies to media audiences. He defines convergence as 'the flow of content across multiple media platforms, the cooperation between multiple media industries, and the migratory behaviour of media audiences who will go almost anywhere in search of the kinds of entertainment experiences they want'.[109] Jenkins contends that media industries have responded to increasingly active, aware and participatory audiences by offering their content in as many forms and through as many technologies as possible. He explains that the demands of the modern consumer are themselves facilitated by digital technologies: 'digitisation set the conditions for convergence; corporate conglomerates created its imperative'.[110] On a separate but important point, Jenkins rejects a 'survival of the fittest' trajectory in media history, arguing that media rarely die out in the face of competing technologies and experiences, but find new applications:

> A medium's content may shift (as occurred when television displaced radio as a storytelling medium, freeing radio to become the primary showcase for rock and roll), its audience may change (as occurs when comics moved from a mainstream medium in the 1950s to a niche medium today), and its social status may rise or fall (as occurs when theatre moves from a popular form to an elite one), but once a medium establishes itself as satisfying some core human demand, it continues to function within the larger system of communication options … Printed words did not kill spoken words. Cinema did not kill theatre. Television did not kill radio. Each old medium was forced to coexist within the emerging media.[111]

There are limitations to the convergence model. The implication that media forms are gravitating towards a hypothetical singularity (a multipurpose 'black box'), does not accord with reality. If anything, between smartphones, tablet devices, VR headsets and smartwatches, we are witnessing a shift towards subdivision rather than recombination. Not to mention the irksome tendency of competing streaming platforms (Netflix, Amazon Prime, Disney+, etc.) to leverage exclusive content in their permanent scramble for market dominance, forcing audiences to hold multiple subscriptions to access all their favourite movies and shows. Nevertheless, convergence aptly describes the ways in which cultural experiences constantly transform and remediate one another. Despite concerns from some quarters, it seems unlikely that opera cinema will kill the auditorium experience; instead, the two phenomena will be forced to coexist and interact. And especially at the time of writing, with lockdowns and social distancing an ever-present spectre, this mutual co-dependence is actually a matter of survival.

At this point, I think it would be useful to review some terminology. There will necessarily have to be some flexibility and permeability here, and I do not presume to necessarily establish agreed nomenclature for other researchers. But not all these concepts have been consistently defined elsewhere (though I do borrow a few useful terms), and for the sake of comprehension we must start somewhere! So: we have *opera cinema* (live opera transmitted to movie houses), *event cinema* (any kind of live content transmitted to cinemas) and *live cinema* (a 'normal' film screening with some sort of 'live' theatrical embellishment). More generally, I use the term *medium* and *art form* interchangeably to mean an established form of aesthetic experience, with well-defined technical characteristics and reception practices (literature, cinema, music, etc.) While I will not dwell on the complex subject of *genre*,[112] I basically regard this as a category, within a medium, defined by common formal and aesthetic conventions (e.g. *opera buffa* is a genre of the medium of opera). Not everything can be an art form, or the term loses all meaning. There are also *remediations*, when one medium is presented in another form, like a photograph of a painting, or a recording of an opera. There are also *cultural experiences* or *cultural phenomena*, which are less-institutionalized aesthetic experiences and events that remediate other art forms, but currently lack a defined formal identity, audience recognition and well-established reception practices. I think opera cinema is one of these. I believe that audience recognition is necessary to define an art form as such. At the point when audiences generally no longer perceive opera cinema as a way of seeing opera, but as something in its own right, then it will have acquired this status.

History and liveness

In researching the history of simulcasting (critical to elaborating its ontology), I stake my position as a Marxist, and therefore a historical materialist. This methodology proposes that society is fundamentally determined and driven forward by the development of the productive forces, the motor force which is struggle between social classes. To be clear, I take an orthodox view of the Marxist theory and methodology. It is not the purpose of this book to weigh the merits of the many reinterpretations of Marxism offered by the various post- and neo-Marxists that have occupied twentieth-century academia. Suffice it to say, I haven't much that is positive to say about any of these.

There is an unfortunate tendency to caricature Marxist historical materialism as economic determinism: suggesting that all the complexity of social relations and human behaviour can be explained by looking at economics alone, disregarding factors like culture, tradition, social phenomena and so on. This was stridently denied by both Marx and Engels during their lifetimes. As the latter wrote in a testy letter to Joseph Bloch: 'According to the materialist conception of history, the ultimate determining element in history is the production and reproduction of life ... if somebody twists this into saying that the economic element is the only determining one, he transforms that proposition into a meaningless, abstract and senseless phrase.'[113] Moreover, nowhere do Marx or Engels suggest that economic forces determine society or human relations at a granular level: as if we were automata carrying out our social roles unthinkingly. Rather, men and women make their own histories according to their own will, but economic imperatives set in motion and motivate the general processes and overarching trends in history and class society. People act freely, but within limits set by the societies into which they are born.

Similarly, the development of art and culture involves many complex factors but is fundamentally determined (and limited) by the development of the productive forces. It is no accident that opera – the apotheosis of the European classical music tradition – emerged at the height of the Renaissance in the wealthy Italian city states. Nor that it began to struggle under brute market logic of capitalism, where this incredibly lavish and expensive art form suddenly lacked the patronage of princes and aristocrats that had formerly kept it afloat. Nevertheless, under capitalism, opera retained its elitist reputation, reflecting its origins as the pastime of nobility – despite the bourgeois-dominated modern auditoria.[114] What capitalism currently portends for opera, and indeed all the arts, in its state of total chaos and degeneration,[115] is frankly frightful to contemplate. The mass sackings and threatened collapse of thousands of theatres, galleries and museums in Britain inspire little confidence in the future.

Looking at history, we can see how social and economic forces motivated the development of opera cinema. Its emergence in the last few decades was only made possible by digital technologies developed relatively recently – earlier attempts at live cinema proved unworkable due to the primitive technologies involved.[116] But at the same time, screen opera's move away from experimental studio productions to formally conservative live transmissions correlated with the period of economic stagnation starting in the 1970s. What resulted in the 1980s was a shift away from state-funded cultural production and dissemination to an ethos of privatization and individual consumer-choice under the Margaret Thatcher and Ronald Reagan governments in the UK and United States. These developments resulted in a general downturn in the creative development of stage opera, which became increasingly reliant on old repertoire; and whose audiences started to rapidly age and decline. All these factors meant opera was slow to recruit new and more diverse audiences to refresh its ranks. This all left an indelible mark on opera cinema as we know it today: they inform the kind of work that tends to be broadcast, the function of these broadcasts and whom they cater towards. This point, about how economic trends express themselves at the level of cultural production, will be elaborated on later in the book.

Before introducing my research, I will end this section with the aspect of opera cinema that has received perhaps the greatest scrutiny from both academic and commercial researchers: liveness. Interestingly, some research suggests that liveness is not a very significant aspect of the opera cinema experience for audiences. According to a study conducted by John Holmes (on behalf of the English Touring Opera), just 17 per cent of opera cinema attendees surveyed regarded liveness as 'very important', while 33 per cent thought it was 'somewhat important'.[117] It is worth pointing out that the ETO has had a negative view of opera cinema historically, which might have informed these results. Also, there is also evidence to the contrary. For example, non-live forms of opera have existed in cinemas for years but have never been as successful as simulcasting. Furthermore, the Royal Opera House screens pre-recorded 'encore' performances in the cinema but these are far less popular than simulcasts. This suggests that, despite what Holmes's respondents claimed, the liveness of opera cinema is a central aspect of its appeal. The discrepancy might be down to the fact that liveness is more complex than it first appears.

Certainly, liveness has been a subject of interest for academics from many different fields. Understandably, it is a prevailing concern for theorists of theatre, often serving as a defining ontological feature of the art form. When Artaud wrote his manifesto *The Theatre and Its Double* in 1937, he delved into the essence of theatre by making the physical, material space of performance a central tenet of the medium.[118] Importantly, Artaud regarded cinema as theatre's natural enemy, arguing the former's 'violent gratification' he felt appealed to the worst instincts of the masses and drew their custom away from theatres.[119] This view of competition between 'live' theatre and 'mediated' art reoccurs across the whole history of media studies, and has rarely been especially productive.

Two interweaving traditions have shaped this debate, one operating mostly in continental Europe and the other in Britain and America. Theatre historian Patrice Pavis charts the beginning of first tradition of dramaturgical analysis back to Denis Diderot and Gotthold Lessing. These eighteenth-century, radical philosophers provided 'remarkable descriptions of acting and stage effects' that had a profound influence, centuries later, on the writings of dramatist, activist and philosopher, Berthold Brecht.[120] Like Artaud, Brecht regarded liveness as a central feature of theatre's ontology, as evidenced by his 1948 description of theatre as 'live representations of reported or invented happenings between human beings and doing so with a view to entertainment'.[121] This basically became the common sense definition of theatre to this day.

These early ideas were developed in the 1960s, particularly in France, where the field of dramaturgical analysis was profoundly influenced by the linguistic-semiotic philosophies of Roland Barthes and Bernard Dort, with structuralism later establishing itself as the dominant paradigm in the 1970s.[122] The structuralists, originating from linguistics, reduced everything to language: from art, to politics and to the development of the human psyche. Therefore, they argued that theatre should be treated as an autonomous language, distinct from other related media like literature by dint of its particular characteristics of communication.[123] This reductive and lopsided perspective was critiqued in the 1980s by proponents of post-structuralism and phenomenology, who swung hard in the other direction, to the point of solipsism. Forgetting that theatre is generally textual to some degree, these theorists argued for a 'return to the concrete, material realities of the stage, a de-sublimated return to the body of the performance'.[124] Rather than treating dramaturgy as an assemblage of linguistic signs, they conceived of performance as a material event that is felt more than read. This perspective made for a very insular, individualist view of theatre that sidelined not only texts, but the social factors that influence and prefigure theatre. These ideas also laid the basis for an uncompromising 'cult of liveness', entrenching a strict division between live theatre and mediated experiences like film and television, which tended to come with an unexamined snobbery towards 'mass' audiences. Under this rubric, anything that is any way recorded can never be a 'performance'.[125] Needless to say, philosophers from this tradition would likely take a dim view of opera cinema.

Meanwhile, a different tradition opened up in the Anglosphere: theatre studies. Historian Christopher Balme delineates three stages in the history of theatre studies in Britain and North America, beginning with its introduction to the Carnegie Institute of Technology in 1914. From the outset, the field had a vocational, performative focus, as many early theorists were also practitioners.[126] This phase was followed by an academic paradigm shift in the 1970s towards scholarly research, precipitating the rise of performance studies in the 1980s, led by New York academic Richard Schechner.[127] This field treated performance holistically, extending beyond theatre to the performance of identity, political discourse, ritual, ceremony and so forth. In Schechner's 2012 text, *Performance Studies: An Introduction*, the theatrical event is *one kind of performance* among many, characterized by explicit suspension of the course of everyday life, which necessitates an audience converging upon a specified location at a given time. By this yardstick, not only opera cinema but cinema in general could be construed as a form of theatre, which feels a bit too broad to be useful. Much like structuralism and phenomenology, performance and theatre studies overreached their remit. While all social intercourse might involve aspects of performance and theatre, it cannot be reduced to these without making the terms basically meaningless.

Meanwhile, in media studies, theoretical treatments of liveness and presence in culture often take a pessimistic view that media simulacra and spectacle erase or replace reality and live experience.[128] On the more historiographical side (considering the work of Andrew Crisell, Thomas Elsaesser and Stephanie Marriott), liveness is generally bound up with broadcasting.[129] Consequently, television and radio are widely assumed to be ontologically 'live' media, even though pre-recorded content is frequently transmitted through both.[130] Nevertheless, as historian Jeffrey Sconce points out, all broadcasts in the early history of television were live and television retains an 'aesthetic of liveness', based on certain conventions like direct address of the audience: '"Don't go away, we'll be right back," rings the perpetual refrain of network broadcasting as it attempts to position us in a series of interpersonally live situations.'[131] The aesthetic of liveness depends in this case on the assumption of a 'centre' from which live events are instantly communicated to the audience. In the book *Media Events*, social theorists Daniel Dayan and Elihu Katz explain how television broadcasting constructs this conceptual centre, through their description of 'media events', which are instances when broadcast media suspend 'the normal flow of broadcasting and our lives'[132] and win the attention of extremely large audiences.[133] The coronation of Elizabeth II in 1953, the Olympics and instances of dramatic human tragedy like 9/11 qualify for this designation. The 'power' of these events, Dayan and Katz contend, is their capacity both to 'insert messages into social networks' while simultaneously creating those networks, turning all eyes towards the centre.[134] Because, in the last century, events like these have tended to be primarily communicated through TV, audiences are conditioned to recognize the aesthetic of liveness as *televisual*, regardless of the actual delivery system. I have found that, in the case of opera cinema, the direct address of the celebrity host, the countdown graphic before curtain-up and the capacity of the satellite to fail, resulting in the promise 'we'll be right back', are indeed perceived as televisual. They prime audiences for engagement with a live performance emanating from the 'centre' – Covent Garden or the Lincoln Centre, for example.

By contrast, Nick Couldry argues that liveness is not a defining feature of television, radio or any other media form but a 'fundamental category (in Émile Durkheim's sense) that contributes to underlying conceptions of how media are involved in social organisation through their provision of privileged access to central social "realities"'.[135] According to Durkheim's theories of ritual practices, a category is an organizing social concept that motivates human behaviour.[136] However, Couldry argues that liveness is not a 'natural category' but a 'constructed term' that rests, not on a technological fact, but on the following chain of ideas:

1. We gain access through liveness to something of broader, 'central', significance, which is worth accessing *now*.
2. Those who gain live access are 'not random, but a representative social group' – this is to say that potentially the entire public could access the live event.
3. The media (as opposed to some other social mechanism) is the privileged means for obtaining that access.[137]

Couldry slips into philosophical idealism here, apparently arguing that liveness exists entirely as *only* a social fact and has no concrete, material or technological basis. But liveness clearly has an objective basis in simultaneous broadcast technologies. Couldry's third point even illustrates a contradiction in his position, because if liveness necessitates media as a mechanism for obtaining access to live events, then it must depend on some kind of technological apparatus or delivery system. However, I think he is correct that liveness also constitutes a social dimension that extends beyond the technological. Furthermore, he correctly identifies that live media and broadcast events powerfully influence human behaviour across enormous populations, drawing our collective attention to sociocultural 'hubs', such as Downing Street on election night, and the Royal Opera House during a simulcast.

In the 1990s, a schism opened between theatre and media theorists concerning liveness. In her famous work on the ontology of performance, theatre scholar Peggy Phelan made a pugnacious and politicized case for liveness as the ontological essence of theatrical performance:

> Performance's only life is in the present. Performance cannot be saved, recorded, documented, or otherwise participate in the circulation of representations of representations. Once it does so, it becomes something other than performance. To the degree that performance attempts to enter the economy of reproduction it betrays and lessens the promise of its own ontology.[138]

She further contended that live performance 'clogs the smooth machinery of reproductive representation necessary to the circulation of capital'.[139] For Phelan, all attempts at technological remediation rob performance of its progressive power and authenticity. Phelan's argument has been especially influential on the study of liveness in opera. Indeed, *Opera Quarterly* editor Christopher Morris notes that Phelan's thesis stands 'like theatre's line in the sand, beyond which media technology holds no sway'.[140] He describes the prevailing view that, in screen opera the camera's selective representation of the mise en scène results in 'the loss of a variable and unknowable temporality of the live' to a 'congealed representation of the past', resulting in the 'lack of the presence of the performer'.[141] Morris suggests that the chief contention for opera studies is that live performance is spontaneous, risky and thus inherently more valuable than recording, which reduces opera performances to pristine but ultimately lifeless products. However, he argues that modern, 'live' opera is actually more prone to repetition than other forms of performance:

> Companies rely on the capacity of singers to fly from city to city to rehearse and perform, while the demand (and fees) for the services of the elite singers is boosted by this international demand. This has led to a degree of standardization, partly because in-demand singers (especially for difficult-to-cast parts) will typically perform the same role repeatedly in several venues ... Another constraint on spontaneity ... comes in the form of the contemporary culture of 'director's theatre' ... the choreography and gestural vocabulary introduced by one of today's celebrated directors may be open to negotiation during rehearsal, but it is rarely the singer's prerogative to improvise from performance to performance.[142]

Morris describes several aspects of live performance that theatre scholars tend to emphasize. These include the communal aspects of performance, the buzz of the co-present audience and their empathy with the materially present performers.[143] However, he points out that 'theatre is predicated on the separation between performer and audience' and collapsing this distance would short-circuit the very 'experience of fracture' that fuels the theatrical event.[144] The integrity of the narrative is usually dependent upon the fourth wall that separates the audience from the stage action. Therefore, live performance demands distance as much as it is on community and presence. Morris also argues that, with the advent of opera cinema and its 'audience of dispersed gatherings',[145] live opera is in a sense liberated from a fixed exhibition space. Morris argues the simulcast changes the live performance, but does not negate it because 'there are other ways of conceptualizing presence, and not all insist on a binary between the live and the mediated'.[146]

Meanwhile, in the influential text *Liveness: Performance in a Mediatised Culture*, theorist Phillip Auslander defines liveness strictly in opposition to mediation. Indeed, he points out that recording technologies in a sense brought liveness into being, because before recording was possible, nothing was live and everything was.[147] He dismisses Phelan's romanticized view of the inherent progressivism of live performance as ahistorical, disputing the notion that 'any cultural discourse can actually stand outside the ideologies of capital and reproduction that define a mediatized culture or should be expected to do so'.[148] The thrust of his argument is that the relationship between live and mediatized performance is one of competition 'at the level of cultural economy'.[149] This opposition does not derive from the 'intrinsic characteristics of live and mediatized forms' but rather is determined by 'cultural and historical contingencies'.[150] Auslander argues that live and mediatized performance compete on a similar field, both requiring the attention (and money) of the same pool of consumers. Recorded and electronically reproduced cultural forms better suit the requirements of a globalized capitalist economy than co-present live performance. As a result, in this battle for supremacy, liveness is losing to mediation.[151] In his original thesis, published in the 1990s, Auslander posited television as the key battleground between live and mediated performance, a role he later attributed to digital media.[152]

Despite justifiably critiquing Phelan's ahistoricism, Auslander's pessimism is still not based on any concrete evidence. Notably, neither he nor Phelan actually engage with real audiences. Media scholar Matthew Reason suggests that this means Auslander 'ultimately seems uninterested in exploring what experiential distinctions might exist [between forms of live experience], even in the particular historical context in which he is writing'.[153] Additionally, as Barker points out, Auslander loses sight of the potential for enhancing (or at least altering) a sense of live participation through technological means.[154] In the case of opera cinema, the incorporation of cinematic visuals and editing creates a different and (for some) a more immersive form of engagement with the performance than traditional auditoria can provide. Furthermore, Auslander's view that mediated performance will eventually displace and devalue liveness seems farfetched. There is arguably a greater proliferation of mediatized experiences now than at any time in history, and perhaps even because of this, we see a surge of events that place their liveness front and centre as a unique selling point. Tickets for Secret Cinema's *Star Wars* events would not sell for £75 apiece if perceptions of liveness did not retain a degree of cultural cachet. Rather than being mortal enemies, it is perhaps truer to say that liveness and mediation dialectically condition one another – they bring one another into being.

My position on liveness draws heavily on research by Barker, who tested aspects of Auslander's thesis in a series of experiments, conducted in the 1990s in Aberystwyth, Wales. His research subjects viewed two adaptations of G. Ballard's novel *Crash*: a student play and David Cronenberg's 1996 film. Barker describes his subjects' perception of liveness as 'an unspoken "contract" between theatre and their audiences'.[155] The audience defined the terms of this contract through negative comparison with cinema, which was categorically defined as 'not live'.[156] However, these conditions are not fixed for all time – they are context specific. For instance, *Live to Your Local Cinema* discusses the form of liveness facilitated by opera cinema. This time, Barker's respondents expressed a variety of views on liveness, with some understanding it in a 'traditional way' (i.e. 'Nothing can replace being there in the house'), whereas others were content to dispense with the contractual condition of physical co-presence and embrace the experience as a new form of live opera.[157] Barker describes five aspects of liveness in opera cinema:

1. Immediacy: connected to the fact that the event is unfolding in real time and to the sense of being able to 'interact with performers or communicate responses to the event'.
2. Intimacy: a feeling of closeness to the performers and the action.
3. Buzz: awareness of other audience members as 'engaged, excited, moved, and sharing the pleasure of the performance'.
4. Expanding oneself: knowing that one might derive intellectual, cultural or spiritual improvement from the event.
5. Being (in) the audience: an element of self-awareness in knowing how to respond appropriately to a given performance type; etiquette, dress, etc.[158]

Most importantly, Barker's approach to liveness considers it in context, rather than as a fixed, abstract category. Audience researcher Matthew Reason further demonstrated the value of this approach by inviting students from the University of Edinburgh to watch a production of a new play, *Olga*, and then write down their main likes and dislikes over the course of a free-flowing discussion.[159] Reason's respondents tended to compare their experiences of theatre to other media, and articulated a sense of liveness in some events that are 'not strictly speaking or entirely live'.[160] For instance, liveness was associated with 'heightened social-spatial environments (cinema, public presentations and gatherings and so forth) or [events] with some degree of temporal determinacy (live broadcasts, premieres, newsflashes)'.[161] Meanwhile, Mike Weed found that football fans will travel long distances simply to watch a match in the host city on television in a local pub or bar, which made the game feel experientially 'more live/present'.[162] All these examples demonstrate how contextual and ritual factors can influence audiences' negotiation of liveness. Therefore, audience experience of liveness must be factored into our understanding of opera cinema.

Social science

I will briefly engage with key debates in the social sciences, couching this book within the field of audience and reception studies. My research into audience experience aims to capture a snapshot of opera cinema as an emergent, complex phenomenon. I owe much to Martin Barker's audience research methodologies in taking this grounded approach, who was in turn informed by the likes of Barney Glaser and Anselm Strauss.[163] I am particularly influenced by Barker's concept of audience viewing strategies, which describe the relationship between individual behaviours and social conventions around media engagement.

Complexity theory is a scientific framework that helped draw together the various threads of thought in my audience research, and became an important influence on my project design. Some influential philosophers of science, notably Karl Popper, argue that social science is a fruitless endeavour, due to its untestable and unfalsifiable claims.[164] However, I share Goldmann's view that: 'Unlike the facts discovered by physics and chemistry, facts concerning man cannot be found out impersonally, from the outside, and by methods which exclude value judgements and practical considerations.'[165] However, given the complexity of the social world, I concur with complexity theorists David Byrne and Gillian Callaghan that the future of all useful social science is 'at the very least interdisciplinary and probably post-disciplinary'.[166] The authors state that a logic of 'dialectical synthesis' underpins the interdisciplinarity of complexity: a process of 'drawing together ideas and accounts of reality from a range of sources and setting them against each other in order to derive a new and improved understanding'.[167]

Complexity asserts that the material world consists of intricate, dynamic and interrelated systems and must be understood as such - it calls for more than just methodological triangulation. All human systems (including cultural formations, media industries and audiences) are complex and non-linear: in that the interaction of elements within them can result in dramatic and unexpected developments, transitions and pattern formations - unlike a simple, linear system where causal relationships produce predictable outcomes. The influence of Marxist dialectics over scientific complexity is clear. Engels's explanation in *Anti-Dühring: Herr Eugen Dühring's Revolution in Science* describes the material world as an 'endless entanglement of relations and reactions in which nothing remains what, where and as it was, but everything moves, changes, comes into being and passes away'.[168] The classical Greek philosopher Heraclitus arrived at a primitive version of the same conclusion some 4,000 years prior, stating: 'everything is and is not'.[169] Complexity and dialectics therefore strive to make sense of an intricate social world in a state of perpetual change and motion. Contrasting the positivistic and dialectical approach to culture, Goldman concludes that 'the two methods consider the actual texts to be both the starting-point and the conclusion of their researches, but whereas one method offers the opportunity of understanding the more or less coherent meaning of these texts, the other does not'.[170]

What does any of this have to do with opera cinema? First of all, the development of media forms, their ritualistic practices and their audiences' behaviours are not random, but evolve as a result of what Gregoire Nicols describes as 'deterministic chaos', wherein the complex interaction of elements progresses towards increasing complexity.[171] This process sees incremental change that can appear random or chaotic (*morphosis*) eventually culminate in radical, rapid, transformation (*metamorphosis*) that nonetheless does not terminate the existence of the underlying system[172] – or in dialectical materialist parlance, the transition from quantity into quality. Change builds upon the existing base system rather than completely supplanting it, resulting in the return of comparable historical phenomena at higher planes of development. In Hegelian dialectics, this is called a negation of the negation.[173] Such a process can be seen in the relationship between primitive theatre television technologies from the 1940s and 1950s and modern, digital event cinema, for example. The basic idea was the same, but it re-emerged in a more developed form at a later stage. As I will explain in Chapter 2, grasping the ontology of any medium necessitates an understanding of its evolutionary lineage, which in turn permits us to explain when and why it diverged from its antecedents and developed its particular characteristics. And similarly, audience viewing strategies and behavioural codes develop over time in tandem with the evolution of media technologies, and are equally subject to the complex, material forces of political economy.

Secondly, complexity urges us not to consider our object of research in isolation, but as part of a larger whole. My subjects did not experience opera for the first time in a vacuum, but as part of a complex social world, with pre-existing expectations about what opera (and cinema) are and how they should be engaged with. These other factors impacted their encounters with opera cinema, and I have tried to develop my methodology in such a way to take account of this non-linear interplay between opera cinema and wider society.

My research seeks to overcome what Kim Schrøder, Kristen Drotner, Stephen Kline and Catherine Murray describe as the qualitative/quantitative division and disciplinary siloing in the social sciences. The authors identify a 'knee-jerk' mutual distrust between fields, fostered by 'widespread ignorance [about] the methodological Other'.[174] The adherents to each paradigm speak from opposing epistemological and political foundations, 'on the one hand, a positivist, administrative and functionalist conceptualisation of knowledge and science, and a phenomenological, hermeneutic and critical conceptualisation on the other'.[175] Klaus Jensen and Karl Rosengren characterize this binary as a humanistic type versus a social science type.[176] Quantitative approaches predominate in most European media and communication research traditions, with the notable exception of Britain and the Netherlands, wherein the two paradigms have historically been of roughly equal strength. In North American communication research, quantitative research was the dominant paradigm up until the 1990s, after which there was something of a qualitative turn. Denmark stands alone in that its dominant humanistic and cultural studies tradition eclipses an almost non-existent quantitative paradigm.[177]

Critics of the positivist school contend that it carries an individualistic bias and treats subjects as rationally motivated individuals, driven by personal, intellectual or psychological needs rather than responding to socially differentiated needs created by social formations. Goldman lays out the limits of this approach in the following terms:

> The main error of most psychological theories has been to concentrate too frequently on the individual as absolute and sole reality, and to study other men only in so far as they play the part of objects in the individual's ideas and activities ... this implicit concept of man primarily as an isolated individual, which dominates modern non-dialectical philosophy and psychology, is quite simply wrong. The simplest empirical observation is enough to reveal its inaccuracy. Almost no human actions are performed by isolated individuals for the subject performing the action is a group, a 'We', and not an 'I' ... this is the communal relationship which I shall call the 'We', the expression which an action assumes when it is exercised on an object by a group of men acting in common. Naturally, in modern society every individual is engaged in a number of activities of this type. He takes part in different activities in different groups, with the result that each activity has a greater or lesser influence on his consciousness and behaviour.[178]

Also, individual experience is rather difficult to quantify. As James Lull states in response to a study of young people's gratification obtained from music concerts, there is 'simply no way to represent numerically the essence of what thousands of young people had experienced during the concert or what the cultural meaning of music is to them generally'.[179] By contrast, humanist research tends to be more self-reflexive, acknowledging the presence and intrusion of the researcher as an inevitable (even desirable) feature of investigating the personal and subjective nature of media use. Then again, it has been criticized for its anecdotal nature, boiling down data to a series of 'interesting stories', which might be individually rich, but contribute little to our overall understanding.[180]

In sum, the quantitative school boasts measurement precision and generalizability, whereas qualitative research is seen as strong on depth and validity. The main thing in my view is not about the general efficacy of this or that methodology, but about having the right tools for the job. Larger data sets are useful for deriving general insights and predictions about large groups of people, but it is very difficult to reduce a more subjective experience in ways that would make sense on a questionnaire issued to thousands of respondents. Of course, there are many instances where a combined approach can be informative, such as by elucidating larger, shallower collections of data with deep impressions from a select group of subjects. I have tried to do this to some extent by grounding my findings alongside the bigger research projects cited above, and by examining the history of opera cinema.

But where exactly does my research sit in the various traditions of audience research? In *Rethinking the Media Audience*, Pertti Alasuutari discusses the history of reception studies and audience research in terms of three loose 'generations'.[181] The influential Frankfurt School (founded in the Weimar Republic in the interwar period), along with the uses and gratifications theory (UGT) in the 1940s collectively mark a sort of year zero. The former is considered seminal, but its view of audiences as passively steered by mass media messaging, readily brainwashed by capitalist commercialism and the propaganda, has a very particular historical context. It reflects the prejudices of disgruntled Marxist (and ex-Marxist) academics from the 1920s–30s, with ebbing faith in the revolutionary destiny of the working class, frustrated with the authoritarian turn of the Soviet Union, alarmed at the rise of fascism in Europe, and wary of the influence of media conditioning over impressionable audiences. Antonio Gramsci's theory of 'cultural hegemony', in which the ruling economic class enforces its rule through control of media messaging, further developed this idea of cultural conditioning from above.[182] UGT flipped these models on their head, instead viewing audiences as active agents in seeking out media to fulfil specific needs: whether to inform or entertain. In so doing, the emphasis shifted to the individual, and the role of culture, society and politics were downplayed.[183] In my view, both these approaches are rather mechanical, one-way schema for understanding how audiences affect and are affected by culture.

The first generation of reception studies to build on these schools was dominated by Stuart Hall's influential 'encoding–decoding' model (developed in the 1970s), which posits that ideological messages (particularly television programming) are encoded into media artefacts at the point of production and decoded by audiences at the point of reception.[184] In this way, Hall tried to make both social influences and individual agency part of the reception equation. The 'second generation' constituted an ethnographic turn in audience research in the 1980s, exemplified by David Morley's groundbreaking *Nationwide* project and subsequent research into family television viewing. Morley's research empirically interrogated the extent to which audiences of differing socio-economic and ethnic backgrounds accorded with, negotiated or rejected the messages of the popular British news programme, *Nationwide*.[185] This highly influential study resulted in a spate of ethnographic work on media audiences (particularly centred around romantic serials) by figures such as Ien Ang, Dorothy Hobson, Daniel Dayan and Elihu Katz.[186] This trend of audience reception studies is characterised by researchers obtaining qualitative impressions from their subjects by embedding themselves in their 'interpretive communities.'[187]

Finally, a third, post-structuralist generation emerged out of a corpus of work that criticized the ethnographic paradigm, led by such figures as Martin Allor and Lawrence Grossberg.[188] These writers contended that 'the audience' is, fundamentally, a 'discursive construct produced by a particular analytic gaze' rather than a discrete entity or group of entities. Researchers in this movement shifted their emphasis from the reception strategies of particular audiences towards an investigation of how media messages and their audiences fit within a larger media culture. Alasuutari characterizes the third generation in audience research and reception studies with the following traits:

1. An emphasis on a 'media culture' and its role within everyday life.
2. A resumed interest in media texts as an element in everyday life, rather than a discrete object of interest to be examined in isolation.
3. A degree of reflexivity in research that takes account of audiences' perception of themselves as audiences engaged in the process of reception.[189]

The grounding of media use in everyday practices was an important development in the field of audience research. However, much like Couldry's view of liveness as a discursive concept, I take issue with presenting the audience as merely as a function of language. The study of media history demonstrates that audience formations long preceded the development of mass marketing and demographic segmentation, for example.

My own research design is largely inspired by Martin Barker's Film, Television and Media Research Group at Aberystwyth University. The 'Aberystwyth school' arguably marks a fourth (albeit short-lived) generation in reception studies. At the 2003 Versailles conference on the future of audience research, Barker illustrated the ethos of this school in a biting polemic that identified three limiting tendencies in field.[190] Firstly, he criticized the singularizing of audience as an abstract entity with established characteristics, based on no (or little) empirical evidence.[191] Secondly, he questioned the 'textual-analytic tendency' to regard audience research as a threat to the intellectual purity of pure theory, and noted the lack of cooperative development between theorists and empirical researchers.[192] Finally, he excoriated British Cultural Studies' slavish attachment to Hall's encoding–decoding model.[193] Barker contends audience researchers after Hall 'started from scratch', abandoning the Marx-inspired, cultural hegemonic model of the Frankfurt School without actually resolving any of its limitations - such as its aforementioned simplistic model of top-down, passive dissemination of false consciousness by capitalist state institutions.[194]

Furthermore, at Versailles, Barker argued that the adoption of the Hall model occurred with no 'elaborated conceptual framework of what is meant by "an audience"' and no 'settled – and therefore checkable – methodologies' for interrogating it.[195] Subsequently, the field has been content with vague concepts such as the active/passive audience, while methodological sophistication has not developed to a sufficient level of rigor to purposefully test the validity of such concepts.[196] He stressed that both individuals and audience communities (fandoms, aficionados, online gamers, etc.) engage with texts according to particular tastes and strategies, but this engagement is not isolated from a wider world. Instead, these interpretive communities exist in dialectical relation to society and one another. This can be demonstrated in the way that audiences import public media practices (e.g. watching films in silent darkness) into the domestic sphere. Barker concluded his polemical lecture by recommending that audience researchers strive to rigorously explore how interpretive communities are actively developed, both internally and in response to external influences.[197] He described the resultant behavioural patterns emerging from individuals embedded in interpretive communities as 'viewing strategies'.[198] Barker's conception of viewing strategies expresses the dialectical synthesis between the social world and individual behaviours: resulting in patterns of engagement that are neither directly determined nor wholly individuated. My research aims to describe a viewing strategy for opera cinema, which is only lately beginning to take shape.

Several audience research projects have served as inspiration for my own project design - particularly those with an emphasis on audience experience, and that employ mixed-methodological designs. I was especially influenced by Florin Vladica's 2013 research on opera cinema audiences. Identifying opera cinema with the public service tradition of television and radio relays, Vladica concedes that the experience of a live broadcast is clearly 'different' and 'possibly inferior' to that of the live stage performance.[199] He also groups opera cinema along with ancillary media like DVD recordings and that are still regarded as 'complementary products for those whose tastes for opera have already been formed, rather than as products that recruit new consumers to the art form'.[200] As will become apparent, my own research arrives at comparable conclusions. Vladica's chief methodological tool is Q Methodology, through which he segments his sample of *Live from the Met* attendees into the following four 'viewpoints':

- Avant-garde: audience members who considered opera cinema to be a legitimate cultural form; an art form in its own right.
- Classical: attendees for whom an opera performance on a cinema screen provided an immersive experience that was sufficiently moving and lifelike to induce behaviour that would have been appropriate in a live theatre, such as applause.
- Worthwhile: these audience members felt that the quality of the experience was *at least* equal to the time and money required to consume it, considering simulcasting to be an affordable and convenient means of participating in live opera.
- Grateful: this last factor attended live streams in part to support a perceived 'good cause', regarding the digitally expanded operatic

platform as a compelling vehicle for 'spreading opera to the masses'.[201]

These findings suggested to me that existing opera cinema audiences generally regard simulcasting as a worthy cultural experience, but that the majority probably do not consider the phenomenon to be a discrete medium. Rather, they see it as a viable way to engage with opera without having to attend a stage performance. Vladica's research became the blueprint for my own methodological design, but I sought to determine whether similar viewpoints would emerge from a sample of novice audiences. I questioned whether the preponderant attitude towards opera cinema as an ancillary experience was a consequence of Vladica's (presumably) opera-literate sample. Moreover, Vladica's methodology seemed appropriate to inductive research, in that it generated compelling and detailed results with a small data set. My own work applies Vladica's methodology to novice respondents, whom I hoped would provide a novel perspective on opera cinema.

I was also informed by John Tulloch's *Shakespeare and Chekhov in Production and Reception: Theatrical Events and Their Audiences*. Tulloch begins from Susan Bennett's premise that, before any encounter between the audience and a theatrical work can take place, audience engagement is already directed by 'the material conditions of production and the positioning of the world on stage vis-à-vis its extratheatrical referents'.[202] This encompasses such factors as the audience's past experiences, the geographical positioning of the theatre and its architectural characteristics and the co-presence of other spectators. Acknowledging this, Tulloch notes that any 'flat' methodology, such as quantitative theatre audience surveys, will be 'likely to miss important aspects of the "live" relationship of negotiation between occasion and place'.[203] Consequently, Tulloch combines qualitative interview data and quantitative data from questionnaires to analyse audience experience as a process, wherein multiple horizons of expectations are renegotiated 'before, during, and after the theatrical performance'.[204] This approach influenced my analysis of the way my subjects structured their engagement with opera cinema (a novel experience) based on their past experiences, the material parameters of the cinema and the external pressures of opera's elite reputation.

Finally, Claudio E. Benzecry's eighteen-month ethnographic enquiry into the behaviour of opera fans in Buenos Aires demonstrates the devotional practices of this community.[205] He demonstrates how 'expert fans' facilitate awareness of 'appropriate engagement' for newcomers to the form.[206] Benzecry explains how new opera fans are coercively introduced to the rules of operatic engagement, with experienced attendees conspicuously hissing and applauding at appropriate moments – some going so far as to police the auditorium by hushing inappropriate exaltations.[207] Despite the different national cultural context, several of my respondents (particularly younger individuals) were subject to similar involuntary education. The intense devotion of experienced operagoers that Benzecry depicts proved useful in understanding the simultaneous feelings of awe and discomfort experienced by my subjects – especially those in the first round of data collection, who attended a performance at Covent Garden. Moreover, Benzecry's study framed the unusual level of influence opera fans have exerted over the formal strategies of remediated opera – roundly rejecting 'excessive' reinterpretation of the sacred art form.[208]

This is opera cinema

Hopefully, in sketching the constellations of thought around opera cinema, I have already demonstrated that we cannot simply write it off as merely another way to see opera – even if some audiences do. The rest of the book will introduce my own research, using historical analysis and the wisdom of opera virgins to elucidate the various aspects of opera cinema touched on thus far. More than simply illuminating a fascinating and evolving media phenomenon, I hope that this book – in some small way – makes a case for understanding all media in social, technological and experiential terms. I consider this to be especially pertinent in an era where media are simultaneously more intrinsic to our lives than ever before, and yet somehow harder to grasp.

Chapter 2 constitutes a historical account of opera cinema, a phenomenon that represents the culmination of nearly a century of evolution, stretching right back to the 1910s, when inventor Lee de Forest stuck radio a transmitter on the roof of the Metropolitan Opera House in New York and beamed a Caruso performance to the surrounding neighbourhood. Starting from here, the chapter investigates electronic theatre television from the 1930s to the 1950s; television opera productions in the post-war period and televised relays from the 1980s, which established the benchmark for modern simulcasts. It also explains how cinema digitization gave the impetus to the development event cinema, and how this phenomenon eventually turned into a multi-billion-dollar arm of the cinema industry. Additionally, the chapter explores the political dimensions of opera cinema, which is inherently limited by the need to serve as an advertisement for the stage – presenting an idealized simulation of 'a night at the opera', rather than striving to creatively reinterpret the source material.

Chapter 3 will investigate opera cinema's distinguishing formal characteristics, which advance it beyond the status of a mere transmission or remediation to a unique cultural experience. I propose four major features of opera cinema: double-direction, liveness, multimediality and collective participation. I provide evidence that opera cinema is deliberately constructed and sold as the next-best-thing to the stage, and this subordinate status is embedded in its artistic strategies. However, unique social and ritualistic aspects of opera cinema attendance are beginning to take shape. Just as event cinema hybridizes formal elements from a range of media, its audiences also exhibit hybrid viewing practices – falling somewhere between what you would expect at the opera house and the cinema. Such novel patterns of behaviour give a sense of an embryonic, hybrid medium struggling to eventually emerge out of opera cinema.

Chapter 4 will report on my audience research project. A major problem with existing audience research on opera cinema is that it focuses on the veteran attendees who make up the bulk of the current audience. These experienced opera fans tend to frame their impressions of opera cinema through comparison with the stage, rather than seeing it as something unique. I set out to address this by engaging with novice subjects ('opera virgins'), who are relatively free of such biases and expectations. My field work started in 2015, with twenty subjects invited to watch *The Rise and Fall of the City of Mahagonny* in both the Covent Garden auditorium and a cinema of their choosing. In 2016, I invited several more groups of subjects to watch simulcasts of *Boris Godunov*, *Lucia di Lammermoor* and *Werther* in two separate locations and two categories of cinema: a multiplex and an independent or art house venue. The chapter uses my subjects' insights to inform my ontological analysis of opera cinema. Conversely, it also discusses my subjects' attitudes towards the experience: how their preconceptions of opera were challenged, changed or confirmed during the project.

The book concludes by summarizing my main findings and theoretical insights, as well as suggesting new questions and directions for further research. It posits that a medium's ontology must be addressed through a sociological and historical lens – determining where it fits into a larger cultural landscape. This book has admittedly only begun to scratch the surface of opera cinema's theoretical significance. Future research could (for example) investigate the different types of experience it facilitates in various national contexts, where different time zones, attitudes towards opera and exhibition conventions impose unique conditions on simulcast audiences. Further comparison with other forms of event cinema (such as spoken-word theatre) could also be very informative. I sincerely hope that other researchers will train a spotlight on opera cinema, to see whether it develops into the medium that I believe it deserves to be.

Notes

1   Martin Barker, *Live to Your Local Cinema: The Remarkable Rise of Livecasting* (Basingstoke: Palgrave Macmillan, 2013).
2   Paul Heyer, 'Live from the Met: Digital Broadcast Cinema, Medium Theory, and Opera for the Masses', *Canadian Journal of Communication* 33 (2008): 592.

3 Bernadette Cochrane and Frances Bonner, 'Screening from the Met, the NT, or the House: What Changes with the Live Relay', *Adaptation* 7.2 (2014): 122.
4 'Who We Are', *Event Cinema Association*, accessed 6 June 2017, https://www.eventcinemaassociation.org/who-we-are.html.
5 Sarah Atkinson, *Beyond the Screen: Emerging Cinema and Engaging Audiences* (London: Bloomsbury, 2014), 228.
6 'Exploring the Market for Live to Digital Arts', *MTM*, March 2015, 10.
7 James Steichen, 'The Metropolitan Opera Goes Public: Peter Gelb and the Institutional Dramaturgy of the Met: Live in HD', *Music and the Moving Image* 2.2 (2009): 453.
8 Ibid., 457.
9 Alexandra Coghlan, 'Why Arias in the Multiplex Fall Flat', *Independent*, last modified 4 December 2012, accessed 13 June 2021, http://www.independent.co.uk/arts-entertainment/classical/features/why-arias-in-the-multiplex-fall-flat-8376326.html.
10 Ibid.
11 Brent Karpf Reidy, Becky Shutt, Deborah Abramson, Antoni Durski and Laura Castle, 'From Live-to-Digital', *AEA Consulting for Arts Council England and Society of London Theatre* (October 2016): 84; Fiona Tuck, 'Understanding the Impact of Event Cinema: An Evidence Review', *Arts Council England and British Film Institute* (January 2016).
12 Ibid.
13 'Opera Cinema: A New Cultural Experience?', Symposium at King's College London, 16 June 2017.
14 Carly Abbate and Roger Parker, *A History of Opera: The Last Four Hundred Years* (London: Penguin Group, 2012), 202.
15 Herbert Lindenberger, *Opera: The Extravagant Art* (London: Cornell University Press, 1984), 234.
16 Marcia J. Citron, 'Operatic Style in Coppola's *Godfather* Trilogy', in *Opera on Screen* (New Haven, CT: Yale University Press, 2000), 41–2.
17 Sam Abel, *Opera in the Flesh* (Colorado: Westview Press, 1996), 165.
18 Steichen, 453.
19 Citron, 20.
20 Lesley Stern, 'The Tales of Hoffman: An Instance of Operality', in *In Between Opera and Cinema*, edited by Jeongwon Joe and Rose Theresa (New York: Routledge, 2002), 45–6.
21 Claudio E. Benzecry, *The Opera Fanatic: Ethnography of an Obsession* (Chicago: University of Chicago Press, 2011), 18.
22 Abbate and Parker, 8.
23 John Holmes, 'Opera in Cinemas – Audiences Outside London', *English Touring Opera*, 2014.
24 Barker, 34.

25 Christopher Morris, 'Digital Diva: Opera on Video', *Opera Quarterly* 26.1 (2010): 109–10.
26 Heyer, 602.
27 Joseph Attard, 'The Opera Virgins Project: Operatic Event Cinema as New Cultural Experience', in *Live Cinema Cultures, Economies, Aesthetics*, edited by Sarah Atkinson and Helen Kennedy (New York: Bloomsbury, 2017).
28 Steichen, 'HD Opera: A Love/Hate Story. Staging the Backstage at Carmen, Live in HD', *Opera Quarterly* 27.4 (2011): 25.
29 Ibid., 27.
30 Ibid.
31 Barker, 4–5.
32 Ibid., 2.
33 Ibid., 35.
34 Ibid., 36.
35 Ibid., 29.
36 Ibid.
37 Ibid., 11.
38 Ibid.
39 Ibid.
40 Ibid., 13–14.
41 Ibid., 21.
42 Ibid., 79.
43 'Royal Opera House Live Cinema Season 2017/18; Broadcast Live to the Memo', *Memo Arts Centre*, accessed 16 December 2017, https://www.memoartscentre.co.uk/royal-opera-house-live-cinema-season-201718-broadcast-live-to-the-memo/.
44 Sarah Cooper, 'Event Cinema on Growth Curve', *Screen Daily*, last updated 16 October 2013, accessed 16 December 2017, http://www.screendaily.com/news/event-cinema-on-growth-curve/5062554.article.
45 'Cinema Audience Distribution in the United Kingdom (UK) as of 2014, by Age and Gender', *Statistica*, accessed 1 September 2015, http://www.statista.com/statistics/296240/age-and-gender-of-the-cinema-audience-uk/.
46 Amanda Fallows, 'Royal Opera House Cinema Research', Royal Opera House research data, October 2014.
47 Ibid.
48 Ibid.
49 Jen Harvie, 'Funding, Philanthropy, Structural Inequality and Decline in England's Theatre Ecology', *Cultural Trends* 24.1 (2015): 56.
50 Arts Council of Great Britain, *ACGB Report 1949/50* (1950): 29.
51 Karpf Reidy et al., 35.

52 John Holmes, 'Opera in Cinemas – Audiences Outside London', *English Touring Opera*, 2014.
53 Karpf Reidy et al., 315.
54 Ibid., 315.
55 Ibid.
56 Hasan Bakhshi, Juan Mateos-Garcia and David Throsby, 'Beyond Live: Digital Innovation in the Performing Arts' (London: NESTA [National Endowment for Science, Technology and the Arts], research briefing, 2010), 2–7.
57 Matt Trueman, 'English National Opera Chief Attacks Live Cinema Broadcasts', *Guardian*, 10 May 2012, accessed 16 December 2017, https://www.theguardian.com/music/2012/may/10/eno-director-hits-live-broadcasts.
58 Karen Wise, 'Opera in Cinemas', report for ETO and Guildhall School of Music & Drama (London, 2013), 19.
59 Tom Service, 'Opera in Cinemas: Is It Creating New Audiences?', *Guardian*, 30 May 2014, accessed 16 December 2017, https://www.theguardian.com/music/tomserviceblog/2014/may/30/opera-in-cinemas-creating-new-audiences.
60 Andrew Clark, 'Royal Opera House Head Rejects "Democratising Art"', *Financial Times*, 31 March 2014, accessed 16 December 2017, accessed 12 May 2018, https://www.ft.com/content/8fc034fe-b8f2-11e3-98c5-00144feabdc0.
61 Fallows.
62 Wise.
63 Bakhshi, Mateos-Garcia and Throsby, 5–7.
64 Susan Bennett, *Theatre Audiences: A Theory of Production and Reception*, 2nd edn (London: Routledge, 1997), 89.
65 Richard Schechner, *Public Domain: Essays on the Theater* (Indianapolis, IN: Bobbs-Merrill, 1969), 34.
66 Bennett, 89.
67 Professor Jonathan Neelands, Eleonora Belfiore, Catriona Firth, Natalie Hart, Liese Perrin, Susan Brock, Dominic Holdaway and Jane Woddis, 'The 2015 Report by the Warwick Commission on the Future of Cultural Value – Enriching Britain: Culture, Creativity and Growth' (Warwick: University of Warwick, 2015).
68 Ibid.
69 Catherine Bell, *Ritual Theory, Ritual Practice* (New York: Oxford University Press, 1992), 221.
70 Kevin J. Corbett, 'The Big Picture: Theatrical Moviegoing, Digital Television, and Beyond the Substitution Effect', *Cinema Journal* 40.2 (Winter, 2001).
71 Roger Silverstone, *Television and Everyday Life* (London: Routledge, 1994).
72 Daniel Snowman, *The Gilded Stage: A Social History of Opera* (London: Grove Atlantic, 2009).

73 Lisa Gitelman, *Always Already New: Media, History, and the Data of Culture* (Cambridge, MA: MIT Press, 2008), 8.
74 Barbara Klinger, 'Foreword', in *Live Cinema: Cultures, Economies, Aesthetics* (New York: Bloomsbury, 2017), xvi.
75 Marshall McLuhan, *Understanding Media: The Extensions of Man* (London: Ark Paperbacks, 1964), 7.
76 Ibid.
77 Raymond Williams, *Television: Technology and Cultural Form* (London: Collins, 1974), 5.
78 Paolo Cherchi Usai, 'Origins and Survival', in *The Oxford History of World Cinema*, edited by Geoffrey Nowell-Smith (Oxford: Oxford University Press, 1996), 6.
79 Joshua Meyrowitz, 'Medium Theory', in *Communication Theory Today*, edited by David J. Crowley and David Mitchell (Palo Alto, CA: Stanford University Press, 1994), 50.
80 Ibid., 51.
81 Martin Lister, Jon Dovey, Seth Giddings, Iain Grant and Kieran Kelly, *New Media: A Critical Introduction*, 2nd edn (Abingdon, UK: Routledge, 2009), 77.
82 Lucien Goldmann, *The Hidden God: A Study of Tragic Vision in the of Pascal and the Tragedies of Racine* (New York: Routledge, 2013), 7.
83 Tom Gunning, 'The Cinema of Attraction[s]: Early Film, Its Spectator and the Avant-Garde', in *Early Cinema: Space, Frame, Narrative*, edited by Thomas Elsaesser (London: British Film Institute, 1990), 52.
84 Roberta Pearson, 'Transitional Cinema', in *The Oxford History of World Cinema*, edited by Geoffrey Nowell-Smith (Oxford: Oxford University Press, 1996), 23.
85 Ibid., 42.
86 Ibid.
87 Ibid.
88 Jay David Bolter and Richard Grusin, 'Remediation', *Configurations* 3 (1996): 346.
89 Linda Hutcheon, 'Beginning to Theorize Adaptation', *A Theory of Adaptation* (New York: Routledge, 2006), 9.
90 Bolter and Grusin, 'Remediation', 315.
91 Bolter and Grusin, *Remediation: Understanding New Media* (Cambridge, MA: MIT Press, 1991), 5.
92 Ibid., 25.
93 Bolter and Grusin, 'Remediation', 346.
94 Ibid., 340.
95 Ibid.

96   Jane Feuer, 'The Concept of Live Television: Ontology as Ideology', in *Regarding Television: Critical Approaches: An Anthology*, edited by E. Ann Kaplan (Frederick, MD: University Publications of America, 1983), 13.
97   Klinger, xiv.
98   John Ellis, *Visible Fictions: Cinema, Television, Video*, rev. edn (1982; reprint, London: Routledge, 1992), 12.
99   Ibid., 12.
100 Ibid., 11.
101 Ibid., 25.
102 Carolyn Marvin, *When Old Technologies Were New: Thinking About Electric Communication in the Late Nineteenth Century* (New York: Oxford University Press, 1988), 8; Gitelman, 15.
103 William Boddy, 'A Century of Electronic Cinema', *Screen* 49.2 (2008): 142.
104 Sarah Atkinson, *Beyond the Screen: Emerging Cinema and Engaging Audiences* (London: Bloomsbury, 2014), 5.
105 Ibid.
106 Norman Taylor, *Cinematic Perspectives on Digital Culture: Consorting with the Machine* (London: Palgrave MacMillan, 2012), 14.
107 Douglas Gomery, 'Theatre Television: The Missing Link of Technological Change in the US Motion Picture Industry', *Velvet Light Trap* 21 (1985).
108 Ithiel de Sola Pool, *Technologies of Freedom: On Free Speech in an Electronic Age* (Cambridge, MA: Harvard University Press, 1983), 23.
109 Henry Jenkins, *Convergence Culture: Where Old and New Media Collide* (New York: New York University Press, 2006), 2.
110 Ibid., 10–11.
111 Ibid., 14.
112 Daniel Chandler, 'An Introduction to Genre Theory', *Visual Memory* (1997), accessed 13 June 2021, http://visual-memory.co.uk/daniel/Documents/intgenre/.
113 Freidrich Engels, 'Engels to J. Bloch in Königsberg', in *Historical Materialism*, by Engels and Karl Marx (Berlin: Der sozialistische Akademiker, 1895), online edition accessed on Marxist Internet Archive, 16 December 2017, https://www.marxists.org/archive/marx/works/1890/letters/90_09_21.htm.
114 Herbert Lindenberger, *Opera: The Extravagant Art* (London: Cornell University Press, 1984), 239.
115 Gita Gopinath, 'The Great Lockdown: Worst Economic Downturn since the Great Depression', *IMFBlogs*, 14 April 2020, accessed 13 June 2021, https://blogs.imf.org/2020/04/14/the-great-lockdown-worst-economic-downturn-since-the-great-depression/.
116 Douglas Gomery, 'Theatre Television: The Missing Link of Technological Change in the US Motion Picture Industry', *Velvet Light Trap* 21 (1985): 122.

117 Holmes, 13.
118 Artin Artaud, *The Theatre and Its Double*, trans. Victor Corti (London: Alma Classics, 1978), 26.
119 Ibid., 60.
120 Patrice Pavis, *Performance: Theatre, Dance, and Film*, 4th edn (Michigan: University of Michigan Press, 1996), 7.
121 John Willet, *Brecht on Theatre* (New York: Hill and Wang, 1964).
122 Pavis, 7–12.
123 Ibid., 12.
124 Ibid., 19.
125 Roger Copeland, 'The Presence of Mediation', *TDR (The Drama Review)* 34.4 (1990): 29.
126 Christopher Balme, 'Surrogate Stages: Theatre, Performance and the Challenge of New Media', *Performance Research: A Journal of the Performing Arts* 13.2 (2008): 11.
127 Ibid., 11–12.
128 Guy Debord, *The Society of the Spectacle* (London: Zone Books, 1994), 2; Jean Baudrillard, *Simulacra and Simulation* (Lansing: University of Michigan Press, 1994), 1.
129 Andrew Crisell, *Liveness and Recording in the Media* (London: Palgrave Macmillan, 2012), 1.
130 Jane Feuer, 'The Concept of Live Television: Ontology as Ideology', in *Regarding Television*, edited by E. Ann Kaplan (Fredrick, MD: University Publications of America, 1983); Stephen Heath and Gillian Skirrow, 'Television: A World in Action', *Screen* 18.2 (1977); John Ellis, *Seeing Things: Television in the Age of Uncertainty* (London: I. B. Tauris, 2002); Jeffrey Sconce, *Haunted Media: Electronic Presence from Telegraphy to Television* (Durham, NC: Duke University Press, 2000).
131 Sconce, 173.
132 Daniel Dayan and Elihu Katz, *Media Events: The Live Broadcasting of History* (Cambridge, MA: Harvard University Press, 1992), 5.
133 Ibid.
134 Ibid., 15–16.
135 Nick Couldry, 'Liveness, "Reality" and the Mediated Habitus from Television to Mobile Phone', *Communication Review* 7:3 (2004): 353.
136 Couldry, *Media Rituals: A Critical Approach* (London: Routledge, 2003), 3.
137 Ibid., 356.
138 Peggy Phelan, *Unmarked: The Politics of Performance* (London: Routledge, 1993), 146.
139 Ibid., 148.

140 Christopher Morris, 'Digital Diva: Opera on Video', *Opera Quarterly* 26.1 (2010): 96.
141 Ibid.
142 Ibid., 101.
143 Ibid., 104–5.
144 Ibid., 105.
145 Ibid., 107.
146 Ibid., 114.
147 Philip Auslander, 'Afterword: Is There Life after Liveness?', *Performance and Technology: Practices of Virtual Embodiment and Interactivity*, edited by Susan Broadhurst and Josephine Machon (Basingstoke: Palgrave Macmillan, 2006), 44.
148 Ibid., 45.
149 Philip Auslander, *Liveness: Performance in a Mediatised Culture*, 2nd edn (London: Routledge, 2008), 9.
150 Ibid., 11.
151 Ibid., 7.
152 Auslander, 'Afterword', 196.
153 Matthew Reason, 'Theatre Audiences and Perceptions of "Liveness" in Performance', *Participations* 1.2 (2004), accessed 22 January 2022, https://ray.yorksj.ac.uk/id/eprint/912/1/1_02_reason_article.htm.
154 Martin Barker, 'CRASH, Theatre, Audiences, and the Idea of "Liveness"', *Studies in Theatre and Performance* 23.1 (2003): 35.
155 Ibid., 28.
156 Ibid.
157 Barker, *Remarkable Rise of Livecasting*, 13.
158 Ibid., 65–6.
159 Reason.
160 Ibid.
161 Ibid.
162 Mike Weed, 'Sport Fans and Travel – Is "Being There" Always Important?', *Journal of Sport and Tourism* 15.2 (2010): 104–6.
163 Barney Glaser and Anslem Strauss, *The Discovery of Grounded Theory: Strategies for Qualitative Research* (Chicago: Aldine, 1967); Barker, 'CRASH, Theatre, Audiences, and the Idea of "Liveness"'.
164 Karl Popper, *The Myth of the Framework: In Defence of Science and Rationality* (New York: Routledge, 1994).
165 Goldmann, x.
166 Ibid., 3.

167 David Byrne and Gill Callaghan, *Complexity Theory and the Social Sciences* (London: Routledge, 2013), 13–14.
168 Frederick Engels, *Anti-Dühring. Herr Eugen Dühring's Revolution in Science* (Moscow: Progress Publishers, 1947), accessed 8 October 2016, https://www.marxists.org/archive/marx/works/1877/anti-duhring/.
169 Ibid.
170 Goldmann, 8.
171 Gregoire Nicolis, *Introduction to Nonlinear Science* (Cambridge, MA: Cambridge University Press, 22 June 1995), 1–2.
172 Byrne and Callaghan, 21.
173 Georg Wilhelm Friedrich Hegel, *The Logic: Encyclopaedia of the Philosophical Sciences*, 2nd edn (London: Oxford University Press, 1874), §93.
174 Kim Schrøder, KristenDrotner, Stephen Kline and Catherine Murray, *Researching Audiences* (New York: Oxford University Press, 2006), viii–ix.
175 Ibid., 26–7.
176 Klaus Bruhn Jensen and Karl Erik Rosengren, 'Five Traditions in Search of the Audience', *European Journal of Communication* 5.2 (1990): 214–19.
177 Ibid.
178 Goldmann, 16.
179 James Lull, 'On the Communicative Properties of Music', *Sage Journals* (1985): 219.
180 Barker, *Remarkable Rise of Livecasting*, 5.
181 Pertti Alasuutari, 'Introduction: Three Phases of Reception Studies', in *Rethinking the Media Audience*, edited by Pertti Alasuutari (London: Sage 1999).
182 Antonio Gramsci, *Prison Notebooks*, edited by Joe Buttigieg (New York City: Columbia University Press, 1992), 233–8.
183 Elihu Katz, 'Mass Communications Research and the Study of Popular Culture: An Editorial Note on a Possible Future for This Journal', *Studies in Public Communication*, 2.1–6 (1959), 4.
184 Stuart Hall, 'Encoding, decoding', in *The Cultural Studies Reader*, edited by Simon During (London: Routledge, 2007), 94.
185 David Morley and Carlotte Brundson, *The Nationwide Audience* (London: Routledge, 1980).
186 Ien Ang, *Watching Dallas: Soap Opera and the Melodramatic Imagination* (London: Methuen, 1985); Dorothy Hobson, *Soap Opera* (London: Wiley, 2003); Daniel Dayan and Elihu Katz, *Media Events: The Live Broadcasting of History* (Cambridge, MA: Harvard University Press, 1992).
187 Alasuutari, 5.

188 Martin Allor, 'Relocating the Site of the Audience', *Critical Studies in Mass Communication* 5.3 (1988); Lawrence Grossberg, *The Audience and Its Landscapes* (Colorado: Westview Press, 1996).
189 Alasuutari, 8–13.
190 Martin Barker, 'I Have Seen the Future and It Is Not Here Yet; or, on Being Ambitious for Audience Research', *Communication Review* 9 (2006).
191 Ibid., 1–2.
192 Ibid., 1.
193 Ibid., 5.
194 Ibid., 4.
195 Ibid., 4–5.
196 Ibid.
197 Ibid., 6–10.
198 Ibid., 9.
199 Florin Vladica, 'Value Propositions of Opera and Theater Live in Cinema', from monograph collection of papers presented at World Media Economics & Management Conference (Thessaloniki, Greece, 23–7 May 2012), 4.
200 Ibid., 4.
201 Vladica, 11–15.
202 Bennett, 33.
203 John Tulloch, *Shakespeare and Chekhov in Production and Reception: Theatrical Events and Their Audiences* (Iowa: University of Iowa Press, 2005), 7.
204 Bennett, 106.
205 Benzecry, 94.
206 Ibid., 94–8.
207 Ibid., 98.
208 Morris, 109–10.

2

The history of opera cinema

Audience research is necessary to understand the distinct experience facilitated by opera cinema. But that is not the end of the story. Media experiences do not emerge fully formed onto the scene. When defining the ontology of media phenomena, we have to understand where they came from, how they developed and identify points of departure from other, related media forms. Opera and cinema similarly emerged from pre-existing arts (classical music, theatre, vaudeville, photography, etc.), eventually coalescing into unique mediums with their own special conventions. As part of the cultural superstructure, art and media are ultimately a product of the forces of production, distribution and exchange that move human society. As such, a historical materialist method is necessary to understand the economic, social and political impetus behind cultural products. This method helps explain why media develop in certain ways at particular junctures, and allow us to make predictions about where they are going. My approach is partly inspired by the New Film History. This tradition, beginning in the 1980s, moved away from looking at films as merely texts, and drew attention to social and economic factors underpinning media histories – emphasizing the role of technologies, institutional interests and political currents.[1]

Opera cinema has a rich and unique evolutionary path, encompassing (but not limited to) the phonograph, telegraphy, radio and television relays. Therefore, this chapter synthesizes historiographies of radio, screen and television opera into a historical narrative that, to my knowledge, has not been illustrated elsewhere. I further argue that the development of opera cinema is inexplicable without attention to underlying economic trends that have informed the development of remediated opera more generally. In the aftermath of the Second World War, state-sponsored efforts to promote cultural access resulted in a flowering of creativity in the realm of screen opera. By contrast, opera cinema emerged from a more recent period of Thatcherian/Reaganite privatization and commercialism in the cultural sector, compounded by economic crisis and austerity. The primary motivators behind opera cinema are helping major opera companies to build their international profiles, appease ageing operaphile constituencies and justify dwindling public subsidies. I argue this has direct aesthetic and formal implications, with opera cinema being more artistically conservative than earlier forms of operatic remediation. As a cultural experience, it is stymied by the same economic and creative impasse that afflicts opera more generally – and is also to some extent a product of that impasse. Cause becomes effect, and effect becomes cause. This is partly why I do not consider opera cinema to be a medium in its own right, despite its great potential.

The first half of the chapter charts opera cinema's main predecessors and technical development, while the latter describes currents in the political economy pertinent to opera cinema in particular. Unfortunately, the period 2019–21 constitutes something of a blank space, due to the impact of the coronavirus pandemic over this period, which has effectively imposed a pause on opera cinema worldwide. The chapter concludes by interrogating the vexed notion of cultural democratization, and speculates as to why opera cinema has struggled to broaden and diversify opera audiences.

Early experiments and radio opera

Opera cinema has existed for less than two decades, but its lineage stretches right back to early developments in telegraphy and radio. As an *idea*, it predates even this. For example, John Wyver traces the earliest known mention of image transmission technology to an 1878 article by Louis Figuier. The article describes a theoretical device called 'Le Télectroscope' (essentially television), which would permit a user in San Francisco to watch a live opera performance 5,560 miles away in Paris.[2] It is not by accident that Figuier envisioned opera as the natural partner to his imagined broadcast machine: opera's cultural esteem means it is often envisioned as an inaugurator of new cultural and communication technologies. No lesser figure than Thomas Edison wrote in the *New York Times* that his intention was to 'have such a happy combination of photography and electricity that a man can sit in his own parlor, see depicted upon a curtain the forms of the players in opera upon a distant stage and hear the voices of the singers'.[3] That Edison envisioned his device specifically as a vehicle for opera further demonstrates that - then as now - the art form was considered a priority for novel methods of remediation and electronic dissemination.

This came to pass in 1881, when the Théâtrephone and its British counterpart, the Electrophone, connected home audiences to live musical and opera performances via a licensed telephone line – albeit with rudimentary sound quality.[4] The great French novelist and essayist Marcel Proust (a notorious introvert who hated going outdoors, but loved music) was an enthusiastic Théâtrephone subscriber.[5] These transmissions soon became an international enterprise, with the Théâtrephone company transmitting the Grand Opéra's 1913 production of *Faust* directly to Electrophone subscribers across the channel, and the British company reciprocated with excerpts of *Tosca* from Covent Garden.[6] This was a niche fancy for wealthy and middle-class music lovers, not a mass broadcast by any means.

Services like the Théâtrephone were eventually supplanted by wireless broadcasts, although these began in a relatively inauspicious fashion. Paul Heyer identifies an ambitious experiment by American inventor and entrepreneur Lee de Forest as a direct precursor to the audience-building objectives of contemporary opera cinema.[7] In 1910, de Forest persuaded the Metropolitan Opera House in New York to mount a transmitter on its roof, and on two successive nights, a handful of radio hams in Manhattan and New Jersey received a garbled transmission of a live Enrico Caruso performance.[8] The Met's general manager at the time, Giulio Gatti-Casazza, tuned in for the transmission but was unimpressed by the virtually unintelligible broadcast of the world's greatest voice.[9] While an aesthetic and commercial failure, de Forest's pioneering transmission is notable for being the first mass wireless broadcast by a major opera company, not to mention the first entertainment radio broadcast in the United States.[10] Moreover, despite the technical limitations, de Forest was motivated by an earnest desire to 'bring opera to the masses'. This objective characterized mass dissemination of opera for the next several decades and continues to figure heavily in debates on the merits of opera cinema.[11]

Only in the aftermath of the First World War were mass transmissions attempted with seriousness, correlating with rapid urbanisation in the United States and Western Europe, which coupled with technological advances (partly motivated by the experience of war), facilitated the development of commercial radio into a mass medium. From across the Atlantic in June 1920, soprano Dame Nellie Melba sang a few pieces of repertoire that were broadcast via radio from the Marconi plant in Chelmsford, Essex, to London. The transmission could allegedly be picked up on the continent.[12] This modest accomplishment was a huge leap forward upon de Forest's attempt a decade prior. A few months later, the incomparable coloratura soprano, Luisa Tetrazzini, broadcast a short performance from her hotel suite in New York, aiming at 'ships within a radius of 400 miles'.[13] From this point, the sophistication and frequency of opera broadcasts increased apace, in line with the economic boom underpinning the 'Roaring Twenties'.

In January 1923, the recently founded British Broadcasting Company relayed a full performance of *Hänsel und Gretel* from the stage of the Royal Opera House in Covent Garden, followed a few weeks later by *Bohéme*, with Melba.[14] Not to be outdone, the Americans set about broadcasting full operas across the nation, with live performances often introduced by a young, part-time singer named Milton Cross. Cross would later find fame as the presenter of the Met's series of in-house broadcasts, the name of which endured in one form of another for the next century: *Live from the Metropolitan Opera House*.[15] In this period, the number of commercial radios in circulation ballooned from half a million sets in 1923 to two million in 1925, then twelve million in 1928.[16] A massive potential audience for a variety of broadcast content, including opera, was emerging. This audience found its way to the art form through mass broadcasting, in many cases for the first time.

The economic collapse of 1929 was bookended by two important radio opera series. In 1925, at the height of the Jazz Age, the NBC-created National Grand Opera Company launched a series of abridged operas for radio under conductor, arranger and former music director at the Edison Phonograph Company, Cesare Sodero.[17] Sodero was, in many ways, a comparable figure to Peter Gelb, general manager of the Met who is often credited as the progenitor of opera cinema.[18] Like Gelb, Sodero hailed from a media background, rather than one that was exclusively musical, and brought his expertize and penchant for showmanship to bear on the world of opera, to significant success. Sodero's choice of programming evinced a shrewd understanding of his target audience. Editing an exhaustive range of operas down to sixty-minute, late-night slots proved challenging for artists but was a hit with audiences, and the series ran for five years.[19] Despite Sodero's accomplishments, the Met was slow to follow suit. The impetus for inaugurating the Met's regular radio series actually came from head of NBC, Merlyn H. Aylsworth, who had approached Gatti-Casazza with the idea several times but had always been rebuffed.[20] Perhaps remembering de Forest's experiment, Gatti-Casazza was initially unconvinced that radio broadcasts could ever do justice to opera. A successful rehearsal transmission of *Madama Butterfly* from the Met stage on 23 December 1931 finally allayed his fears, and the Met went fully 'live' with *Hänsel und Gretel*.[21] The calamitous effects of the Great Depression, which cost the Met 30 per cent of its subscribers and particularly impacted sales for the more expensive seats, were also key in convincing Gatti-Casazza to relent.[22] Like Gelb eighty years later, Gatti-Casazza seized upon technological remediation to pull the Met out of the throes of dwindling attendance, earning the company a desperately needed $150,000 and establishing a broadcast series that runs to this day, whose Saturday matinee transmissions initiated a generation of opera fans.[23] *Live from the Met* was a crucial series for this reason, but also because it confirmed the existence of a reliable, mass audience for live, remediated opera.

The early history of radio opera laid the foundation for opera cinema. The brand name, *Live from the Met*, spans the history of live, remediated opera. Even at this early stage, one can see the institutional urge to broaden and diversify opera audiences and the use of remediation to financially reinvigorate the art form – under the pressure of economic crisis. These were both important considerations for remediated opera for the ensuing decades. Very similar conditions would result in the initial boom of cinema simulcasting in the mid-2000s. Moreover, many of the operaphiles created by the *Live from the Met* radio broadcasts transitioned into the core audience for television relays in the latter half of the century. This in turn provided the basis for opera cinema's core audience. Therefore, the kernel of opera cinema's audience was also developed in this period.

Theatre television

Different media histories provide tributaries to the main historical narrative of opera cinema. The direct precursor to event cinema (live content streamed to cinemas) emerged separately to radio opera in the 1930s, in the form of theatre television – live, electronic, sound-image transmissions to cinemas, constituting what Douglas Gomery describes as the 'missing link' between cinema (recorded images projected in an exhibition space) and television (images transmitted from elsewhere, usually to a domestic space).[24] Despite embodying similar commercial and institutional objectives to event cinema, theatre television never evolved into a viable commercial enterprise, and foundered due to material limitations of its day. These were only resolved by digital technologies. In other words, the world was not ready for it.

While television broadcasts (a quintessential domestic media technology) are often presented as public cinema's natural rival, the early history of the two media reveals a more complex and interwoven picture than many realize. In 1925, less than a year after securing the patent for his 'televisual' system, inventor John Logie Baird wrote to a colleague that cinemas would be the first recipients of television, so that 'audiences in all parts of the country will be able to watch the finish of the Derby and other topical events at the moment they are occurring'.[25] He developed a televisual system optimized for cinemas, which he pitched to the BBC in 1937, who rejected the technology because they were concerned about the implications for their public broadcasting monopoly.[26] He later brought his idea to the Post Office, who refused his application for wireless transmission, citing scarcity of bandwidth.[27] Finally, he struck up a deal with the Gaumont-British Picture Corporation and installed an apparatus at Gaumont's Dominion Theatre in Tottenham Court Road that transmitted live images via a landline.[28] Assembled members of the press were moderately impressed by Baird's 150-line picture.[29] Baird next took his system to the Palais-de-Luxe, a Gaumont-British cinema in Bromley, and, on 6 December 1937, illegally picked up BBC transmissions and showed them on the cinema screen to the assembled press.[30] Later that week, he presented a crude colour transmission at the

Dominion, which soon became part of the theatre's regular evening variety bill.[31]

A burgeoning cultural phenomenon - a hybrid of cinema and television - rapidly emerged. Baird faced stiff competition in the summer of 1938 when Solomon Sagall's Scophony company demonstrated its own live, large-screen pictures at a Kensington department store,[32] although the system produced only faint and grainy images.[33] On 23 February 1939, both Baird and Scophony held competing, large-screen cinema presentations of the Eric Boon and Arthur Danahar title fight – the first boxing match ever exhibited on television.[34] The broadcasts were such a success that Oscar Deutsch, owner of the Odeon cinema chain, installed the Scophony system in his flagship cinema in Leicester Square.[35] Later, he announced his intention to mount Scophony big-screen television systems in all sixty of his London Odeons, while Gaumont-British placed large-screen television systems in five of its London cinemas with a combined capacity of 7,000 seats.[36]

The year 1939 marked an early peak for theatre television that was interrupted by the outbreak of war, when television at home and at cinemas was diverted to state propaganda and news from the front.[37] The phenomenon's return in 1946 suffered a major setback when Baird's large-screen showing of the Victory Parade on 6 June was a total technical flop.[38] Moreover, the BBC continued to oppose theatre television, citing its public broadcasting monopoly. Eventually, the author of Clement Atlee's post-war economic programme, William Beveridge, took the side of Paramount, Granada and other theatre television supporters, and permitted the Postmaster General to license wavelengths for the use of big-screen broadcasts. However, he introduced the caveat that the BBC should have the opportunity to screen any original programming first.[39] Subsequently, The Rank Company, Paramount and Granada presented well-received public screenings at the Festival of Britain in 1951, but were under increasing pressure given relatively low demand, the rapid growth of the home television market and the inability to create new content.[40] These were not, however, the fundamental reasons theatre television began to struggle in the early 1950s: the technology involved was simply too expensive and nobody was making money.[41] Even today, the high costs of simulcasts mean they rarely turn a direct profit for arts companies, although they constitute a lucrative arm of the cinema industry.[42] Though it eventually fizzled out, all the elements of modern event cinema existed in Britain (in analogue form) well before the advent of digital technologies, and certainly before the Royal Opera appeared live on cinema screens. The germ of event cinema has long since inhabited the British film and television industries.

Meanwhile, theatre television in America used similar tactics to contemporary event cinema, emphasizing live content to defend cinema's status against perceived competition from domestic media technologies - in this case, home television.[43] Even prior to the Second World War, there were discussions amongst the oligarchical movie studios in America about how to deal with the anticipated threat of television. In 1938, the major studios established a committee via the Academy of Motion Picture Arts and Sciences to study television and develop plans for how to innovate and compete.[44] One suggestion floated was to install television in cinemas, or alternatively control television production – co-opting the new technology in the way the majors had already attempted, unsuccessfully, to take over radio.[45] Paramount purchased an interest in television receiver manufacturer DuMont that year, and created its first television station in Chicago in 1940 and another in Los Angeles in 1943, with further purchases in New York and Washington giving it four of the first nine stations in America.[46] All the major studios sought television licenses by end of the war, and there was talk of alliances with NBC, ABC and CBS.[47] The film studios coveted vertical integration comparable to their domination of the film industry, but their ambitions were dashed after the Paramount anti-monopoly case in 1946, which halted their license applications. Their wings clipped, the big cinema capitalists turned away from owning television and returned to their plan of putting live transmissions in their theatres.[48]

The studios initially envisioned using television to showcase major sporting events, virtually expanding the seating capacity of the sports stadiums. Gomery reveals parallels between this relatively primitive technology and modern event cinema, writing that the film industry hoped to 'use theater television to differentiate its offerings and counter home television'.[49] The industry did not immediately settle on one apparatus. As is often the case with novel delivery systems, many technologies were considered and trialled – some of them rather exotic, and none of them entirely satisfactory.

The Swiss Eidophor, which never made it as far as theatres, used an oil-film-and-arc-light technique, bombarding the oil with electrons and creating turbulence, which, when combined with a set of mirrors and lenses, could create a clearer and more brilliant image than anything possible from a mechanical system like Scophony.[50] By contrast, the RCA Corporation developed a cathode ray tube system that dwarfed those used for home sets, housed in a barrel two-and-a-half foot in diameter and three-foot long. As with Eidophor, a reflection mechanism was used to magnify the image. According to Gomery, the image quality was 'acceptable', but far from the standard of thirty-five milometer celluloid.[51] Recognizing these limitations, RCA employed the system only in front of audiences of a hundred or fewer. Perhaps most outlandish of all was the Paramount intermediate file system, which used a standard television receiver to obtain a video signal, which was then transferred onto motion-picture film – a process that took sixty-six seconds.[52] The ambitious technology required two cathode-ray tubes: one that provided a monitor, and a special, aluminium-backed, flat-faced screen with reversed polarity that functioned as the recording screen. A film camera was synchronized with this second screen, and recorded the electronic message, while exposed thirty-five milometer film passed through a chute into a processing unit to be developed, washed, dried and projected.[53]

As one might expect, these systems were unreliable and absurdly expensive to install, operate and maintain. Nevertheless, Warner trialled its own version of the RCA system in 1948 to 3,000 guests, showing the Joe Louis versus Jersey Joe Walcott heavyweight boxing match.[54] During the same summer, Paramount demonstrated its intermediate file system to a full house at Paramount Theatre on Broadway - a success that led the company to plan a national chain of theatre televisions.[55] Paramount hoped to make Chicago its seat of operations, and organized a spectacular launch event for 16 June 1948 at its flagship theatre to inaugurate its theatre television initiative. Television cameras recorded a variety of vaudeville acts in a studio across the street and transmitted them live to the theatre.[56] In a remarkable instance of multivalent historical convergence, the theatrical, vaudeville and roadshow attractions that characterized early cinema screenings returned to the movie house - via television. Moreover, as an additional treat, attendees were filmed entering the theatre, allowing the audience to see themselves on the screen – a precursor to the modern convention of filming the opera house interior as the audience shuffles in.[57] Variety bills of this kind were largely supplanted by much more lucrative major sporting events, particularly boxing and baseball.[58] The former became theatre television's most durable form of programming.[59] The year 1952 was a peak for theatre television in America, 102 theatres were equipped with the technology, and major theatre chains still hoped they could increase profits given declining movie going, due to suburban living patterns and the popularity of domestic television.[60] When these profits failed to materialize, the majors abandoned the idea of beating television at its own game, turning to technologies designed to augment recorded cinema, like colour film, 3D and Cinemascope.[61]

Aside from a handful of championship boxing matches, which were screened into the 1960s, and a broadcast of Elizabeth II's coronation (not coincidentally regarded as the birth of modern television in Great Britain), live content nearly vanished from cinema screens in the late 1950s.[62] It would remain for digital technologies to make live cinema sustainable, half a century later. In Hegelian terms, the relationship between theatre television and digital simulcasting is a negation of the negation - the same basic idea re-emerged at a new historical juncture at a higher plane of technological development. Even the self-reflexive institutional dramaturgy of modern event cinema was beginning to take shape around this time, with the 1948 Paramount showcase acknowledging the presence of the virtual audience. Notably, like event cinema today, theatre television was a 'novelty among many', rather than developing into an art form in its own right. This case study is instructive as to why not every novel media phenomenon should be considered a medium.

Opera on television

While the institutional basis for event cinema can be glimpsed in theatre television, the aesthetic and formal properties of opera cinema are indebted to the small screen. Remediated opera found its most enduring success on television, and televised opera provided the aesthetic blueprint for simulcasting today.

After the Second World War, a combination of home television, together with a new Keynesian 'consensus' in the capitalist west in favour of state spending (predicated on a historic upswing in production), resulted in a centralized drive to bring high culture 'to the masses'. Early advocates of television opera, such as Austrian composer and former director of productions at the Met, Herbert Graf, hoped home media could be used to elevate public tastes, and bring more people into the operatic fold.[63] For decades after, televised opera deliberately and consistently targeted new audiences, and furthermore displayed a high degree of artistic experimentation.

Marcia Citron defines three main types of television opera: the studio production, the made-for-television film and relays (live or delayed) direct from an opera house.[64] While this is a helpful taxonomy, its boundaries can be ambiguous. For instance, Ingmar Bergman's *The Magic Flute* was originally produced for television and subsequently shown in movie theatres.[65] This example cautions against sharp ontological distinctions between different cultural experiences, and against simple definitions of liveness. Indeed, 'live opera' has never had a categorical definition. Different forms of remediated opera have been live to varying degrees, and to this day opera cinema is broadcast with a tape delay to account for mishaps or time zone differences. However, these three different types of television opera were dominant at different times. For reasons I will explain, the live relay eventually emerged as the main mode of remediated opera, eclipsing the studio production and directed, made-for-television films.

In 1944, Graf was hired by NBC to create productions for television.[66] He soon found that certain formal conventions – including English translation, sensitive camerawork and naturalistic acting – worked well on television and adopted them as a default.[67] In so doing, he laid the aesthetic foundations for populist screen opera, a tradition to which opera cinema belongs. The relative strength of organized labour in the post-war period exerted an influence over screen opera, since those representing performers had differing ideas of what should and should not be shown. This was due in part to varied interpretations of 'live performance'. For instance, the so-called Petrillo Ban on live music on American television, due to an agreement struck with the Musician's Union in 1948,[68] meant all musical performances were overdubbed in post-production.[69] In Britain, a different labour agreement produced the opposite effect: the British Musician's Union insisted on live music for all television recordings. This meant that when the BBC began broadcasting operas from Covent Garden, starting in 1947, the music was beamed directly from the stage.[70] Meanwhile, on the continent, liveness was eschewed altogether. Italy and Germany both favoured pre-recorded productions, while the latter had singers overdub professional screen actors.[71] Then as now, opera lovers in the press denounced television opera as no substitute for the 'real thing', and critics cruelly mocked singers for their appearance and occasionally limited acting abilities.[72] Nevertheless, televised opera began to cultivate a significant following, building on the audience developed by radio relays in the first part of the century.

A major turning point came when ABC telecast the opening night of the Met's 1948 production of *Otello* to an audience of 500,000 – a huge success, given the relatively low penetration of home television at the time.[73] Despite a number of technical shortcomings, including dim lighting, excessive long shots that made performers even more difficult to see and poor synchronization between the editing and on-stage action, the telecast was an acceptable proof of concept.[74] Opening nights at the Met ran on television for a further two years, until high costs for ABC led the Met to pursue closed-circuit broadcasting as an alternative.[75] Other studios sought a piece of the action, and NBC took the lead with its in-house NBC Opera Theatre, which launched a series of studio productions that lasted fifteen seasons from 1949 to 1964. Under the leadership of Hungarian-born conductor Peter Adler, who was eager to 'develop a new kind of opera' and felt television could 'bridge the gap between the mass audience and the opera house', NBC Opera's series was a great success.[76] Adler's ambition to facilitate a true-blue American opera led to a number of new commissions for the series, including *Amahl and the Night Visitors* (1951) and *Labyrinth* (1963) both by Gian Menotti, and Lukas Foss's *Griffelkin* (1955), which became a holiday favourite.[77] Adler did not shy from controversy, offering a full version of *Salome* (complete with striptease) in 1954.[78] The series also introduced Americans to newly composed repertoire from overseas, including Benjamin Britten's *Billy Budd*. The 1952 telecast marked the first time a Britten opera had been aired on television.[79] CBS's Opera Television Theatre was less successful. Despite opening with a well-received production of *Carmen*, it ran for only one year between 1949 and 1950 due to sponsors pulling out.[80]

Nevertheless, the aesthetic and commercial maturity of television opera was confirmed with the creation of the Salzburg Prize in 1959. The accolade specifically rewarded the best new operas written for television, with recipients including Paul Angerer's *Passkontrolle*, performed in 1959, and Ingvar Lidholm's *Holländarn* in 1967.[81] After NBC Opera folded, the Ford Foundation, which had previously sponsored opera through the 1953 televised cultural variety show, *Omnibus*, approached Adler to draft recommendations for opera on non-commercial television, leading to the creation of the NET Opera Company.[82] A substantially reworked version of Leos Janacek's *From the House of the Dead* inaugurated the series in 1969, but the most significant work for NET was Benjamin Britten's entirely new opera for television *Owen Wingrave*, released on 16 May 1971.[83] Unfortunately, high costs and unconventional staging meant the new production alienated affiliates, which ultimately killed the series. This concluded the peak of screen opera's aesthetic ambition and critical acclaim. But, in the decades since Lee de Forest first beamed Caruso from the Met's roof, remediated opera had proved its capacity to cultivate a mass audience, and push opera into new artistic territory. Other fruitful endeavours continued, however. For example, one of the most important opera directors in history, Jean-Pierre Ponnelle, enjoyed a successful relationship with German media company Unitel, producing sixteen screen operas for television between 1972 and his death in 1988.[84] Citron describes Ponnelle as an 'activist behind the camera', who not only relished experimentation, but saw the camera as a distinctive musical element. He stated in 1983:

> To me, the language of the camera is like added lines in the score [Partitur]. That means that one can and must master this technique musically. I see analogies between the vocabulary of music and that of film. Dynamics in music are similar to tracking shots ['Travellings'], camera movements, zooms, etc., in film. Harmony in music, the vertical, relates to color in film [and] variety in focal adjustment from the whole to the close-up. Musical rhythm corresponds to cutting, which must follow exactly from the score ... It's [important] to preserve the primacy of music. One can also proceed contrapuntally, dialectically.[85]

However, opera cinema as we know it today is a product of the next period, which saw the financial bottom line assert itself in a big way. The high costs of studio productions and falling costs of live recording equipment meant that live relays started to become the main format for televised opera in America.[86] By this point, relays were specifically tailored to celebrate the opera house as much as the performance – shifting away from creative reinterpretation of texts towards brand-building. The *Live from Lincoln Centre* series was inaugurated in the spring of 1976 with Douglas Moore's *The Ballad of Baby Doe*, and televised relays from the Metropolitan opera house commenced in 1977, with *La Bohéme*.[87] These relays became the natural successor to the Met's popular radio series from the 1920s. In its 1979–80 season, *Live from the Met* utilized tape-delayed relays: a practice that soon became standard.[88] The studio opera was still favoured in Europe well into the 1980s, but the final transition was assisted by improvements in video recording technology, and – starting in 1985 – home video playback.[89] Citron names two relays as watersheds. The first was the 1987 Met Telecast of *Turandot*, which established the formal default for the modern telecast, and, by extension, opera cinema:

> The lavish [Franco] Zeffirelli production received a nuanced and idiomatic interpretation for the small screen ... The telecast also features typical trappings of the relay. Viewers feel the sense of occasion in sharing a night at the opera house, seeing first a lengthy exterior view of the Met and the foundation on the plaza. *Turandot*, the cast and conductor, and Zeffirelli-Browning may appear to be the stars; but the Metropolitan Opera as a mecca of high culture is celebrated as well.[90]

The emphasis on virtual presence, the celebration of the opera house and the interspersion of stage action with shots of the conductor, the audience and the opera house itself evince the emergence of the institutional dramaturgy that defines modern simulcasts – promoting the institution-building agendas of major opera houses by selling an idealized, virtual night at the opera.[91]

By contrast, a spectacular telecast production of *Tosca* in 1992 demonstrated the artistic potential of live relay technology to transform the art form. The production was broadcast from various locales in Rome at the times of day appropriate to the opera's narrative. One had to tune in at three different times over a twenty-four-hour period to consume the entire 'live film'.[92] To permit freedom of movement for the cameras, the orchestra was placed in a remote location, the singers and conductor Zubin Mehta used television monitors to coordinate with one another and voices were picked up using body microphones linked via a form of microwave-based transmission.[93] The relay profoundly challenged the meaning of 'live' opera and demonstrated emphatically the creative potential of live telecasting as a hybridized art form in its own right.[94] However, exorbitant costs and an unforgiving viewing schedule meant this kind of *tour-de-force* has remained the exception rather than the rule. The formal conventions concretized in the 1987 *Turandot* have proved objectively far more influential in the development of opera cinema. The economic shift towards privatization, brand development and commercialism in the cultural realm culminated in a dominant form of remediated opera that was more of an advertisement for the stage than an artistic reinterpretation of form.

Opera and cinema

The special historical relationship between opera and cinema forms an important aspect of the evolution of opera cinema, explored here. The connection between these two art forms emerged as an object of study with Jeremy Tambling's influential *Opera, Ideology and Film* (1987), and consolidated by Marcia Citron's *Opera on Screen* in 2000, and the edited collection of essays *Between Opera and Cinema* in 2004. In general, this area of inquiry is still relatively underexplored. Understanding the interplay between these art forms is key to comprehending opera cinema, which is arguably their most successful synthesis – at least in terms of audience figures. Interestingly, opera failed to make its mark on cinema after the introduction of sound cinema. However, opera inspired many of cinema's conventions.

For example, the design and 'twilight reverie' of the movie theatre[95] owes much to Richard Wagner's Bayreuth Festival Theatre, which was designed to neutralize all disruptions to Wagner's unity of music and drama (*gesamtkunstwerk*). The orchestra pit was covered, rendering it invisible to the audience, and the director insisted on complete darkness to promote silent absorption throughout performances.[96] Prior to these innovations, aristocratic audiences would show up halfway through the show to catch the highlights, chat and play chess in the boxes and spit on the heads of the commons below.[97] Wagner's insistence on darkness, silence and continuous viewing anticipated the discipline the cinema industry had to impose on its own audiences in its evolution from a sideshow attraction to a mass theatrical medium.[98] Moreover, unlike the tiered horseshoe of most opera houses, in which ones' wealth generally correlates with a better view (or at least displays one's wealth more effectively), the seats of the Bayreuth Festival Theatre are organized in egalitarian rows, aligned on a steep wedge. This arrangement gave everyone a roughly equal view of the stage and was later adopted by movie houses. It is arguable that cinema began to fill opera's shoes in some respects at the turn of the twentieth century. Little-used opera houses in the late 1900s were sometimes adopted as exhibition spaces for cinema shows.[99] Even where this was not the case, many early cinemas were euphemistically called 'opera houses' to skirt over the less-than-salubrious connotations of this populist pastime where genders, races and social classes would mix in a darkened room. By the sound era, many movie palaces had the lavish feel of European opera houses.[100]

Snowman goes so far as to argue that the cinema 'took over' from opera in the early twentieth century as the dominant popular entertainment form.[101] Even on a formal level, film philosopher Stanley Cavell has identified film as the successor to opera.[102] Both media combine many art forms into a cohesive whole (*gesamtkunstwerk*, to use Wagner's term) and, particularly in the case of early cinema, favour larger-than-life acting styles.[103] Some authors have even pointed to anticipations of filmic techniques in opera, such as Siegfried's journey down the Rhine, which Snowman argues is a prototypical transition scene.[104] Moreover, film scores are heavily indebted to the emotional intensity of late nineteenth-century *verismo* opera and Wagner's *leitmotif*. Famed film composers like Max Steiner, Miklos Rosza and Bernard Hermann all relied on operatic idioms.[105] John Williams's use of the convention was noted by film reviewers in the 1970s, including Roger Angell, who called *Star Wars flick gotterdammerung*, while Pauline

Kale praised Irvin Kirchner, director of *The Empire Strikes Back* for the film's 'Wagnerian' quality.[106] Citron goes into further detail, describing the wedding scene at the beginning of *The Godfather* (1972) as

> quintessentially operatic: moments of drama and intrigue enacted during a large celebration. This is an archetypal First Act with all the appropriate elements: a narrator to provide background to the story (Michael); the reigning monarch holding court, benevolently granting all requests (Don Vito Corleone); the trusted councillor (Tom); the predictable tension from the adversaries (FBI); the seduction of the bridesmaid (Sonny); and even the comic basso (Luca Brasi).[107]

She goes on to explore the *Godfather* trilogy's use of the leitmotif, with common elements including the minor mode, 'folk-like rhythms and melodic turns, modal harmonies, and an affinity for the Neapolitan flatted-second degree'.[108] She concludes that the trilogy as a whole 'is an operatic film saga that partakes of verismo, melodrama, grand opera, epic, and the German ideal of transcendent instrumental music: a catholic vision that represents a magnificent juncture of film and opera'.[109] However, despite these comparisons, opera was never a popular medium in the true sense and did not share cinema's early, plebeian history as a sideshow attraction. This has had a clear influence over opera cinema's reception and development.

The dialectical relationship between cinema and opera cuts both ways. For instance, after the Second World War, Adorno commented on the lack of monumentality in the rebuilt German opera houses, complaining they had the appearance of cinemas.[110] Film has also influenced twentieth-century opera aesthetically. Citron contends that Alban Berg's *Wozeck* (1925) suggests cinematic montage in its juxtaposition of snapshot-like scenes, while his later opera *Lulu* (1937) includes an actual filmed sequence.[111] Additionally, opera and opera singers (including Caruso and Geraldine Farrer) appeared on film very early in cinema's history. *Faust* became a favoured subject for silent cinema, with a number of adaptations, including a 1903 version of *Faust aux enfers* based on Hector Berlioz's *Damnation of Faust* and a 1904 thirteen-minute *Damnation du Docteur Faust* based on Charles Gounod's *Faust*, both by the great French film pioneer Georges Méliès.[112] Although, of course, they contained no music, the films were distributed with scores that included film cues for the piano accompanist.[113] Edison's company produced an ambitious version of *Parsifal* in 1904, directed by Edwin S. Porter that had accompanying phonograph records to be played alongside the images.[114] Such operatic adaptations enjoyed a certain vogue from 1908 through 1910: of the 150 opera-related titles produced before 1926, nearly half were released during these years.[115] Other notable releases include an American-made *Manon Lescaut* (1914), with Emilio Cavalieri and Lucien Muratore, based on Prévost's novel.[116] Farrar also appeared in a film version of *Carmen* in 1915, directed by Cecil B. DeMille, which became a big hit,[117] and went on to further make fifteen films by 1921.[118]

Opera began to retreat from the movies at the beginning of the sound era. By this time, Citron writes, Hollywood preferred opera in small doses – as a scene or aria inserted into a film, or to add a classy backdrop to other genres: from tragic romance, as in *Letter from an Unknown Woman*, to the comic capers of the Marx Brothers.[119] Europe still produced opera films, but many of these were 'in prose' (containing no music, and therefore essentially literary adaptations).[120] The Soviet Union produced several opera films, somewhat ironically, to glorify Russia's imperial history and rich operatic lineage. Throughout the 1950s and 1960s, the Soviets produced lavish adaptations of *Boris Godunov, Khovanshchina* and *Eugene Onegin*.[121] However, Paul Czinner's version of *Der Rosenkavalier* (1960) served as a capstone to the first half-century of opera on film, which petered out in the latter-half of the century.[122] Even Ingmar Bergman's *The Magic Flute*, a modest success, was originally intended for television.

The matter of opera's lacklustre performance on film was addressed at the 2005 'Opera Goes to the Movies' festival in Washington, DC, by Philip Kennicott, a writer for the *Washington Post*.[123] Reflecting on a lack of 'great opera films', he argued that the art form never overcame the 'tongue and teeth' problem of filmic remediation, and stated that the over-the-top emotionality of the form does not lend itself to the big screen, looking a little cartoonish.[124] However, Kennicott's explanation does not account for why these problems did not hamper the movie musical, which – despite a decline from the 1960s onwards – bounced back in recent years with star vehicles like *Les Misérables* (2012) and *La La Land* (2017).[125] While purists might sneer at the comparison, the former is a sung-through, ensemble musical – with copious shots containing Hugh Jackman's tongue-and-teeth. It represented the closest thing to opera to grace cinema screens in decades, and was a wild success. Of course, the film benefitted from a star-studded cast, but surely demonstrates that opera's poor performance in Hollywood has little to do with the art form's essential characteristics. It is not as though there were no successful opera adaptations in the late twentieth century. The 1980s were a productive decade, perhaps assisted by the global recognition of stars like Pavarotti at the time. For instance, Zeffirelli's *La Traviata* (1982) did well at the box office and appeared in regular theatres as well as art houses, as did Luigi Comencini's *La Bohéme* (1988).[126] In 1987, British producer Don Boyd released *Aria*: an intriguing operatic film that comprises ten vignettes, all ten minutes in length, and drawn from different works, with a different director behind each (including the likes of Jean-Luc Godard, Robert Altman and Ken Russell), creating visualizations of the music that explicitly avoid traditional renditions of the narrative. While an interesting artistic experiment, it would be generous to call *Aria* a crossover success. There was nevertheless a brief spike in academic interest in film opera in the 1980s, with two major journals: *L'Avant-Scéne Opéra* and *Revue du Cinéma*, devoting special issues to opera on film in 1987, concurrent with the *Turandot* relay.[127] The same year, a special session on opera and film took place at the fortieth Cannes Festival.[128] More recently, I co-edited a special edition of *The Opera Quarterly* specifically on the subject of opera at the cinema, published in 2018.[129]

However, it is undeniable that, prior to simulcasting, opera was not a major presence in cinema from the 1930s onwards, and had nearly vanished by the 1970s. The explanation for this situation is probably prosaic: just as television studios gravitated away from expensive, experimental studio productions of opera to the telecast, so film opera suffered from financial considerations. Moreover, while the likes of Ryan Gosling can manage show tunes, the decades of training required to master opera singing can hardly be expected of most Hollywood actors, depriving film opera of star power. Perhaps opera's reputation as an elite art form, entrenched in recent decades, is off-putting to economically diverse cinema audiences. Citron also proposes that generational changeover affected opera's performance in cinema: an audience enraptured by Caruso recordings and Metropolitan Opera radio relays was replaced by offspring raised on the Beatles, then the Walkman, then MTV and finally digital distribution.[130] That live relays became the default mode of remediated opera both on television and in the movie house is telling. The digital simulcast has exceeded all previous attempts to unite opera and cinema in terms of the sheer scale of its audience, but it is arguably the least productive synthesis on an aesthetic level. Today, the cinema provides a gateway to a beloved art form, not, in the main, an arena for artistic reinterpretation. Opera cinema's formal characteristics are thus directly explicable by looking at its historical development - demonstrating the need to factor historical context into any ontological analysis.

Event cinema

Contemporary event cinema is a media phenomenon that encompasses opera cinema, and inherits the shift away from aesthetic experimentation and state support towards formal conservatism and privatization. It must be acknowledged that theatre television - event cinema's predecessor from the post-war period - was also driven by the commercial bottom line. Indeed, the introduction of theatre television and event cinema occurred under comparable circumstances: with the incursion of new home media technologies, Hollywood was compelled to compete for audiences' attention with novel theatrical experiences. This demonstrates the salience of the materialist conception of history, revealing how similar social and cultural phenomena emerge in response to similar economic conditions. However, where theatre television failed in the 1950s due to unreliable technologies, live cinema content became a viable, commercial arm of the film industry. At least until the economic turmoil unleashed by the Covid-19 pandemic took a wrecking ball to the culture sector, and right-wing governments proved unwilling to pick up the pieces.

In the 2000s, digital technology provided both the means and the impetus for event cinema. Digital units were cheaper than film stock, costing as little as $300 compared with $1,800 per unit for celluloid.[131] However, the up-front cost of installation was very high. As Barker writes, '"Alternative content" [live, digitally streamed events] became a device to persuade investors to bite the digital bullet.'[132] Much like theatre television, digital simulcasting was initially envisioned as a vehicle for major sporting events, pop concerts, even (for early enthusiasts at Fox Faith) to distribute religious films but certainly not opera.[133] Nevertheless, opera was instrumental in its general adoption - which as we have seen, is not the first example of opera pioneering a new distribution channel.

Like Graf before him, the Met's manager Peter Gelb, who joined the company from Sony, pushed for a new mode of remediated opera in response to worrying developments for the opera house. In 2006, ticket sales had fallen below 75 per cent, traditional sponsorship sources were drying up as wealthy patrons either died or took their finances elsewhere, and the average age of auditorium attendees had reached sixty-five.[134] Gelb saw his challenge as to 'attract a younger, more hip, audience to opera ... the intellectually curious arts consumer, people in their 30s or 40s who, for example, like art-house cinema'.[135] While the high initial outlay made for a risky gambit from the Met's point of view, the premium $17.95 ticket price was a strong incentive for cinemas. Gelb's *Live from the Met in HD* series launched with a simulcast of *The Magic Flute* in 2006. The production was abridged, visually arresting and performed in the English language: all characteristics that Graf had successfully adopted for screen opera decades prior. The relay was transmitted via satellite to cinema and television screens in the United States, Canada, the UK, Norway and (via tape-delay) Japan.[136] The sell-out response led to new cinemas being added throughout a four-month, six-opera run to accommodate audience demand. The season also included Bellini's *I Puritani*, the world premiere of Tan Dun's *The First Emperor*, Tchaikovsky's *Eugene Onegin* and Rossini's *The Barber of Seville*.[137] Overall, an aggregate audience of 325,000 people worldwide watched the relays, leading the Met to immediately announce an expansion of the scheme for the following season.[138] In December 2007, a *Roméo et Juliet* relay (starring Anna Netebko) reached a worldwide cinema audience of nearly 100,000 on 600 screens.[139]

The press was initially enthusiastic about the Met's simulcasts, which were briefly touted as opera's saving grace. *Newsweek* hailed Gelb's bold effort 'to popularize opera and perhaps save it from obscurity', while *Variety* wrote that 'after years on the ropes, high art is battling back [by] cribbing moves from the pop culture playbook'.[140] The *Washington Post* described the events as 'one of the more fascinating cultural hybrids to appear recently'.[141] The *Los Angeles Times* went further still, announcing the advent of a new art form entirely: 'Filmed operas have been around for quite a while ... but they were never like this. The Met has reinvented the form. Or, rather, it has created a new art form.'[142] Despite the financial risk, other companies soon followed suit, including the San Francisco Opera, Milan's La Scala, the Royal Shakespeare Company, the National Theatre and, in 2008 with *Don Giovanni*, the Royal Opera House (Royal Opera House). Partnered with Arts Alliance Media as go-between with its cinema partners, The Royal Opera House led the way in Britain just as the Met had done in America, catering at their peak to well over 1,500 sites across fifty-five territories to an audience of millions, when factoring live-to-digital and big screen public shows.[143]

While opera remains the most common form of event cinema, it was soon outflanked by theatre in terms of box office revenue: 45 per cent of the 4.3 million tickets sold by the National Theatre in 2013/14 were for *NT Live*, for example. Opera cinema does not come near these numbers.[144] As a sub-sector of the film industry, event cinema overall has boasted impressive figures. The year 2019, the eve of the pandemic, was a record year for event cinema in the UK, for example, with record box office takings of £53.7 million from 130 titles. The event cinema audience increased by 30-even per cent on the previous year, constituting 3 per cent of all cinema tickets sold.[145] This might seem like peanuts compared to tent pole Hollywood releases, but the single-night model (excluding pre-recorded shows on subsequent nights) ought to put these numbers in context. The average event cinema production in the UK generates over £230,000 in box office revenue. For comparison, 62 per cent of UK and Ireland film releases produce less than £100,000 on their opening night.[146] The growth in event cinema is facilitated by 94 per cent of the world's cinemas being equipped for digital projection.[147] The UK became a world leader in this industry, with thirty-five distributors and the world's only trade body for the phenomenon: the Event Cinema Association.[148] Britain's geographical position results in favourable time differences with multiple key markets, making it viable to distribute and receive programming from the US and Russia, for instance.[149] The UK also has several globally visible organizations (all those with the royal charter, for instance) and full digital adoption by a strong cinema network.[150] More recently, the industry experimented with augmented reality and 4K technologies.[151] The National Theatre, in partnership with Sony and the Vue, captured the world's first multisite live 4K transmission in autumn 2015 with Benedict Cumberbatch's *Hamlet*, which became the fastest selling show in London's theatre history.[152] Its 2019 production of *Fleabag* became the biggest event cinema show of all time, taking in £4.3 million at the box office.[153]

However, event cinema's emphasis on theatre, opera and ballet has been criticized from some quarters for inhibiting its potential to accrue a youth and working-class audience. As Sarah Cooper remarks, a 'combination of premium ticket prices and content such as opera and ballet, continues to attract, primarily, an older, wealthier type of audience member, with the sector agreeing that more needs to be done to attract youth audiences, in the form [for example] of concert films'.[154] Moreover, simulcasts do not tend to generate income for arts organizations. This is partly due to the high up-front costs (each relay can cost in the region of £250,000),[155] and also because half the box office revenue goes to cinema partners, with a further portion to 'middleman' organizations like Arts Alliance Media. It is generally accepted that the primary function of simulcasting for arts companies is not direct income generation, but the promotion of brand visibility and audience acquisition.[156] Opera cinema has notably struggled in the latter regard, but other forms of event cinema have successfully grown and diversified stage audiences. The additional reach created by simulcasting permitted the National Theatre to grow its audience by over 50 per cent in 2013–14,[157] and it went on to grab half of the top ten best-selling event cinema shows of 2019.[158] Of course, the National Theatre is a very different organization than the Royal Opera House and benefits from a more stable economic position, which in turn permits greater experimentation and innovation in simulcasting. The National Theatre boasts more of an economy of scale, with longer theatrical runs, lower costs-per-show and a larger percentage of overall income received from the box office, and is thus less sensitive to reductions in government support.[159] It is also less reliant on donations and can take greater financial and creative risks.[160] For instance, during the relay night for *NT Live*, theatre tickets are sold at reduced prices and a compere explains to the audience in advance that there will be some intrusions. This permits the presence of tracks, rails, cranes and mobile cameras on the stage, which allows for greater versatility in the filming process, and in turn perhaps permits *NT Live* to assert itself as more of an art form in its own right than opera cinema.

Nevertheless, opera cinema draws together the various historical threads introduced in this chapter: the evangelizing streak of early remediated opera, the digital re-emergence of theatre television, the evolving relationship between opera and cinema and the effect of economics over remediated opera. It adopts the aesthetic conventions of the opera telecast refined and consolidated by the 1987 *Tosca* relay, which have become the dominant mode of opera remediation. It represents an important new development in the historical relationship between opera and cinema, as the first stable and lucrative hybrid between the two art forms. Using digital technology, it fulfils the institutional ambition for live, electronic cinema that was thwarted by objective factors in the post-war period. Finally, it confirms the transition that began in the 1980s away from attempts at democratizing opera through remediation and towards primarily commercial motivations.

Opera cinema and arts funding

While research exists on opera cinema's influence over the cultural ecology, no attempt has yet been made to explain how the effect of broader economic and political trends have shaped opera cinema to date. I argue that the development of opera cinema, as with all social phenomena, is motivated fundamentally by underlying economic imperatives. These trends must be explored to illustrate opera cinema's social and historical situation, which is partly constitutive of its ontology. As with its technological lineage, the economic currents pertinent to opera cinema began well before the first simulcast in 2006. Opera has always been especially sensitive to sociopolitical turbulence, and the emergence and function of opera cinema as a virtual gateway for established audiences reflects the precarious position of opera in the current economic climate. These two final parts of this chapter will explain how opera cinema is connected to a longer history of stage and screen opera under capitalism. Event cinema emerged under post-Thatcherite arts policy, partly to justify state subsidy by fulfilling opera companies' commitment to audience diversification. The related, sensitive issue of audience democratization explains why opera cinema has thus far failed to accrue new audiences. For the sake of concision and due to my own knowledge base, I will focus on the situation in the UK.

As a product of the late feudal era, opera has never sat comfortably under capitalism. It is a lavish and expensive art form that came out of a tradition of aristocratic patronage, where a small number of wealthy nobles would pay for its composition and production. Under a market economy, opera cannot consistently turn a profit under its own power.[161] However, the cultural esteem afforded to opera grants it additional income streams, and in the past century the medium has balanced awkwardly between government subsidy, donations and the box office to survive. Opera has tended to be a favoured art form of the political establishment, and from its relaunch in 1946, Covent Garden received a lion's share of arts grants.[162] A dramatic change occurred under Margaret Thatcher's Conservative government. While previous, patrician Tory governments took a certain pleasure in lavishing state support on the Royal Opera, under Thatcher's monetarist economic principles, the institution was seen as little more than a pompous drain on the public purse. As such, she aimed to give it a quick blast of the market economy. Her government began squeezing opera and ballet funding, which exerted a deleterious effect on repertoire, with a notable shift towards 'warhorses' (crowd-pleasing, canon works). The trend continued under John Major and the subsequent so-called New Labour governments of Tony Blair and Gordon Brown.[163] Arts Council grants to the Royal Opera House rose from £1.4 million to £20 million between 1970 and 1997, but inflation meant the actual purchasing value of the grant halved.[164] The right-wing tabloids, which had never previously voiced any particular interest in opera, chose this period to denounce its claim to public money.[165] Where once the government had provided 60 per cent of the Royal Opera House's costs, it now covers 22 per cent, which is still high relative to the state support given to other organizations.[166]

The Thatcher government exerted an effect beyond funding cuts: it also began insisting that subsidized organizations justify any public money received. In truth, this amounted to measuring the 'quality' and 'impact' of arts in terms that make sense on a spreadsheet.[167] Blair's New Labour government left much of Thatcher's economic policy intact, but coupled it with a newfound obsession with spin, image and 'optics'. In 1997, the Arts Council demanded that all projects be evaluated in terms of 'measurable success factors' to determine the accomplishments of organizations in which they had made an investment. These factors included social inclusion, widening access and artistic quality.[168] This is not an objection to the principle of ensuring democratic accountability over public spending and striving for inclusivity. However, real-terms funding cuts meant the actual outcome was a general withering of the cultural ecology across the board. These policies failed to produce a perceptible increase in participation in the arts, which precipitated a change of direction in 2010 under the Tory–Liberal Democrat Coalition government. The Arts Council argued that direct funding of social objectives had caused 'excellence and innovation' to suffer – as opposed to three decades of funding cuts.[169] The bureaucracy attached to public funding was not removed, but the funding was yet again reduced, and the government privatized the burden of assessment by shifting the responsibility to arts organizations.[170]

In the wake of the 2008 financial crash, the term 'cultural value' was coined to describe all the types of value generated by cultural activities, including their economic benefits. It has now entered political parlance and demonstrates the enduring legacy of the metrics-based allocation of funding for the arts under Thatcher and Blair.[171] The tendency was accelerated by austerity measures following the 2008 recession. The period saw cultural organizations gravitate towards audience development rather than product development, particularly with the use of new technologies to cultivate new arts consumers.[172] Demonstrating innovative means of disseminating ones' product is a way of tacitly justifying continued subsidy in an era of austerity. This reflects a political basis for widespread adoption of digital distribution methods by arts organizations in recent years, which has coalesced with the general digital changeover at cinemas and the greater reliability of satellite transmission technologies.

The connection between new communication technologies and provision of public money is explained in a 2012 article by Hasan Bahkshi and David Throsby for the *International Journal of Cultural Policy*, entitled

'New technologies in cultural institutions: theory, evidence and policy implications', in which they specifically reference simulcasting:

> The emergence of the creative industries as a central element in cultural policy formation over recent years has been importantly driven by the application of new technologies in cultural production, distribution and consumption ... Innovation in audience reach relates to the generation of new audiences, including through use of digital technologies such as live high-definition (HD) broadcasts in the case of theatre and opera companies, and providing online access to collections in the case of art galleries and museums ... The need for arts and cultural organisations to experiment with new business models requires new funding streams with an appetite for risk. In cases where there is a strong commercial prospect this may involve arts organisations working out new project finance structures which compensate private investors for the risk they take. Where the risks are too great to attract private financiers, but the sector stands to gain from the experiment (through wider lessons, for example), cultural organisations need to negotiate new funding streams with arts funders.[173]

The authors conclude that 'the link between new communications technologies and cultural policy has been acknowledged for some time'.[174] Given the historic controversy over state funding for 'elite' culture, it is hardly surprising that the Royal Opera House (which still receives more state funding than any other British arts institution, despite a 3 per cent cut in 2018/19, prior to Covid-recovery efforts)[175] has led the way in Britain in terms of institutional self-assessment – as noted by Jackie Bailey and Lance Richardson in *Cultural Trends*.[176] It is also no accident that the Royal Opera House was the first chartered organization to attempt simulcasting.

Whereas remediated opera thrived artistically in the post-war period of unprecedented state-sponsorship, opera cinema is a means to keep opera afloat in the recent era of privatization – a fact reflected in its aesthetic conservatism. Radio and television opera came on the crest of a productive boom that saw a general uptick in the standard of living, disposable income and leisure time for most of the British population, whereas opera cinema came about in a period of economic stagnation. Where state subsidies under the post-war consensus promoted a diverse artistic ecology, which in turn incentivized creative risks, the withering of state support in the present period of capitalist crisis has caused opera companies to fall back on reliable, canon productions. At the same time, the pressure to demonstrate accountability and the problem of ageing audiences have forced opera companies to grasp at digital dissemination to justify their relevance to state funders. These objective imperatives are reflected on an aesthetic level. Opera cinema is marketed at and is deliberately constructed to appeal to experienced audiences, upon whom opera companies depend for survival. Moreover, opera companies cannot readily risk the large financial outlay of conducting a cinema simulcast with an untested new repertoire, and this circumstance entrenches old favourites. These factors partly explain why simulcasting has not established itself as a discrete art form.

Democratization

Another contradiction in the ontological character of opera cinema is that, despite originating in part to meet social inclusion objectives, opera cinema's capacity to democratize audiences has been both limited and politically controversial. First, we must put matters in wider context.

As John Storey explains, since the Royal Opera House UK first received government support via Arts Council subsidies in 1946, the company has 'talked about reducing seat prices in order to make opera more accessible to a broader social mix'.[177] At the height of Thatcherism, in 1983, then chairman of the Royal Opera House Sir Charles Moser claimed, 'we are desperately trying to widen access … if we get more money, we will reduce seat prices. That's our top priority at the moment, and to widen access.'[178] This pledge was repeated in 1995 by the then chairman Sir Angus Stirling, who stated 'we are doing everything we can to bring seat prices down'.[179] His successor, Sir Colin Southgate, made the same promise in 1998: 'We have been asked to make the Royal Opera House less elitist and to bring ticket prices down. We want to do this, but we can't without money. It's a circle we cannot square.'[180] The main thing to understand here is the *quid quo pro* dynamic, where commitments to widening access comes in exchange for funding. Storey (citing Norman Lebrecht) questions whether the rebuilding of the Royal Opera House (paid for by a National Lottery grant of £78.5 million) showed genuine commitment to bringing in wider layers of audiences, given that it did not considerably increase its number of seats, unlike both the Met and the Bastille, who had kept tickets affordable by building new houses with significantly increased seating. This was justified by Southgate, who explained: 'We mustn't downgrade the opera house. I don't want to sit next to somebody in a singlet, a pair of shorts and a smelly pair of trainers. I'm a relaxed individual, but I'm passionate about standards of behaviour.'[181] The point is opera houses have always talked about widening access, but the combined pressures of inclusivity (which justifies essential state support) while also maintaining 'standards' (in the eyes of operaphiles, critics and stars) applies a countervailing pressure. All these dynamics found a new lease on life in the 2000s and 2010s through the rubric of digital distribution.

Chief executive of the Royal Opera House, Tony Hall, went on record in a 2010 interview with the *Independent* to specifically highlight the democratizing effect of simulcasting as justification for public expenditure on opera. Despite facing 'spending cuts that would have made Mrs Thatcher blush', Hall stated his commitment to bringing the 'most notoriously elitist art form to the masses'.[182] Hall is quoted as saying: 'We have to keep looking for ways of reaching people, but we have to reach out to where people are. We can't just be passive and ask them to come to us … If we are taking money from the public, then it is absolutely right that we try to reach as many people as want us.'[183] Intuitively, it seems that opera cinema should have the capacity to diversify opera audiences. It is generally cheaper and more convenient than auditorium attendance, particularly for those who live outside of metropolitan centres, and it has a greater geographic reach than stage opera. It is also clear that audience diversification was high on the Royal Opera House's list of priorities when it adopted digital simulcasting. However, the Royal Opera's research data indicate that it mostly caters to an older and more experienced cross-section of its existing audience: it is reaching more of the same people, rather than newcomers.[184]

A related controversy surrounding opera simulcasting concerns its potentially deleterious impact on staged opera by cannibalizing audiences from the auditorium. Every new channel for distributing opera has been met with this criticism.[185] As far as I can tell, there is limited concrete evidence of cannibalization.[186] An investigation by Brent Karpf Reidy, Becky Shutt, Deborah Abramson, Antoni Durski and Laura Castle indicates that Live-to-Digital online streaming might have a small effect on the success or length of local and touring runs, but found no such trend for simulcasting.[187] Research on simulcasting by Karen Wise for the Guildhall and English Touring Opera sparked a minor controversy when the mainstream press reported that it provided positive proof of cannibalization.[188] In fact, Wise's findings merely implied some first-time opera cinema attendees in her small-scale research project were more motivated to attend future simulcasts, and their intention to attend further stage performances was broadly unchanged.[189] It is possible the findings were selectively represented by ETO, who took a very strong anti-simulcast position at the time. The present consensus is that opera cinema neither meaningfully cannibalizes existing audiences nor creates new ones.[190]

However, it is certainly true that the rise of opera cinema correlated with a reduction of the artistic ecology, given cuts to state subsidies and concentration of support for the arts in urban centres.[191] In the period of 2010 to 2014, the Arts Council's budget was cut by £100 million and its portfolio of subsidized organizations fell by 140, with an additional 5 per cent cut in 2018.[192] Many of the organizations affected closed their doors, while many more are at an imminent risk of closure. Regional authorities have also come under the knife, which has dramatically reduced Britain's arts ecology, as confirmed by the Arts Council itself.[193] By contrast, five metropolitan organizations (including the Royal Opera House) receive 30 per cent of the Arts Council's entire funding expenditure, with 600 other organizations sharing the remaining 70 per cent.[194] At the time of writing, in the aftermath of the Covid-19 pandemic, these trends are likely to continue.[195] In sum, simulcasting increases the visibility of chartered companies at the perceived expense of regional companies and the high up-front costs associated with simulcasting mean they are strictly the domain of national organizations. The issue is not fundamentally one of distribution, but production. Namely, a crisis of overproduction that brought on a protracted period of crisis and austerity. This is primarily to blame for the dire straits of the culture sector, rather than event cinema per se.

The next chapter for opera cinema

No cultural experience can be understood either in the abstract, or with audience data alone. Opera cinema is a unique cultural experience that draws together numerous historical narratives, including the tension between popular and elite culture, the relationship between cinema and opera, the democratizing effect of technology and the pressure of socio-economic factors. Furthermore, opera cinema must not be homogenized within the event cinema umbrella as it is distinct from other forms of event cinema in terms of its social position, technical and experiential characteristics. This distinctiveness can be partly illustrated through historical analysis. The evolutionary process charted here demonstrates how opera cinema emerged out of the interaction and hybridization of various media forms across the twentieth century. There is a direct line to be drawn between the primitive experiments conducted by Lee de Forest from the roof of the Metropolitan Opera House in 1910, through radio broadcasts, to theatre television, to live telecasts and to modern event cinema. The latter fulfils a particular institutional objective, strengthened by competition from domestic media, to transmit live images to the movie house. Digital technology has facilitated this ambition as a stable and lucrative phenomenon.

Relative to earlier forms of remediated opera, opera cinema is less concerned with spreading high culture 'to the masses', and instead reflects a commercial, institution-building imperative that began to define remediated opera in the 1970s, being consolidated by the modern opera telecast. Opera cinema adopts most of its technical conventions from the telecast, whose default aesthetic was established by the Met's 1987 relay of *Turandot* - an opera that is still a popular choice for contemporary simulcasting. The phenomenon also represents an important development in the close and complex relationship between cinema and opera. While the movies are in many ways indebted to opera on both an aesthetic and institutional level, the latter has generally performed better on radio and television than the big screen. The simulcast is the first consistently successful hybrid of sound cinema and opera, achieved by combining televisual elements with digital communication.

Furthermore, opera cinema is not currently a means to build and diversify opera audiences, although there is no convincing evidence that it is hampering opera in this regard either. Where the telecasts of the post-war period, to a certain extent, reflected a principle of treating culture as a public good (albeit one based on liberal Keynesian economics rather than sustainable socialist economic planning), opera cinema has emerged at a time of stagnation that has forced opera companies to find new means of survival. Therefore, where television opera in the 1950s and 1960s displayed much experimentation with staging, style and repertoire, opera cinema evinces opera's current reliance on established audiences and repertoire, giving rise to accusations that it has become a museum art.[196] In the main, opera cinema serves to promote the profile of major opera companies and justify government subsidies by proving these companies' commitment to inclusion. This in turn reflects the increasing scarcity of arts funding since the 1980s, and the shift towards 'accountability', amounting to metricisation and increasing corporatisation of the arts. These objective factors are crucial to understanding opera cinema as they inflect its composition and the experience it facilitates, as I demonstrate through the impressions of my research subjects in the following chapters.

At the time of writing, the event cinema industry is reeling from the Covid-19 pandemic and successive lockdowns across the world, under which doors were closed for months at a time. The Event Cinema Association has received a chunk of the government's emergency relief fund for the culture sector.[197] In Britain, the Royal Opera House leaned on different forms of digital distribution to keep the lights on: re-releasing old productions via its website for a small fee, and making recordings available on their YouTube channel for a limited time. It is experimenting with the possibilities of rehearsing and staging new productions in lockdown conditions, though it is not clear whether these are intended for broadcast. In a brief (and inadvisable) national reprieve between lockdowns in the summer of 2020, the Royal Opera House facilitated a handful of drive-in nights to showcase some of its older programming: a fascinating revival of a vintage exhibition practice under peculiar circumstances. However, for now, opera cinema remains in limbo: like so many other cultural forms, it is a victim of circumstances entirely beyond its control. Whether it will enjoy the 'V-shaped recovery' optimistically anticipated by financial and political pundits for the rest of the economy remains to be seen. With the culture sector hollowed out by mass unemployment, it seems doubtful that any 'return to normality' can be expected. The new normal will have to take account of the severe damage dealt to the arts across the board, but also the public's greater familiarity with home viewing and live, digital distribution. We can only speculate as to whether this portends good or ill for opera cinema, but I suspect online, at-home distribution will be the main beneficiary of any altered patterns of audience behaviour. The jury is out on opera cinema. One way or another, screen opera will continue to feature heavily in the art form's destiny.

Notes

1. Robert C. Allen and Douglas Gomery, *Film History: Theory and Practice* (New York: McGraw Hill, 1985).
2. John Wyver, 'The Early Imaginary of Event Cinema, 1878–1953', paper presented at Live Theatre Broadcast Symposium at University of York (York: University of York, 25 June 2015).
3. Marcia J. Citron, *Opera on Screen* (New Haven, CT: Yale University Press, 2000), 25.
4. Daniel Snowman, *The Gilded Stage: A Social History of Opera* (London: Atlantic Books, 2009), 282.
5. Ibid., 282.
6. Ibid.
7. Paul Heyer, 'Live from the Met: Digital Broadcast Cinema, Medium Theory, and Opera for the Masses', *Canadian Journal of Communication* 33 (2008): 592.
8. Snowman, 282.
9. Ibid.
10. Heyer, 592.
11. Ibid.
12. Snowman, 282.
13. Ibid.
14. Ibid.
15. Ibid.
16. Ibid., 282–3.
17. Ibid., 283.
18. Martin Barker, *Live to Your Local Cinema: The Remarkable Rise of Livecasting* (Basingstoke: Palgrave Macmillan, 2013), 2.
19. Snowman, 283.
20. Ibid., 284.
21. Ibid.
22. Ibid.
23. Ibid.

24 Douglas Gomery, 'Theatre Television: The Missing Link of Technological Change in the US Motion Picture Industry', *Velvet Light Trap* 21 (1985): 54.
25 Wyver.
26 Ibid.
27 Ibid.
28 Ibid.
29 Ibid.
30 Ibid.
31 Ibid.
32 Ibid.
33 Ibid.
34 Gomery, 120.
35 Wyver.
36 Ibid.
37 Ibid.
38 Ibid.
39 Wyver.
40 Ibid.
41 Gomery, 122.
42 Fiona Tuck, 'Understanding the Impact of Event Cinema: An Evidence Review', *Arts Council England and British Film Institute*, January 2016.
43 Gomery, 120.
44 Ibid.
45 Ibid.
46 Ibid.
47 Ibid.
48 Ibid.
49 Ibid.
50 Ibid., 120–1.
51 Ibid., 121.
52 Ibid.
53 Ibid.
54 Ibid.
55 Ibid.
56 Ibid.
57 Ibid.
58 Ibid., 121–2.

59 Luke Brown, 'Floyd Mayweather vs Conor McGregor to Be Shown Live at Cinemas for Far Less Money than the PPV Cost', *Independent*, 27 July 2017, accessed 7 June 2018, https://www.independent.co.uk/sport/general/boxing/mayweather-mcgregor/floyd-mayweather-vs-conor-mcgregor-live-fight-watch-cinemas-movie-theatres-ppv-cost-a7862816.html.
60 Gomery, 122.
61 Ibid.
62 Wyver.
63 Citron, *Opera on Screen*, 41–2.
64 Ibid., 41.
65 Ibid., 42.
66 Ibid.
67 Ibid., 43.
68 Jennifer Barnes, 'Television Opera: A Non-History', in *A Night in at the Opera: Media Representations of Opera* (Luton: University of Luton Press, 1994), 40–1.
69 Citron, 43.
70 Ibid.
71 Barnes, 42.
72 Barnes, 40–3.
73 Citron, 43.
74 Ibid.
75 Ibid.
76 Ibid., 43–5.
77 Ibid., 44.
78 Ibid., 45.
79 Ibid.
80 Ibid.
81 Ibid., 45–6.
82 Ibid., 47.
83 Ibid.
84 Marcia Citron, 'Subjectivity in the Opera Films of Jean-Pierre Ponnelle', in *When Opera Meets Film*, edited by Citron (New York: Cambridge University Press, 2010), 97.
85 Ibid., 99.
86 Citron, *Opera on Screen*, 46.
87 Ibid., 47–8.
88 Ibid., 48.
89 Ibid., 47.

90 Ibid., 49.
91 James Steichen, 'HD Opera: A Love/Hate Story. Staging the Backstage at Carmen, Live in HD', *Opera Quarterly* 27.4 (2011): 27.
92 Citron, *Opera on Screen*, 64.
93 Ibid.
94 Ibid., 63–5.
95 Roland Barthes, 'Leaving a Movie Theatre', in *The Rustle of Language*, edited by Roland Barthes (Toronto: Collins Publishers, 1986), 346.
96 Carolyn Abbate and Roger Parker, *A History of Opera: The Last Four Hundred Years* (London: Penguin Group, 2012), 19, 31, 356–72; Snowman, 196–7.
97 Snowman, 46.
98 Snowman, 45; Charles Acland, *Screen Traffic: Movies, Multiplexes, and Global Culture* (Durham, NC: Duke University Press, 2003), 20.
99 Snowman, 286.
100 Citron, *Opera on Screen*, 30.
101 Snowman, 286.
102 Marcia J. Citron, 'Operatic Style in Coppola's *Godfather* Trilogy', in *When Opera Meets Film* (Cambridge: Cambridge University Press, 2010), 57.
103 Snowman, 24.
104 Ibid., 287.
105 Claudio E. Benzecry, *The Opera Fanatic: Ethnography of an Obsession* (Chicago: University of Chicago Press, 2011), 18; Snowman, 287; Citron, 'Operatic Style in Coppola's Godfather trilogy', 31.
106 David Schroeder, *Cinema's Illusions, Opera's Allure: The Operatic Impulse in Film* (New York: Bloomsbury, 2016), 214.
107 Citron, 'Operatic Style in Coppola's *Godfather* trilogy', 23.
108 Ibid., 37.
109 Ibid., 57.
110 Herbert Lindenberger, *Opera: The Extravagant Art* (London: Cornell University Press, 1984), 239.
111 Ibid., 22–3.
112 Ibid., 26.
113 Ibid.
114 Snowman, 284.
115 Rose Theresa, 'From Méphistophélès to Méliès: Spectacle and Narrative in Opera and Early Film', in *Between Opera and Cinema*, edited by Jeongwon Joe and Rose Theresa (New York: Routledge, 2002), 7.
116 Ibid., 7.
117 Snowman, 287.

118 Citron, *Opera on Screen*, 26–7.
119 Ibid., 32.
120 Ibid., 33–5.
121 Ibid., 39.
122 Ibid.
123 James Steichen, 'The Metropolitan Opera Goes Public: Peter Gelb and the Institutional Dramaturgy of the Met: Live in HD', *Music and the Moving Image* 2.2 (2009): 24.
124 Ibid., 21.
125 Melina Esse, 'Don't Look Now: Opera, Liveness, and the Televisual', *Opera Quarterly* 26 (2010): 81.
126 Citron, *Opera on Screen*, 61.
127 Ibid.
128 Ibid.
129 Joseph Attard, 'Opera in the Multiplex', *Opera Quarterly* 34.4 (2018): 284–305.
130 Ibid., 63.
131 Barker, 3.
132 Ibid., 4–5.
133 Ibid., 4.
134 Ibid., 2–3.
135 Ibid., 3.
136 Ibid., 2.
137 Ibid.
138 Snowman, 421.
139 Ibid.
140 Steichen, 24.
141 Ibid.
142 Ibid., 24–5.
143 'Live from the Royal Opera House 2017/18 – 12 Blockbuster Titles, One Cinema Season', *Trafalgar Releasing*, accessed 7 June 2018, https://www.trafalgar-releasing.com/news/live-from-the-royal-opera-house-201718-12-blockbuster-titles-one-cinema-season/.
144 Tuck, 7.
145 'Event Cinema Box Office', *Event Cinema Association*, accessed 13 June 2021, https://eventcinemaassociation.org/news/event-cinema-box-office/.
146 Tuck, 10.
147 Ibid., 19.

148 'Who We Are', *Event Cinema Association*, accessed 6 June 2017, https://www.eventcinemaassociation.org/who-we-are.html.
149 Tuck, 24.
150 Ibid.
151 Brent Karpf Reidy, Becky Shutt, Deborah Abramson, Antoni Durski and Laura Castle, 'From Live-to-Digital', *AEA Consulting for Arts Council England and Society of London Theatre*, October 2016, 84; Tuck, 25.
152 Karpf Reidy et al., 85.
153 'Event Cinema Box Office'.
154 Sarah Cooper, 'Event Cinema on Growth Curve', *Screen Daily*, 16 October 2013, accessed 13 June 2021, http://www.screendaily.com/news/event-cinema-on-growth-curve/5062554.article.
155 Tuck, 8.
156 Karpf Reidy et al.; Tuck, 38.
157 Tuck, 7.
158 'Event Cinema Box Office'.
159 'Arts Council England Analysis of Theatre in England', *Final Report by BOP Consulting & Graham Devlin Associates*, 13 September 2016.
160 'Arts Council England Analysis of Theatre in England'; 'National Theatre: Key Facts and Figures', *National Theatre*, accessed 13 June 2021, https://www.nationaltheatre.org.uk/about-the-national/key-facts-and-figures.
161 Snowman, 139.
162 Andrew Sinclair, *Arts and Cultures: The History of the 50 Years of the Arts Council of Great Britain* (London: Sinclair-Stevenson, 1995), 110–11.
163 Ibid., 382.
164 Snowman, 414.
165 Ibid., 414–15.
166 Alex Beard, 'Arts Council England: National Portfolio and Bridge Funding Announced', *The Royal Opera House*, 1 July 2014, accessed 13 June 2021, http://www.roh.org.uk/news/authors/alex-beard.
167 Olivia Turnbull, *Bringing Down the House: The Crisis in Britain's Regional Theatres* (Bristol: Intellect Books, 2008), 48.
168 Ibid., 193.
169 Ibid., 184.
170 Ibid., 200.
171 Hasan Bakhshi, Juan Mateos-Garcia and David Throsby, 'Beyond Live: Digital Innovation in the Performing Arts' (London: National Endowment for Science, Technology and the Arts, 2010): 211.
172 Ibid.
173 Bakhshi, Mateos-Garcia and Throsby, 205–12.

174 Ibid., 212.
175 Alex Beard, 'Royal Opera House to Continue Receiving Government Investment until 2022', *Royal Opera House Online*, 27 June 2017, accessed 6 June 2018, http://www.roh.org.uk/news/royal-opera-house-to-continue-receiving-government-investment-until-2022.
176 Jackie Bailey and Lance Richardson, 'Meaningful Measurement: A Literature Review and Australian and British Case Studies of Arts Organizations Conducting Artistic Self-Assessment', *Cultural Trends* 19.4 (2010): 297.
177 John Storey, '"Expecting Rain": Opera as Popular Culture?', in *High-Pop: Making Culture into Popular Entertainment*, edited by Jim Collins (London: Wiley-Blackwell, 2002), 45.
178 Ibid.
179 Ibid.
180 Norman Lebrecht, *Covent Garden, the Untold Story* (Boston, MA: Northeastern University Press, 2001), 458.
181 Ibid., 455.
182 Sarah Arnott, 'Taking High Culture to the Mass Market', *Independent*, 12 August 2010, accessed 13 June 2021, http://www.independent.co.uk/news/business/analysis-and-features/tony-hall-taking-high-culture-to-the-mass-market-2050088.html.
183 Ibid.
184 Amanda Fallows, 'Royal Opera House Cinema Research', Royal Opera House research data, October 2014.
185 Snowman, 281–4.
186 Hasan Bakhshi and Andrew Whitby, 'Estimating the Impact of Live Simulcast on Theatre Attendance: An Application to London's National Theatre', *NESTA* 14.4 (2014).
187 Karpf Reidy et al., 82.
188 Tom Service, 'Opera in Cinemas: Is It Creating New Audiences?', *Guardian*, 30 May 2014, accessed 13 June 2021, https://www.theguardian.com/music/tomserviceblog/2014/may/30/opera-in-cinemas-creating-new-audiences.
189 Karen Wise, 'Opera in Cinemas', report for ETO and Guildhall School of Music & Drama (London, 2013).
190 Tuck, 30.
191 Turnbull, 201.
192 Beard, 'Arts Council England: National Portfolio and Bridge Funding Announced', *Royal Opera House*, 1 July 2014, accessed 13 June 2021, http://www.roh.org.uk/news/arts-council-england-national-portfolio-and-bridge-funding-announced; Jen Harvie, 'Funding, Philanthropy, Structural Inequality and Decline in England's Theatre Ecology', *Cultural Trends* 24.1 (2015): 56.
193 'Arts Council England Analysis of Theatre in England'.
194 Harvie, 57.

195 'Context for Our Approach to Investment in 2018–22', Arts Council England, accessed 13 June 2021, http://www.artscouncil.org.uk/sites/default/files/Context-for-our-approach-to-our-investment_2018-22.pdf.
196 Snowman, 424.
197 'ECA to Receive Culture Recovery Fund Support', *Event Cinema Association*, last updated 2 April 2020, accessed 13 June 2021, https://eventcinemaassociation.org/news/eca-to-receive-culture-recovery-fund-support/.

3

What makes it opera cinema?

Now we have looked at the history of opera cinema, we will focus on its distinguishing formal, aesthetic and experiential aspects. We need to understand how these events are made, how they look and how they feel. This dimension of opera cinema's ontology is obviously not a closed question. The conventions of simulcasting have developed over time and vary across different opera houses and directors. For instance, the BBC-credited director I interviewed during my PhD research contrasted his work for the Royal Opera House (ROH) with Andy Morahan's filming of *Peter Grimes* for the English National Opera (ENO) in 2014. Morahan did not have a background in classical music, but was an experienced director of popular music videos (for the likes of Guns'N'Roses and Michael Jackson) and concert recordings. The ENO, who pride themselves on their edgier approach to the medium (and who had previously disparaged opera cinema),[1] wanted their relays to be done differently to their competitors. The result – a largely improvised visual approach consisting of 'multiple camera angles, ultra-bright lights, plenty of movement and extreme close-ups' – enjoyed a mixed reception, with fair reviews but complaints from some audience members that the production made them feel 'nauseous'.[2] Nevertheless, this kind of experimentation remains the exception rather than the rule. As discussed in Chapter 2, there is strong institutional and commercial pressure for directors not to push things 'too far' on the aesthetic front. The Royal Opera House's meticulous, arguably more cautious approach to their relays are probably closer to the norm.

    I will be drawing on information obtained over the course of my PhD project, during which I interviewed various artists, technicians and behind-the-scenes personnel, sat in on rehearsals and watched a relay being conducted. This provided me with a wealth of material, but in order to preserve anonymity I will not be citing my interviewees directly. As these discussions and observations took place some time ago, it is possible that aspects of the production process have moved on, but I still hope to provide a decent picture of what goes into putting on these events. I will also slightly pre-empt Chapter 4 by touching on my own audience research data, where appropriate. Throughout, I will continue to engage with the theoretical debates raised by the unique and evolving cultural experience of opera cinema. Also, while I will make some comparisons between the Royal Opera House and other opera companies, the bulk of my research has been with Covent Garden, which puts a certain slant on my impressions. I can only invite future researchers to fill any gaps in my work.

As a digital experience, opera cinema is necessarily implicated in new media debates surrounding medium specificity – which generally fall into either technical or social determinist paradigms. While the basis for technological lines of demarcation between media types has been blurred by digitization, there are nevertheless qualities particular to opera cinema that inform its ontology. As Rob King argues, 'the forms and strategies of [media] have among their conditions of possibility the technological properties ... by which they are produced and circulated.'[3] In other words, the horizon of experience for opera cinema audiences is limited and structured by the phenomenon's technological parameters.[4] Simulcasting synthesizes a variety of media forms, while concealing evidence of technological intervention. Opera cinema brings the visual grammar of film and television, networked communication, interactivity and the exhibition practices of cinema to bear upon a centuries-old cultural artefact. It is a gestalt entity, but it is not *merely* a remediation or transmission of existing cultural forms. Although opera cinema upholds the dual logic of remediation (hypermediacy and immediacy), and thus strives for a transparent representation of the stage action, it nevertheless reflects artistic and institutional decision making. The chief visual strategy of opera cinema's double-directed screen action (that hybridizes live performance with the language of cinema) is influenced by simulcasting's early function as an audience building tool. As such, it promotes legibility of the drama through relatively tight camerawork that privileges key points of narrative action and the principal performers. While this superficially implies a more passive and less intellectually and emotionally engaged mode of viewing, the double-direction permits deeper appreciation of performers' facial performances, which opens-up an additional layer of interpretive work. In short, opera cinema changes stage opera into a new cultural experience, with formal characteristics unlike either a stage show or pre-recorded cinema.

The main formal analogue for opera cinema's visual strategies are opera telecasts, which started in earnest in the 1980s onwards. Although the technical parameters of the expanded cinema image have exerted a degree of influence over shot scale and cutting rates. Despite the primarily televisual basis for opera cinema's composition, the exhibition environment means it is primarily interpreted as cinematic by general audiences – and my respondents. It is also marketed along these lines. Posters usually put the principal performers front-and-centre (especially in the case of opera's few international stars, like Jonas Kaufman and Bryn Terfel), while trailers cut together moments of high drama and visual impact. Contrasted with twentieth-century operatic marketing material, which tends to throw emphasis on the title of the opera and the composer – perhaps with stylized imagery lifted from key scenes for the knowing gaze of an experienced audience – opera cinema exploitation casts a wider net. In part, this is necessitated by the fact that these materials are displayed in cinemas, where they must stand alongside Hollywood marketing material. I have spoken to marketing staff who admitted that opera cinema attendees are 'not a digital audience', but nevertheless companies utilize social media channels to promote upcoming relays, and strive for online engagement up to and during broadcasts: with dedicated hashtags and the like. At the time of writing, there has been a notable redoubling of efforts to exploit digital promotion and distribution channels through streams, video 'masterclasses' with the likes of Royal Opera House music director Antonio Pappano, behind-the-scenes footage and snippets of performances. Of course, none of this is specifically promotion for opera cinema, which occupies a 'third pillar' alongside auditorium performances and streaming. In terms of 'conventional' exploitation, the Royal Opera House's past media partners (including the *Telegraph* newspaper) seem to acknowledge a comparatively mature, middle-class audience for opera cinema hinting at its primary function of serving the experienced rather than converting novices.

Regarding novice audiences, the formal characteristics of opera provoked a variety of responses from my research subjects, not all of whom necessarily appreciated the unique elements of simulcasting (as I shall explore in depth in the Chapter 4). However, negative and positive responses to opera cinema's peculiarities are equally valid evidence of its formal specificity. As Wolfgang Ernst states, any media ontologist must begin with a 'close examination of technical media as they actually operate' – which is the objective of the current chapter.[5] I begin with perhaps opera cinema's most distinctive quality: the double-directed screen action. I then tackle the numerous interpretations of liveness presented by these events. I go on to discuss two distinctive aspects of opera cinema: the insight films (short 'making of' documentaries) and celebrity presenters that occupy intervals, and the networked communication encouraged and facilitated during the show. The chapter brings these micro-level characteristics to bear on broader debates around media ontology that arise from the digital cultures that opera cinema typifies, characterized by convergence, hybridity and networked communication. I will then address three features of the simulcasting experience that indicate its subordinate and ancillary status to stage opera. First, I argue the main experiential objective of opera cinema is to create a sense of virtual attendance, promote an opera house's brand

and encourage future auditorium attendance. Secondly, I address the effect of remediation over immersion, and its connection to cultural validity. This is related to the 'cult of liveness', which emphasizes the mystique and value of live performance over recorded or mediated experiences. After which, I address the opera's reputation for elitism, justified or otherwise.

The chapter will proceed by introducing the most salient aspects of opera cinema's burgeoning exhibition practices. I begin by dealing with specific ritual behaviours, etiquette and contextual parameters of opera cinema, before moving on to more general observations about attitudes towards the developing status and function of this new cultural experience. For my theoretical framework for understanding of media use, I draw primarily on Lisa Gitelman's concept of protocols and Martin Barker's notion of viewing registers. I will demonstrate how opera cinema's behavioural codes are enforced from the institutional side, motivated in part by the special technical requirements of simulcasting. Subsequently, I touch on how the mature, opera-savvy audience present during simulcasts prefigure audience engagement with opera cinema. I will focus on a pair of ritual case studies – choice of attire and applause – then theorize the sense of occasion fostered by the simulcast, relating my conclusions to wider debates over the status of 'the event' in contemporary media cultures. I will intervene on the complex, politicized issues of accessibility and audience democratization, broach the related questions of cultural esteem, before discussing the intricate notion of accessibility, which encompasses practical and more subjective aspects. All these features offer evidence of a unique viewing strategy that could take shape for opera cinema, though as yet it remains only as potential.

Double-direction

I was struck by a comment by a member of Royal Opera House staff whom I interviewed in 2014, who said, 'to see a story go to the cinema, to see a performance go to the auditorium'. From the earliest stages of planning my research project, I was fascinated by the simulcast's double-directed screen action: by which I mean the action is directed once for the stage, and again as a cinematic experience for the simulcast. On a theoretical level, this trademark strongly evokes Jay David Bolter and Richard Grusin's remediation: the process of mediation conceals itself, and yet displays a multitude of media forms. Opera cinema hides evidence of its own mediation process, reflecting a shift from reinterpretation to reportage undergone by screen opera from the 1980s onwards, in which elaborate, made-for-screen adaptations of opera were supplanted by live relays. Opera cinema also supports Bolter and Grusin's essential premise that digital media are almost always representations of representations that strive for transparency – *remediations*.[6] However, remediation is never an entirely 'cold' process.

As Emanuele Senici points out, 'even [screen operas] made with only one fixed-position camera ... highlight, hide, confuse, clarify, promote, demote, ignore, contradict, and so on'.[7]

Except in rare cases (like the production of *Peter Grimes* cited above), the camera director for opera cinema is seldom celebrated in promotional material, at least at the Royal Opera House. Their role is assumed to be technical rather than artistic. This is reflected at a production level. In the rehearsals, I observed the simulcast director was present but occupied a clear subordinate role to the stage director – observing the proceedings largely in silence and planning their shots accordingly. There were rare instances where certain shot choices were communicated to the stage director (particularly group shots), but the process seems less an equal creative collaboration, as specialist brought in to relay an artist's vision. The multi-camera operator whom I interviewed (who was experienced in classical music and had many BBC production credits to his name) explained that he would not expect a stage director to understand the ins and outs of the complex recording process. Instead, he tries to understand the stage director's thought process and realize it in the cinema. The terms frequently utilized were 'cherishing' a production, and 'celebrating the work of the artist', stating that he brought the same ethos to the Royal Opera House as to other houses he has worked with, including ENO and Dresden. However, he attested to variations, explaining that different theatre directors have different perspectives with regards to the involvement of the film director. The stage director does not have to sign off on every shot choice, but some are more concerned than others about the final product. Outside of opera, the National Theatre (NT) and Royal Shakespeare Company (RSC) use a 'paid-for audience' (i.e. theatre attendees offered discounted tickets), allowing the use of tracking shots, cranes and cinematic effects. To do so in the opera house would be prohibitively expensive, due to the listed building, and frowned upon by the audiences present on the night. For this reason, cameras for the simulcast must be positioned unobtrusively, which limits shot options.

As a result, the film director I interviewed explained he will offer small notes to the performers during rehearsals, containing suggestions on how to make their performances more sympathetic to the camera. So, there is a certain amount of reciprocity, wherein the relay has an impact of the stage production. He also explained that attitudes are changing. There is a trend towards more awareness of the remediation process from stage directors, permitting some film directors a degree of creative autonomy. For example, Keith Warner – who directed the Ring cycle for the Royal Opera House – added things intentionally that would've been invisible on stage but visible for screen. In *Valkyrie*, he included a little religious ceremony where a chorus character cut his finger with an axe. This was a contained piece of action in the dark of the auditorium, but highly visible on screen. He also kept action going in musical interludes, knowing this would be visible on the screen.

All of this was done with the blessing of the stage director. The attitude of 'you work on TV, I'm not interested in you' was at one time prevalent, but is apparently waning.

The variations in mise en scene, lighting and so on across different productions means there is no 'one-size-fits-all' approach to filming, but ultimately this process of translation seeks to be as seamless as possible. When it comes to planning shots, the director explained that the craftspeople involved in the production must be represented 'sympathetically': set design, costume, lighting, make-up and so on must all be represented, ignoring no contributions. Following the stage rehearsals, a camera script is developed some weeks before the broadcast, in which shots are meticulously selected and marked on the score and libretto. The script I was privy to was very detailed, and additional suggestions were made in the camera rehearsal I attended to allow the technicians to refine their shots. The score reader, lighting, vision mixer, sound mixer and seven camera-people were present, along with the director, who described those in attendance as 'the finest crew available for this kind of event'. The simulcast crew watched an unedited, continuous take of the dress rehearsal and rehearse every movement, cut and zoom, taking account of narrative issues, character, dynamics of relationships, groupings on stage, location of characters in the mise en scene, anticipation of events, planting a character's presence in the audience's mind, emotional pitch, musical phrasing and so on. Each camera operator had his or her camera card on which their shots were listed, with the lead camera operator calling out cuts.

The quirks of the performers affected these deliberations. For instance, one of the principals had a tendency of raising his hand 'dramatically', which – when done repetitively – looked rather silly on film. Consequently, shots of him were tightened to conceal this tendency. Once the rehearsal was concluded, the director developed a few recommendations for the performers. He explained that the advantages of clarity and drama offered by the grammar of television and cinema must balance with every other aspect of mise en scene. For instance, he explained that he tends to avoid extreme close-ups on artists *in extremis*: straining on a high C, for example, saying this is not fair on the artist; and moreover, making sweat, wig line and head mikes visible destroys the suspension of disbelief for the audience. There is no way to hide the proscenium arch, but the integrity of the drama is preserved as far as possible, with care taken to ensure the broadcast does not 'cheapen the art'.

When I pressed on this value judgement, the director explained that television is still seen as a populist medium, and it is important to avoid any sense of minimization of opera as an art form. This was interesting on several levels. Firstly, it underlines opera cinema's primarily televisual heritage, despite the cinematic exhibition context. This sets the basic parameters for its double-direction. Secondly, these comments show the marginalization of the remediation process from creative considerations, and strongly implies opera cinema's ancillary, supportive status – which has implications in terms of defining its ontology, and in explaining why I do not consider it an art form. And finally, it highlights the longstanding anxiety in the operatic milieu that technological mediation taints or diminishes opera. This charge has been levelled against every form of remediated opera ever to exist, from Adorno's denigration of radio broadcasts and LP recordings, to critical assessments of digital streaming by modern operaphiles.[8] These wider social pressures have a direct impact on opera cinema's formal characteristics. The director explained that the increasingly reciprocal relationship between the stage performance and the simulcast produces anxiety from some members of the opera community, who fear the art is being 'cheapened' by the alien considerations of the camera. In short, film directors working at this level of the industry are forced to perform a delicate balancing act to appease all quarters.

Despite television being the main analogue for opera cinema direction, there are specific considerations for cinema. Firstly, the size of screen and clarity of picture. The director made the comparison between a MacBook Pro and a 5K screen: perception is completely altered in the cinema, as audiences become 'bored' quickly with a low-quality image. Higher quality images affect the cutting rate, as shots can be allowed to sit on the screen for longer. Consequently, the average shot length increases at the cinema compared to TV. I gleaned evidence of the on-going developmental process for opera cinema conventions through our discussions. The director explained that he is starting to revert more to a conventional grammar of faster cutting, rather than allowing medium length shots to linger, or as he put it, 'sitting there and allowing things to happen'. This earlier style of editing can be observed in the Metropolitan Opera House's *Magic Flute* and the Royal Opera's *Don Giovanni* simulcast in 2006 and 2008, respectively.

The problem is that shots that last too long draw attention to the camera's position and elevation, which can take audiences out of the drama. Moreover, the size of the cinema screen draws attention to camera movement, meaning it must be carefully calibrated and judged. If a camera pans from left to right it must finish and hold. If it moves back and adjusts, it looks like a mistake. This can be more easily gotten away with on television. The director will sometimes encourage a camera operator to chase the action for a particular expressive effect, but there can be no adjustment: in an ideal world, the camera should be an 'invisible eye.' Furthermore, the action can be contained much more effectively on a cinema screen, meaning one does not have to direct the audience's attention so aggressively. He explained there is a 'sweet spot' of engagement between subtle direction of the action and obtrusive mediation that shatters audience engagement. One of the biggest considerations is lighting. Cameras are less sensitive than the human eye in dealing with contrast. Very brightly lit areas of the stage will therefore throw everything else into darkness on screen. It is a true art to light the stage without high contrast, so as not to render the image flat. There is therefore a high degree of communication with the Royal Opera House's lighting director, because barely noticeable changes in the auditorium can produce a huge change for the camera.

What is the ultimate effect of this painstaking and highly skilled process? My own subjects' responses suggest double-direction actively promotes legibility - streamlining the stage action by guiding one's view to points of major narrative significance. Curiously, given that simulcasting audiences tend to be experienced opera-goers, this strategy seems tailor-made for novice audiences - helping to 'ease in' the uninitiated. In part, this is probably a vestigial remnant of audience development and democratization objectives that motivated Peter Gelb to initiate simulcasting over a decade ago. Furthermore, despite being a hypermedium (drawing upon a variety of existing media forms) whose closest relative is TV relays, as noted, opera cinema was primarily interpreted as cinematic by my subjects. The legibility of opera cinema is thus twofold: on the one hand, the stage drama is literally streamlined and edited to emphasize key plot points and clarify subtext, and on the other the resemblance to more familiar media results in a more comfortable encounter for people unfamiliar with opera. Both aspects apparently privilege novice audiences.

However, the 'cinematic/televisual' double-direction was not well-received across all my subjects. For some, the clarifying effect of opera cinema came at the expense of their ability to freely interpret the stage action. These comments touch on older academic debates over the agency of screen audiences (or lack thereof). For example, according to apparatus and Frankfurt School models of spectatorship, the cinematic apparatus induces placid subjects, susceptible to interpellation by the ideologically dominant capitalist class.[9] Moreover, the presumed passivity of screen audiences is sometimes utilized as proof of the inferiority of recorded media to the 'unmediated', dramatic arts. Catherine Belsey describes the loss of interpretive freedom in cinema compared to theatre, which she contends arises from cinema's fixed viewing positions and controlled perspective on the dramatic action.[10] These theories of spectatorship and media ontology suffer from constructing spectators out of texts and media technologies, rather than investigating the complex - even skilled - activity of viewing, and using this information to inform media ontology.[11] My own research proceeds from Martin Barker's conception of the act of viewing as active-but-stratified.[12] Audiences actively engage with cultural experiences, but their engagement is not free or random - it is guided by the technical parameters of the experience, the context of viewing and the social formations surrounding given cultural phenomena. Broadly speaking, I see opera cinema direction as inhibiting a holistic interpretation of the dramaturgy, but promoting closer engagement with the performers. These data run counter to contentions by Phillip Auslander that emotional and intellectual engagement is necessarily inversely proportional to mediation.[13]

Emanuele Senici's research on modern screen opera reports that this convention is denigrated by some experienced opera fans as 'porn style': fetishizing the main aspects of the mise en scène and facilitating instant gratification rather than intellectual engagement.[14] Such comments require explication, as opera cinema's legibility does not represent an abstract 'dumbing down' of the stage form but expresses its synthesis with existing media technologies and conventions. The strands of hypermediacy in opera cinema's double-direction can be unpicked by close analysis of its visual strategies and production practices. Despite superficially resembling jumbo-screen presentations at music or sporting matches, and although simulcasts are edited live ('in-the-can'), on a production level opera cinema is distinct from the relatively spontaneous direction involved in such events, at least at the Royal Opera House. As we have seen, the coordination of the film crew by the multi-camera director is as elaborate and scripted a performance as the opera itself. When it came to the night of the broadcast, I was observing in the media room, and the entire process was already a well-oiled machine. The only chaotic factor was the celebrity host, who missed their cue to sit for a two-shot while interviewing the leading man during the interval. With the high cost of Royal Opera House simulcasts, Morahan's risky approach to *Peter Grimes,* for example, remains an outlier. Primarily, opera cinema's visual grammar seeks to facilitate a sense of virtual attendance rather than creatively reinterpret the text. A Jürgen Kühnel writes, the telecast is a 'reportage of a performance' that does not 'narrate' an opera, but rather 'relates' [*referiert*] a performance of an opera, it 're-narrates' it.[15]

Nevertheless, a tentative trend away from straightforward relation can be identified in more recent simulcast, which reflects opera cinema's failure to tempt new audiences into the operatic fold through its established visual conventions. For instance, a simulcast of Thomas Adès's 2017 adaptation of Luis Buñuel's surrealist film, *The Exterminating Angel*, employed unusual high-angle shots to disorientate the viewer and mirror the obfuscating stagecraft. Furthermore, one of my case studies – Katie Mitchell's 2015 adaptation of *Lucia di Lammermoor* – employed a split-stage, in which off-stage events from the original opera (such as Lucia's murder of her unwanted fiancée, Arturo) were acted out as dumb show, in tandem with the main drama. This arrangement was well-suited to the simulcast, permitting cross-cutting between scenes, and resulting in an especially successful synthesis between stage opera and cinematic screen grammar. Whether this was intentional I cannot say, but texts like the *Lucia* simulcast represent the embryo of a genuine hybrid art form, struggling to be born. At present, this kind of synthesis remains the exception rather than the rule. However, *Lucia* demonstrates how the unique ontological characteristics of opera cinema could be harnessed to facilitate a qualitative development in screen opera.

It also (ironically) reveals that some novice respondents find greater merit in creative utilization of cinematic direction than the default, 'legible' screen grammar of opera cinema, if my subjects are anything to go by.

Liveness

Aside from double-direction, the liveness of opera cinema is its other main defining formal characteristic. Even from a purely technological perspective, this designation is complicated. Firstly, the 'live' transmission is conducted with a small tape delay to allow time to pull the plug in the event of major mishaps. And in some territories (like Australia, for example) the Royal Opera House will broadcast with a very considerable delay in order to provide a more favourable timeslot for cinemas. Moreover, not all the show is actually live – the transmission is broken up with pre-recorded content (more on this later). Nevertheless, the live dimension is very strongly foregrounded in marketing material and throughout the show, with constant reminders from the celebrity host that the performance is coming to you 'live from the Royal Opera House'.

Simulcasting reveals the increasingly unstable and complex position of liveness in the early twenty-first century. Obviously, liveness is technologically determined by the more-or-less simultaneity of production and reception. However, that is not the end of the question. As Barker demonstrates, different audience members privilege different aspects of an experience as quintessentially 'live'. For some, only physical co-presence counts (attending a show at a music concert for example). For others, simultaneity is enough. Many of my own research subjects identified liveness in terms of the empathetic connection between spectators and performing subjects – a sense of immediacy that has been claimed by some dramaturgical theorists as the sole ontological domain of co-present theatre. Additionally, the possibility of disaster simultaneously promotes the tension and empathy that permits identification with the performers, and – where mistakes do occur – provides *proof* of liveness that is ordinarily (and paradoxically) concealed at the same time as it is shown. Still other audience members identify liveness with events that cannot be repeated, meaning the 'one-off' nature of the experience is what defines its ontology. This all suggests that we cannot be sloppy with our treatment of live experience if we truly expect to understand it.

In opposition to the static and inflexible ontologies posited by scholars such as Auslander, Erika Fischer-Lichte and Peggy Phelan,[16] Matthew Reason provides a different concept in the form of 'presentness': constituting the experiential, negotiable and subjective nature of liveness – beyond a strict, technical definition.[17] This is a helpful contribution, though I think it leans too far in the subjective direction. Liveness is not just a state of mind, it has a definite, objective aspect – even if it is not as straightforward as it appears at first blush. Developing this idea in relation to audience research, Martin Barker construes liveness as both a technological fact and also an experiential *contract*, in which certain criteria have to be met for an experience to qualify as live in the minds of audiences. This contract is closely bound up with cultural value and esteem. It constitutes an unspoken agreement that exists between the artists behind a live event and their audiences, which is almost ineffable except by distinguishing it from the inferior experience of recorded media such as cinema – 'the "mediated" versus the "immediate"'.[18] It is this value and esteem that permits the likes of the Royal Opera House to charge a higher ticket price for their simulcasts as opposed to pre-recorded cinema content. Barker's emphasis on the perception of liveness is somewhat similar to Stephen Prince's notion of 'perceptual realism' with regards to CGI.[19] Prince argues that digital imagery can be artificially coded with lighting, gravity, texture and shadow that imitate indexical photography, and constitute learned 'cues' for realism by which audiences judge their credibility.[20] In the same way, audiences draw on a set of learned cues for liveness: the direct address, evidence of improvisation, lower image quality and so forth. These conventions have been codified and inculcated into audiences by their exposure to various forms of live media; particularly television, and more recently internet streaming. But while Price portrays these codes of realism as more-or-less fixed and universal, the conditions of Barker's 'liveness contract' vary from person to person. Yet they retain some common features across audiences as well, which is why we cannot reduce liveness to an individualist, subjective impression. I will demonstrate this at greater length in Chapter 4 in relation to my novice audiences.

But do audiences *care* that opera cinema is live? In 2014, Karen Wise provocatively suggested that opera cinema audiences only identify liveness as a meaningful aspect of the simulcast experience when specifically questioned about it.[21] These data were seemingly upheld in 2016 by research conducted on behalf of Arts Council England, which found that just 17 per cent of surveyed event cinema audiences regarded liveness as 'very important' – although sixty-seven regarded it as 'somewhat important.'[22] However, there are a few other things to consider. It strikes me as inconceivable there is no causal relationship between opera's newfound success in cinema and its reincarnation as a live, digital medium. The relatively poor performance of opera on the big screen hitherto – not to mention of recorded, encore screenings compared to simulcasts today – provides some evidence of the significance of liveness to audiences.

How to explain the discrepancy between Wise and the Arts Council's research, and the lacklustre box office performance and perceived inferiority of recorded opera? Firstly, as I have stressed, terms like 'live performance' cannot be deployed without qualification – especially in the present media moment. As Duncan White notes, 'in the early twenty-first century, "liveness" and "immediacy" are taken-for-granted aspects of modern media culture.

A live and instantaneous media network is part and parcel of everyday life'.[23] The fact that most media forms now have some live dimension has made liveness unremarkable, which arguably reinforces the dichotomy between co-present, physical performance and mediated cultural forms – even those based on simultaneous communication. I discussed with one of my subjects (an employee of the Hatfield Odeon) who estimated that 'if you assume the live performance would be sold out then you'd have half full screens at encore'. Moreover, she spoke about the diminished atmosphere and quality of experience at the encore recording: 'People psychologically know that it's pre-recorded so it becomes more like a film. There is no wow factor.' This 'wow factor' could constitute simply a heightened sense of value, but also reflects different exhibition practices. For example, applause occasionally breaks out at simulcasts, but from my experience, never at encores. Clearly, the knowledge of liveness exerts an impact on reception strategies.

That being said, some of my subjects felt the liveness of opera cinema did not significantly affect their viewing experience – in some cases, they did not perceive the simulcast as live at all. I had one subject who claimed that a fire at Holborn station that caused a small disruption in the form of a power outage at Covent Garden served as the only 'proof' the performance of *The Rise and Fall of the City of Mahagonny* they saw in the cinema was actually live. These comments reflected a minority opinion – most of my respondents regarded opera cinema as live in one form or another, and attributed value to this dimension of the experience. However, the risk of disaster was one of the commonest features of my subjects' liveness contracts, although it was parsed in different ways across the sample. The 'danger' of liveness is especially pertinent to opera, which evolved as a showcase for musical virtuosos, and as such is avowedly and deliberately challenging for the performers – especially principal singers. Displaying the range and power of vocal chords has always been central to the art form's appeal. Moments of particular musical virtuosity like *Der Hölle Rache kocht in meinem Herzen* (better known as the 'Queen of the Night's aria') from *The Magic Flute* become beats around which an experienced audience's anticipation hang, and serve to thrill newcomers. As Morris writes, 'the singer's failure to "pull it off" may tellingly reveal the labor involved, may elicit sympathy. It also, however, generates displeasure that will be eagerly, even ruthlessly, flagged in audience reaction and in the critic's pen.'[24] Even this displeasure in failure arguably contains an implicit, sadistic pleasure.

The possibility for failure during a simulcast is twofold. The first pertains to all forms of stage drama; namely, the risk of something going wrong on stage, such as a cast member fudging their performance or a piece of the set collapsing. The latter concerns digital remediation specifically: the danger of technical hitches, such as the satellite signal dropping out. There is a debate amongst audience researchers concerning the importance of failure to the experience of live performance. Reason contends that an audience's perception of liveness hinges in part on 'the possibility of something going wrong', which in turn promotes a sense of presentness by fostering empathetic tension – with the audience willing the cast to succeed.[25] By contrast, Barker is unconvinced by 'untested' notions that 'audiences gain much from a sense of the risks of performance – that performances are unpredictable, might go wrong'.[26] He argues that since audiences generally only attend a single performance, they have 'no measure of what might be "accidental" in it'.[27] This is an uncharacteristically inflexible statement from Barker. His claim that audiences tend to only watch a given performance once is itself untested (at least, he does not provide any proof), and surely audiences can often differentiate deliberate staging from gaffes like dropped props and fluffed lines even on first viewing?

In part, Barker's conclusion is derived from his opposition to Phelan's criticism of the 'sameness' of recorded media versus the spontaneous and unpredictable nature of live performance. As he correctly notes, 'a committed company of players will surely be working towards minimizing random changes between performances.'[28] The peculiarities of opera production (the reliance on a small number of elite singers and the need to promote the opera company's international brand) further ensure consistency across performances, as Morris relates.[29] On this basis, it could be argued that recording and broadcast technologies simply fulfil the perfect consistency for which live operatic performance has always strived. However, Barker may bend the branch too far in the opposite direction. He (along with the likes of Hansen and Barbara Klinger) is correct to say that every screening of event a recorded medium also constitutes a unique event – in which the precise material parameters of viewing will always be different.[30] Nevertheless, audiences clearly draw a distinction between essentially consistent, mechanically reproduced media texts and the unpredictability of simultaneous performance – whether or not it is remediated to a screen. That was certainly the case for my research subjects, a significant cross-section of respondents commented frequently and with great enthusiasm on the possibility of failure as a positive experiential element of live performance.

Part of the problem is that liveness remains a vexed and often poorly theorized term in both media and performance theory. Many theories of liveness by scholars such as Ulrich Gumbrecht, Phelan, Auslander and Fischer-Lichte contend that liveness depends on presence, meaning a direct, spatial relationship between audience and performer.[31] These definitions feel rooted in the past, and are insufficiently flexible to account for the range of live experiences available to contemporary audiences. Musicology has only lately begun to grasp the nettle of live experience, and opera studies last of all. Until comparatively recent, opera scholars dealt with texts, de-emphasizing productions. Theorists of opera did not really deal with staging until the 1990s, under the influence of performance theory. The question of mediation has followed on from this, but only really in the last decade. As a case study, opera cinema thus lies on the bleeding edge of the field. The emergence of these experiences has also provoked a certain backlash, with performance scholars in particular entrenching their defence of the ontological purity of live performance. Christopher Balme offers a three-part explanation of academic fetishizing of the live event as: (1) an attempt to free the subject from an entirely positivist–historicist orientation, (2) to distinguish the theoretical significance of dramaturgical from literary criticism and (3) to draw a 'clear line of demarcation between theatre and the new, technical, audiovisual media'.[32] The likes of Phelan celebrate the ontology of live performance as necessarily progressive, for clogging the smooth machinery of capitalist reproduction. The 'unrepeatability' of the live event runs counter to mechanical reproduction.[33] However, the cult of liveness reflects brute capitalist logic on two levels. Firstly, live performance is itself a saleable, time-limited commodity that usually commands a higher price than recorded media. Secondly, the concept of 'unrepeatability' and eventfulness demands exclusion and asserts the privilege of consumers over one another (those who were 'there', and those who bought the recording). And despite Phelan's attempt to claim live performance as a mode of political resistance to capitalist cultural hegemony, this live/mediated dichotomy is a by-product of the mechanical reproduction of culture - not everyone can afford the money/time to attend the show, some will have to settle for the recording.

The whole point is that primarily middle-class audiences are willing to pay more for an experience that is *not* recorded. In that respect, liveness underlines the haves and have nots, the invited and the uninvited, the co-present and the mass audience. But even this distinction is not a binary. The liveness of opera cinema exists in part to promote the 'true' live experience of attending the auditorium. The 'real' audience depicted on screen occupies a privileged position compared to those sat in a cinema. This situation resonates with Claudio Benzecry's concept of conspicuous consumption, in which culture becomes a confrontational arena where 'art is monopolised as a restricted resource and used as a weapon of distinction and status; art as ideological domination'.[34] This function of art and culture as a 'weapon of class distinction' was operative in my subjects' engagement with opera cinema as a live medium - a contention that extends to live performance more generally. Liveness was heavily bound up in notions of exclusivity for my subjects - the prestige of opera was based on experiencing an event others could not. And most of my subjects saw the opera house as the most exclusive possible way of experiencing opera. Some live performances are apparently more equal than others.

In sum then, the simultaneity of opera cinema is a technological reality, but liveness does not mean - and nor has it ever meant - one thing. Moreover, the majority of formerly recorded or otherwise non-live media forms now incorporate aspects of liveness - from 'instant' televisual streaming services, to e-books downloaded from central databases, and to networked multiplayer videogames, to event cinema. This both reflects a historical trajectory towards convergence and complicates canon media ontologies. The very presence of live content in cinemas reveals the limitations of Bazinian models of cinema, for example, based as they are on indexicality, recording and technological reproduction.[35] As I continue to stress, these changed conditions do not mean we should abandon ontology or categorization altogether; they just demand a nuanced, multi-sided, dialectical approach to the issue.

Multi-mediality

Opera cinema's multi-medial features – specifically the pre-recorded documentaries (called 'insight films' by the Royal Opera House), live interviews with the cast and social media chatter that break up the transmission – are among its least-theorized aspects. Opera cinema not only transforms live opera but introduces new experiential elements, derived from the aesthetic conventions of film and television, and the networked simultaneity of digital communication.

The programme for a live opera broadcast typically begins with a television-style introduction by the celebrity host. British actor Paterson Joseph did the honours for *Mahagonny*, for example. The host warms up the cinema audience with repeated reminders that they are watching a live show. They will usually interview the principal performer during one of the intervals and introduce each act with a reminder of where the story left off. A script will be produced for the celebrity presenters, which is sent away in advance for the talent to make revisions if necessary. The simulcast announces itself as serialized at the end of the show, with the celebrity host reminding audiences of the next transmission in the live season, which carries a flavour of the seminal *Live from the Met* radio broadcast series ('tune in text time!'). The celebrity host also calls to mind a news broadcaster – with the direct address to the audience and reminders that the night's events come to us 'live from the Royal Opera House'. In this way, the celebrity host primes an audience for engagement with a simultaneous event, helping to construct an aesthetic of liveness, as mentioned previously. Stephanie Marriott's analysis of the broadcast event makes this point effectively:

> Electronic telecommunication devices ... permit their users to interact with a simultaneous elsewhere: a distant place in which events are transpiring in tandem with events in an individual's own vicinity. When I switch on the radio or the television, or ring up a friend, my interaction with those devices is predicated upon my belief that it is now in that distant place of enunciation just as it is now in my own. All have in common that they are capable of transmitting instantly or near instantly from a source to

a receiver. Instantaneity, then, is not simply an affordance of electronic media; it would also appear to be ontological, part of the essential nature of such devices ... Furthermore, instantaneity is ... predicted on simultaneity. Electronic communication can only deliver information instantly or near-instantly because everywhere is unfolding at once.[36]

Media technologies like radio and TV are historically associated with live communication; as such, their ontology is partly 'contingent upon the temporal status of the material transmitted'.[37] This is also true of opera cinema. However, few of my subjects actually compared the simulcast to television, and this comparison has not been prevalent in other audience research I've seen, despite all the televisual conventions involved. Aside from the cinematic exhibition context, this is probably because digital imagery and mass communication have significantly blurred the ontological boundaries of television. Between streaming services like Amazon Prime, Netflix and online platforms like YouTube, the conceptual parameters of television as a live, domestic medium have been thoroughly obfuscated. Nevertheless, I identify many old media practices in opera cinema that belie its televisual DNA; and I contend that audiences are primed for a live event through aesthetic strategies that are distinctly televisual.

Additionally, pre-recorded featurettes containing additional information about the opera and the production process play during the breaks. For example, the transmission of *Lucia* contained a lengthy explanation of the significance of the glass harmonica used to musically convey the protagonists' fall into insanity. The Royal Opera House's 'features' material is produced by an entirely separate team to that responsible for the live transmission, who pre-record, edit and then insert them into the relay programme. Evidence from existing audiences reveal a mixed reception for these diversions - many of Wise's respondents considered them a tedious distraction from the drama that ruined their suspension of disbelief.[38] Meanwhile, James Streichen is sharply critical of what he regards as an attempt by opera companies to 'monetize the backstage', making ' "creative content" out of what otherwise would languish behind the scenes'.[39] I posit that these documentary insight films are further evidence of the lingering influence of opera cinema's early history as an audience development initiative. Indeed, my novice respondents were broadly positive about the latter for enhancing their appreciation of the performance. One of them complemented the educative value of the insight films in *Boris Godunov*, commenting: 'I liked the bit at the beginning where he [Bryn Terfel, who performed the lead role] was talking the opera itself and learning all the songs in Russian.'

The multi-medial dimension of opera cinema lies on a wider historical trajectory towards hypermediacy and convergence. Typically of mediatized performance (following Balme's taxonomy) opera cinema is both hypermedial - in that multiple media forms combine to form its unique aesthetic – and intermedial – in that it represents and thematizes other media.[40] The 'extra' features on the simulcast programme support Bolter and Grusin's thesis that digital media are defined by multiplicity of images in one space, following a trajectory towards hypermediacy in post-Renaissance art.[41] They also uphold the essential premise of Henry Jenkins's conception of media convergence – that the pressure of technological development will not negate 'old' media but force them to hybridize with other cultural forms and adapt to new exhibition contexts.[42] They furthermore bear resemblance to Raymond Williams's conception of televisual content flow,[43] and demonstrate opera cinema's predecessors. More specifically, the combination of 'simultaneous' media such as the opera performance and recorded media such as the insight films in the same frame is a broadcasting trope, which presents opera cinema as a broadcast event. These conventions constitute a televisual aesthetic that primes audiences for engagement with live, varied content.

In terms of the impact of all these extra features, several of my subjects considered them to be an attempt to elevate the simulcast with content unavailable to the auditorium audience, suggesting they add 'value for money', or otherwise the Royal Opera House is 'trying to bring [opera cinema] up to the same level as the live experience'. Aside from the value added from the Royal Opera House's side (more on that in Chapter 4), there is also value added on the cinema's side. Samantha Atkinson situates the recent vogue in 'live' experiences at the movies – including event cinema, immersive theatre and live cinema – within a broader historiographical narrative. She argues that 'emerging cinematic practices are compensating for [their] perceived liveness through the recreation of the film's milieu in both virtual and real spaces, which are embedded with a performative dimension for the audience to engage within'.[44] In other words, the recent incursion of live content into cinemas represents the movies struggling for prominence against live media by offering a sense of theatre. The current trend towards theatricality and multi-mediality is nothing new, as Atkinson points out through the historical example of highly ritualized, theatrical engagement with cult films like the *Rocky Horror Picture Show*.[45] William Castle's theatrical gimmicks in the 1950s - including the use of the vibrating motors of aeroplane wing de-icers on the underside of some of the seats to bring to life his titular monster in *The Tingler* - are another point of comparison. Indeed, modern simulcasting has more than a little in common with Castle's cinematic novelties, as an intrusion of a live 'reality' into the exhibition space. On a separate point, television is not the only live communication medium with which opera cinema is hybridized. It also incorporates social media interaction, with tailored hashtags used to facilitate communication between audiences immediately prior to, during and after performances – constituting what Marie Gillespie deigns 'overflow'.[46] The social media elements threaded throughout the simulcast event represent an interesting renegotiation of the public realm, and they resonate with Jenkins's notion of an increasingly networked, active and participatory media culture.[47] This kind of content is also an unusual presence in the cinema, where phones are usually switched off before the show starts.

Furthermore, these elements reflect the institution-building function of simulcasting as part of a global cultural economy. The collective experience of the simulcast audience operates at three levels: the co-present audience sitting in the cinema; the relationship between the cinema audience and the attendees at Covent Garden depicted on screen and the global audience, distantly represented via social media chatter (which is often multilingual). As a Marxist with a dim view of British exceptionalism, I must confess that the latter two forms of collective participation rankle me during simulcasts. What I will call the 'local' broadcast event (i.e. the link between British cinemas and Covent Garden) situates cinema audiences within what Stuart Hall would perhaps describe as the 'imagined community of the nation', to participate in a celebration of the 'best of British opera'.[48] The language of the celebrity host and feature material in particular foregrounding an idealized spectacle of 'the Nation', which puts me in mind of the Last Night of the Proms (though not nearly so egregiously jingoistic). The global participation fostered through social media during the transmission is bound up with the promotion of the Royal Opera House on a global stage. The institutional mothership of Covent Harden - a chartered company and icon of British cultural accomplishment - is situated within a global audience, signified by the multilingual Twitter feed. This was in fact picked upon by some of my own research subjects as creating a sense of national pride. The brilliance of the Royal Opera House becomes an international celebration of British cultural superiority. The event explicitly sells not just an opera, nor even the Royal Opera House, but Britain itself.

The mass, global reach of opera cinema reifies the dual logic of centralization and globalization that characterizes contemporary digital cultures - drawing eyes towards London as the centre of British culture. This is nothing especially new. Opera has always served as a means for wealthy countries to show off on the world stage.[49] But opera cinema offers a new and powerful platform for this objective. The simulcast event becomes a condensed and choreographed representation of relationship between the British culture sector and the rest of the world. During a simulcast event, audiences occupy the familiar exhibition space of a cinema, but are virtually transported to Covent Garden, and also connected via a digital broadcast event to a global audience.

This is not a 'neutral' process. The audience represented on screen is intended to be aspirational, while the tweets that appear on screen are selected by technicians from behind the scenes. The organic 'coming together' of this virtual audience is tightly choreographed, and intended to put the Royal Opera House in the best possible light. Putting it another way, the sense of the virtual audience for opera cinema is a controlled part of the performance. The fact that the Royal Opera House has the financial and cultural clout to present itself in this way is probably part of the reason opera cinema infuriates smaller opera house. This helps to explain anxieties from regional and touring companies about the effect of simulcasting on the British cultural ecology, given the historic antagonism between the capital and the rest of Britain over competition for arts funding and audiences.[50] In sum, the social media elements of opera cinema assist the monopolization of cultural power by major arts institutions with the capital and resources to digitally disseminate their output. In so doing, elite opera companies promote an idealized version of nationhood. Moreover, these events are seen to consolidate the power of a few, powerful opera houses by giving them access to a very privileged vantage point for self-promotion.

Institutional dramaturgy

These issues move us to the related concept of institutional dramaturgy. I argue throughout this book that, despite its unique attributes, simulcasting has not been recognized by audiences as an art form independent of staged opera. The mere existence of new technologies and delivery systems are not sufficient to delineate a new art form. All new media experiences must undergo a process of emergence as a medium or art form, including cinema, for example. As Ann Friedberg relates, the many systems for exhibiting moving images at the turn of the twentieth century 'demonstrated the uncertainty about what the predominant form of the [film] medium would be'.[51] A number of ancillary media to single-frame, montage cinema never attained acknowledgement as discrete media on their own terms and have been largely forgotten by history. Opera cinema's prospects as a medium remain in a state of uncertainty.

Opera cinema occupies a diminished position on what Bolter describes as the 'disintegrating chain of remediation'.[52] As noted, while shadowing rehearsals, I observed the cinema director silently taking notes from the sidelines without ever interacting with the stage director. Despite dozens of BBC credits to his name, he was clearly expected to know his place. This is an eloquent expression of the general status of opera cinema as a support column to stage opera rather than an art form in its own right. It seems that the majority of audience assessments of simulcasting consider it an alternative to opera – not something new, but a lesser version of the existing experience. The basis for this perspective includes certain material limitations (particularly with regards to digital remediation of the human voice), but primarily more subjective interpretations of opera cinema's social and commercial function as a cheaper, more convenient but ultimately lesser alternative or supplement to the stage. This function also has an impact on the aesthetic and formal characteristics of this media experience.

As I explained in Chapter 2, the default style for simulcasting was established by a lavish television broadcast of the Met's *Turandot* in 1987.[53] Notably, in this watershed relay, the Metropolitan Opera House was as much the star of the show as principal vocalist Eva Marton. In this and most modern simulcasts, establishing shots of the house exterior prior to curtain-up visually invite the virtual spectator over an imaginary threshold, while sweeping pans of the interior auditorium provide constant reminders of the presence and materiality of the place of performance. As the overture approaches, the screen director will often cycle between a static, wide-angle shot of the stage, filmed from the back of the house (surveying the backs of attendees' heads) and slow pans of the audience entering the auditorium and settling down. These images are accompanied by 'the dull murmur of conversation mingled with the distant cacophony of the orchestra warming up' – assaulting the virtual attendee with a range of sensory stimuli to evoke feelings of actual, collective participation operating at a national and international level.[54] These tropes constitute the institutional dramaturgy of opera cinema, defined by Steichen as aesthetic strategies that cue the cinema audience to imaginatively inhabit the physical opera house – to not only *see* there, but *be* there. Indeed, many of my own subjects' testimonies indicate they 'forgot' they were at the cinema and became 'absorbed by the event'. Steichen explains that simulcasts remediate, not just the opera, but the entire opera house:

> The Met's HD broadcasts present much more than an afternoon of Donizetti--or a longer afternoon of Wagner, *but rather a dramatization of the experience of attending the actual Metropolitan Opera, effectively doing double duty as opera broadcast and institutional documentary* (or, in less flattering terms, reality television or even an infomercial). The Met's HD broadcasts aim to present to the world not just opera, but Opera, that is, the Metropolitan Opera.[55]

As I have explained, the aesthetic strategies adopted by operatic remediation in the last couple of decades, and especially since digitization, demonstrate a shift away from artistic reinterpretation and to a straight transmission. Strictly speaking, opera cinema's primary commercial purpose – at least from the perspective of opera companies – is not direct revenue generation but advertising and catering to existing audiences. Fiona Tuck's recent survey of sector agents with simulcasting initiatives presents the main commercial application of opera cinema as increasing the 'reach' of work, to 'ensure that as many people as possible in the UK and abroad have the opportunity to experience performances'.[56] Secondarily, opera cinema is intended to build 'the profile and the reputation of cultural brands', which is particularly pertinent to international simulcasting, as noted with regards social media.[57] Opera cinema exploits the holistic auditorium experience by offering a simulacrum of a night at the opera house to 'leverage new media to advance [opera companies'] institution-building agendas'.⁵⁸

This aspect of opera cinema touches on a central concern of new media theory: virtuality. This does not necessarily mean immersive VR (utilizing something like an Oculus Rift headset) but when a media experience creates a facsimile of the real thing. Though I am no fan of the postmodern solipsism underpinning his work, there is certainly something about opera cinema's dreamlike, idealized representation of a night at the opera that appears to resonate with Jean Baudrillard's conception of the simulacrum: a representation without an original.⁵⁹ But as Thomas Elsaesser argues, the virtual space is not really a false reality but 'one of the dimensions of the actual'. Given the ubiquity of networked, interactive and virtual experiences, it's just one more way in which reality is experienced.⁶⁰ Moreover, a virtual experience does not necessarily subordinate or replace the 'real' live experience.⁶¹ In the case of institutional dramaturgy it's actually the opposite. Virtual attendance at the opera house during a simulcast – the constant visual reminders of the glamour and grandeur of the auditorium, the virtual admission, the sense of being close-but-not-quite-there – give the expanded audience a taste of the 'real thing', but by design seeks not to exceed it. If the simulcast was perceived as equal to or better than the staged experience, it would defeat its own commercial purpose.

Despite attaining virtual access to the live performance, opera cinema audiences must endure ceaseless reminders that they are physically removed from a more exclusive, valuable and culturally esteemed event, which attains more cultural capital by dint of the greater availability of opera in a digital form. This constitutes what Steichen describes as opera cinema's 'double-edge':

> [By] leveraging the prestige of the Met and the glamour of figures such as Renée Fleming to win over new opera fans, they can't help but reinforce the inherent exclusivity of the real thing. Peter Gelb has managed to make the Met at once more inclusive and more exclusive. Or, looked at more charitably, the Met has opened up to the public, with the predictable side effect that the original now acquires even more cachet.⁶²

Steichen's thesis must be tempered by acknowledging his personal ambivalence towards simulcasting. In a 2011 article for *Opera Quarterly*, he admits that participating in simulcasts makes him feel as though he is 'cheating on opera'.⁶³ He belies reservations around mediated performance, noting that if 'the very ontology of performing arts non-profits is to curate both aesthetically and economically obsolescent art forms' then it is 'the degree to which they resist incorporation within our market-driven cultural industries that makes them so important'.⁶⁴ In other words, like Phelan, he believes the value of live performance is based on its resistance to capitalist production. Privileging live performance and arbitrarily exonerating certain forms of cultural consumption – usually more expensive ones, associated with middle-class audiences – does not get around the fact that all cultural consumption is based on the same capitalist system of production. When it really comes down to it, the system does not care what you are spending your money on, as long as you're spending.

Moreover, Steichen notes with evident relief that 'most of the [opera cinema] audience is there for the "right" reason, that is, because what we really love is the real thing'.[65] He also affirms opera's cultural validity through negative comparison with cinema, stating that 'when there is an Angelina Jolie blockbuster playing in the theatre next door, a five-hour broadcast of *Don Carlo* feels like an act of principled cultural transgression'.[66] In the same breath as castigating opera cinema for exclusively enhancing the cache of staged opera at the expense of the cinema audience, Steichen attacks cinema as a lower form of art.[67] And while he is sceptical that the next Stephanie Blythe will be discovered on Facebook or YouTube, really, who knows? The wealth of talent available through these social media platforms makes them a potentially plausible route for performers to find mainstream visibility. In truth, the main barriers to entry for world-class opera are the years of exclusive and expensive tutelage necessary to get ahead, rather than the particular mode of distribution.

Steichen's comments are comparable to Sam Abel's reductionist contention that 'the whirlwind of high-technology games puts us in perpetual danger of forgetting the appeal of traditional non-mediated performance, in which performers and audience members occupy the same space at the same time'.[68] The implication is that opera's aura risks desecration through the intrusion of mundane, populist, digital media technologies, which through their effacement of the presence of emoting human bodies robs live performance of its affective and political power. These perspectives emphasize the value of obtaining the views of novice respondents on simulcasting. Melina Esse notes the tendency of opera aficionados to 'confer a special status on live opera, cordoning it off from the commercial pandering to short attention spans represented by cuts and close-ups'.[69] By contrast, as Morris points out, belittling remediated opera as a 'second-hand imitation, supplement, or record of something that happened elsewhere begins to seem hopelessly inadequate' because '[opera's] here and now is increasingly found in its remediated form'.[70] Given the massive proliferation of opera in remediated forms, assuming an absolutist view on opera's ontological status as a stage medium looks increasingly absurd. As noted, opera is far more widely consumed on screen than the stage.

Also, the data I have seen strongly suggest that audiences tend to regard staged opera as a more esteemed and valuable cultural experience than opera cinema, even (as with some of my research subjects) where they lacked direct comparison. Aside from formal and aesthetic issues, there is a cultural and historical aspect to this assessment. An important factor of institutional dramaturgy relates to what Herbert Lindenberger describes as opera's drawing together of the aesthetic and the societal.[71] The opera house represents the pinnacle of cultural production and social power in any society in which it is situated, and opera cinema enhances the impression of opera's grandeur. It deliberately *sells* it. I believe this is especially the case for newcomers to the form. Anecdotally, one of my subjects vividly described the splendour of Royal Opera House, having deliberately arrived early enough to explore the building prior to the show, commenting 'I remember thinking about the history of the building while I was watching'. Ironically, far from demystifying opera - the apotheosis of the European music-drama tradition, the 'last vestige of high style'[72] - remediation has to a certain extent entrenched its mythological status.

Lindenberger notes that the so-called golden age of opera coincided with the invention of the phonograph record, which, even as the opera house adapted to accommodate the ascendant middle-class, permitted a mass audience that lacked the means to access physical auditoria to consume operatic music in comfort and privacy.[73] In so doing, the phonograph isolated operatic aesthetics from the markers of class society. This was what Adorno found so appealing about the medium as a platform for opera, and conversely why he regarded the phoney hullaballoo of television opera with disdain.[74] Television opera introduced a visual dimension to remediated opera, thus reintroducing the unity of opera's aesthetic and societal grandiosity to a mass audience.[75] Opera cinema takes things further, introducing the theatrical dimension to a media audience. I argue that situating these visual and auditory cues within a cinema (a theatrical venue) produces a much more powerful effect than anything achievable via a television relay. Moreover, unlike the opera films and studio productions of the 1950s–70s that often announced their creative reinterpretation, the simulcast conceals the process of remediation. In so doing, it promotes the value of the stage performance at the expense of the remediated experience.

However, despite the power of institutional dramaturgy, opera cinema has proved an ineffective recruitment tool for stage opera. While opera cinema's formal conventions showing the lingering influence of Gelb's audience building initiative, the reality is that it now mostly caters to an experienced audience that (for reasons relating to convenience and/or accessibility) want an alternative way of accessing live opera than the auditorium. This veteran audience arguably consolidates rather than erodes opera's exclusive reputation. Institutional dramaturgy's invitation to vicariously enter the Mecca of high culture thus strengthens perceptions of the opera house's elitism to a far greater extent than previous forms of operatic remediation - emphasizing what Walter Benjamin might describe as opera's cult value.[76] In sum then, institutional dramaturgy enhances the impression of stage opera as an elite, desirable art form, and in so doing disavows the simulcast as a discretely valuable experience. This is an important dimension of opera cinema's ontology.

Immersion

A brief aside on the question of immersion and immediacy, which are pertinent to institutional dramaturgy and key issues in media and audience research. Barker identifies emotional engagement as key to facilitating a sense of immediacy.[77] This pertinent word choice literally means *un-mediated*, referring to uninterrupted engagement between audiences and the cultural event. Therefore, by this measure, a sense of live engagement is negatively correlative with evidence of remediation: intrusive camerawork, special effects, non-diegetic sound and so forth. This was certainly the opinion of the opera cinema director I interviewed. Barker further argues that, in the case of live performance, a sense of immediacy specifically depends on a physically present, human cast. Morris argues that remediation reduces the two-way engagement of live performance, where the cast can at least hear the audiences' applause, to a one-way engagement, arguably encouraging passivity.[78] However, this two-way engagement at the auditorium is rarely realized in truth, especially in the packed, cavernous Covent Garden auditorium, in which individual spectators are lost in the crowd. Nevertheless, for my subjects at least, the presence of the cast made a difference on an emotional level.

The unique function of emotion in opera bears consideration here. Amongst the performing arts, opera is specifically renowned for its emotional fireworks. Indeed, Sinéad O'Neill, Joshua Edelman and John Sloboda conducted research on the precise relationship between opera's cultural value and the emotional response it elicits from audiences, acknowledging the art form's predilection for sentiment.[79] The form's wild histrionics and dramatic flourishes, conventions that Lesley Stern describes as 'operality',[80] are esteemed by acolytes for their emotional impact, even as they are mocked and parodied by opera's detractors. Existing audience data imply a strong negative correlation between emotional engagement and evidence of remediation in opera. For instance, O'Neill, Edelman and Sloboda found that their respondents regarded live broadcast and recorded opera as less emotionally engaging than staged performance. Given that this applied equally to cinema simulcasts and DVD recordings, the authors conclude that 'physical co-presence was a more important aspect of liveness than simultaneity' for their subjects.[81] The lack of emotional engagement during simulcasts does not represent the distanciation of Brechtian theatre, for example, which deliberately obstructs emotional engagement to promote intellectual and emotional engagement.[82] Opera cinema strives to transparently remediate the emotionality of opera, but, at least for these subjects, it fell short.

Based on my research, the visual immersion facilitated by opera cinema is generally considered more effective than the sonic one. Sound capture for opera cinema is usually achieved by means of throat and head mikes (which can very occasionally result in drop-outs if the performers happen to turn their heads towards dead spots). The wet quality (reverberation) of sound captured from a large auditorium is quite unlike the polished and crafted Foley sounds and film scores that accompany commercial cinema. However, the effect of simulcast sound certainly falls short of the 'presentness' and sense of live participation facilitated by uncompressed sound waves interacting with an audience's auditory faculties in a live exhibition space. Several of my subjects from the comparative study described the experience of live opera music as 'overwhelming', comments that evoke the unique potency of operatic music, and resonate with Andrew Tommasini's reflection on the surprising responses of young attendees to the Met's 2006 production of *Die Zauberflöte*:

> [Tommasini] was told repeatedly that the voices were loud, unpleasantly so. Struck by such comments from an audience accustomed to powerful stage amplifiers and high-volume headphones, he reasoned that he perception of loudness wasn't a matter of decibels per se but of raw human decibels: of loudness of without crutches; of a sense of what the sound must be like close to.[83]

Reflecting upon the function of sound during the silent era of cinema, Norman King describes how live accompaniment to silent film strips 'actualised the image', resulting in a 'sense of immediacy and participation' by emphasizing 'the presentness of the performance and the audience'.[84] Consequently, the effect of simulcast sound falls into a curious limbo. It does not fulfil the same narrative and affective function of sound in mainstream narrative cinema, in which the source of non-diegetic music is invisible. By contrast, opera cinema generally presents various shots of the orchestra – and particularly the conductor – throughout simulcast, acknowledging them as part of the performance. Moreover, the musicians are concealed for most of the simulcast, whereas (except for Wagner's tailor-made Bayreuth Festspielhaus) the orchestra pit is open and visible to auditorium attendees. The consequence for opera cinema is a middle ground wherein sounds and their sources are simultaneously present and absent: they are more immediate than in conventional cinema, but not so close as in a live venue.

Elitism

The million-dollar question: is opera 'elitist'? And does this elitism carry over into opera cinema? As John Storey argues in *The Social Life of Opera* (2003), for many people (especially in the UK and the United States) opera represents 'the very embodiment of "high culture"'.[85] This is despite the changing visibility and more convivial role of opera in everyday life due, amongst other things, to opera stars performing at pop concerts and sporting events, and hosting reality shows; and opera's greater presence in advertising and film. Storey argues that it is unfair to simplistically construe opera as an expensive pastime of the upper crust, citing Bernard Zelechow and Henry Raynor to point out that opera was the 'first musical institution to open its doors to the general public ... The first opera house opened in Venice in 1637'. It presented 'commercial opera run for profit ... offering the new, up-to-date entertainment to anyone who could afford a ticket'.[86] Zelechow argues further that, in the United States at least:

> By the late eighteenth century and in the nineteenth century the opera played a preeminent role in the cultural life of Europe. The opera was enjoyed and understood by a broad cross section of urban Europeans and Americans. The opera house became the meeting place of all social classes in society ... The absence of the concept of a classical repertoire is an index of the popularity and vigor of opera as a mode of communication and entertainment. By the 19th century, therefore, opera was established as a widely available form of popular entertainment, consumed by people of all social classes.[87]

Bruce McConachie contends that the isolation of opera from other forms of entertainment was a conscious process by elite social groups in New York, who developed three social strategies 'that gradually separated opera from the everyday world of popular entertainment: the first was to separate it from theatre by establishing buildings specifically for the performance of opera; second, they "also worked to sharpen and objectify a code of behaviour, including a dress code, deemed proper when attending the opera"; and, finally [they] insisted that only foreign-language opera could meet their standards – "standards upheld by behaviour and criticism employing foreign words and specialized language impenetrable to all but the cognoscenti"'.[88] It was only at the end of the nineteenth century in the United States that there was 'growing social acceptance of the insistence that opera was a "higher" form of art demanding a cultivated audience'.[89] By this point, the public were taught to observe opera with 'reverent, informed, disciplined seriousness'.[90]

This process was not overlooked by observers at the time. On the opening night (22 October 1883) of the New York Metropolitan Opera House, an estimate was run in a local paper that the boxes were occupied by people whose combined wealth was in the region of $540 million.[91] The *New York Evening Post* commented the following evening: 'From an artistic and musical point of view, the large boxes in the Metropolitan is [sic] a decided mistake. But as the house was avowedly built for social purposes rather than artistic, it is useless to complain about this.'[92] Janet Wolff argues that a similar process occurred in Britain, where a deliberate institutional agenda was undertaken to drive a wedge between 'the high arts of music, theatre and literature being the province of the upper-middle and middle classes, and the popular cultural forms of music hall, organised sport and popular literature providing the entertainment of the lower classes'.[93] Storey argues that opera did not become unpopular, but rather it was made unpopular. 'It was actively appropriated from its popular audience by elite social groups determined to situate it as the crowning glory of their culture – so-called "high culture". In short, opera was transformed from entertainment enjoyed by the many into culture to be appreciated by the few.'[94]

Something like this might have occurred in the specific cases of the United States and Britain, where opera was imported in relatively recent times, and already carried an elite and exotic reputation. It is true that British opera audiences tend towards the middle and upper end of the socio-economic spectrum, although in fairness this is true of spoken-word theatre as well.[95] It could be argued that this social stratification is as much a consequence of cultural baggage as it is evidence of genuine financial barriers. Certainly, a ticket for the gods, even at the Royal Opera House, is within the reach of most ordinary household budgets as a treat (between £30 and £50 if you book in advance), not to mention cheaper regional and touring performances. But even in its home continent, I would argue opera has never been a populist form.[96] That being said, neither did it cater exclusively to the aristocracy. Much like today, for the commons, it was an expensive evening out. Ticket prices for the opening night of *The Magic Flute* (a 'popular' vaudeville) in 1791 at the Freihaustheater in Vienna were as follows (fl.= Austro-Hungarian gulden, kr.=kreuzer=1/60 fl.):

- The most-expensive box: 6 fl. 50kr.
- A large box for eight: 5fl.
- A small box for four: 2 fl. 30 kr.
- *Parterre noble* and Gallery: 34 kr.
- Seats for commoners: 17 kr.
- Last seats/Entrance to Gallery (probably standing): 7 kr.[97]

For context, this means standing tickets were the equivalent of about half a day's salary for a day labourer. The 'commons' were close to a day's wage.[98] This isn't terribly different from today. While not totally exclusive, this is not the kind of activity ordinary people could enjoy on a daily or even weekly basis, and we are talking about a relatively affordable venue in a city with a strong operatic tradition. In opera's eighteenth-century heyday throughout Europe, the price of tickets meant even the nascent bourgeoisie did not attend regularly, let alone the lower classes – though both would watch a show on occasion. Most regular attendees for opera in Europe in the eighteenth and nineteenth century were wealthy, and paid for their seats on subscription.[99] The presence of boxes and tiered seating are precisely intended to stratify attendees according to wealth. And the social elite were the main financiers for opera, increasingly assisted by the state. Indeed, in some cases, the opposite process to the one Storey describes took place – despite the best efforts of governments to democratize the art form. For instance, in 1884 in the Paris Opera, state-imposed price controls demanded that tickets be made available for twelve (later twenty-four) performances a year, to cater to poorer customers. This was abandoned in 1907, when it turned out that the people snapping up these tickets were not the working classes as intended, but the same middle-class and wealthy audiences as usual.[100]

There are objective reasons for opera's high cost. An enormous amount of labour (and therefore value) goes into the production of opera due to the specialist training received by the performers and the army of musicians necessary to put on a show. While it is certainly true that the ruling classes have generally made a concerted effort to push the masses out of huge swathes of so-called high culture, I disagree with Storey that this is a novel development. Rather, it is an inevitable consequence of the monopolization of power and wealth in few hands, under capitalism, which inevitably leads to the sequestering of the cream of cultural production for a privileged layer. This in turn makes certain forms of culture – like opera – a domain for celebrating and confirming class privilege. And this clearly has an effect on the perception of opera. Fairly or otherwise, the fact remains that I have yet to come across an audience research project on opera (on stage or on screen) that did not bring forward the question of the art form's 'elitism' in one way or another.

The elite perception of even screen and simulcast opera contradict postmodern contentions about a flattened distinction between high and low cultures in the digital age. Norman Taylor, for example, speaks of the 'levelling effect' of digitization as creating an 'egalitarian terrain of producer and consumer-users that spawn new attitudes to screen media'.[101] This notion of digital levelling is also prevalent within convergence models of new media, which presume that a combination of empowered and participatory spectators, coupled with the blurring of ontological boundaries between media forms, have flattened cultural distinction between media forms.[102] On the contrary, opera was strongly associated with cultural distinction by my sample of novice subjects, and the mere existence of digital simulcasting had little impact on this impression. However, it was clear to me that any sense of haughtiness or social distinction were magnified in the opera house, as compared to the cinema.

Some of my subjects' run-ins with experienced opera house attendees evoked the formal process of initiation detailed in Benzecry's ethnography of Argentinian opera fans, whom he affectionately dubs 'opera people'.[103]

Benzecry conducted eighteen months of ethnographic research on opera practices, centred mostly on the upper-floor standing rooms of Buenos Aires's Colón Opera House, one of the most traditional houses in the world and a cornerstone of the international opera circuit. Although Buenos Aires is a very different city to London, there are points of commonality that bear consideration here. For instance, Benzecry describes how experienced opera-goers regulate the behaviour of novice audience members, leading by example (for instance, applauding at appropriate moments) and scolding noisy or unruly patrons to 'socialise the rest of the house into their understanding of opera'.[104] This hierarchical system of self-policing by the audience constitutes a 'complex system whereby rules of civility both constrain and enable emotion and allow for its proper public display'.[105] These rules are learned and adopted from rigorous study that begins years prior to setting foot inside an auditorium:

> [The] highly experiential character of learning makes for a complex system, one that proposes opera as an activity that (a) looks to the past for reference and comparison, (b) demands extensive and intensive attendance, (c) encourages people to attend conferences and lectures, listen to the radio, read related books, and buy records (although these activities are always complementary and never a substitute for attendance), and (d) makes for an almost automatic and informal apprenticeship process in which the older members school the younger ones and are recognised and revered for their knowledge.[106]

What emerges from this complex dynamic is a mode of engagement that Benzecry dubs 'collective connoisseurship', which is composed of 'more and less implicit doses of persuasion and coercion'.[107] In the world of opera, there is no pretence that all fans are equal. Benzecry describes several devotional, ritualistic practices performed by experienced attendees that mark out their status as such; listening with eyes closed, kneeling as if in prayer, enclosing their bodies by moving their chins closer to their chests and trying to move out of their sight 'anything that interrupts their one-on-one relationship with the music'.[108] Such overt devotional displays are less common in Covent Garden, but experienced fans nonetheless distinguish themselves through codes of dress and behaviour. In Durkheimian parlance, opera is sacred to its admirers, assuming a 'non-negotiable, totemic character'.[109] The religious analogy is especially apt for opera, where the experienced layers of fandom behave in a manner almost evoking a clergy, with detailed knowledge of their subject, rapt appreciation for it and a certain disdain for and sense of superiority over the layperson.

Benzecry discusses this arrangement positively, framing the inculcation into collective connoisseurship as an intrinsic part of opera novices' matriculation. My subjects' usually less-than-appreciative response to similar treatment in London might be explained by the fact that they attended their first opera as part of a research project, rather than being self-motivated to see one, and were thus less primed for micromanagement, however well-intentioned. There is also a detectable degree of romanticism on Benzecry's part - I am not convinced that every Argentinian at their first opera enjoys being shushed for opening a candy wrapper at an inopportune moment. It is likely that cultural specificity also plays an important role. Benzecry notes that opera in Buenos Aires is more detached from the national culture than in many Western European cities, mitigating against class-based snobbery and elitism. Indeed, it was partly for this reason that he selected the city as his case study. He contends that the on-going economic crisis that has squeezed the Argentine middle-classes from the 1990s onwards means that 'people from many backgrounds engage with opera in a situation of extended downward mobility, despite economic constraints and lack of a status payoff'.[110]

Based on personal participation, I can confirm that the Covent Garden audience can be extremely stringent about etiquette. I have personally endured the wrath of more experienced attendees for clapping at ill-opportune moments and for my occasionally less-than-formal attire. Conversely, I have also witnessed much generosity of spirit on behalf of the Royal Opera House audience, and particularly its established, loyal audience base. Indeed, this caste is granted special status as 'friends of the Royal Opera House', and invited to general rehearsals. During one such rehearsal, for Wagner's *Der Fliegende Holländer*, a spectacular (but perhaps over-ambitious) stage effect went awry during the overture. Water cascading down the inside of the stage curtain spilled over the lip of the stage into the orchestra pit, prompting a hasty end to proceedings to allow stagehands to hoover up the puddles. The crowd showcased a laudable degree of patience and sympathy, applauding Royal Opera House director Kasper Holten as he sheepishly came onstage to apologize for the disruption. As moments like these attest, it would be an injustice to castigate the Royal Opera House audience as stuffy and intolerant. However, they represent an especially knowledgeable and conscientious taste culture for whom intrusions into their beloved art in the form of inappropriate behaviour from fellow attendees are intolerable. This attitude cannot help but spill over into opera cinema to a certain degree.

Where I *do* agree with Storey are his objections to the likes of sociologist David Evans, who seeks to draw a distinction 'between opera in the opera house and opera as experienced in TV commercials, film soundtracks, sporting events, CD compilations, celebrity concerts by opera "superstars", opera holidays, and so on'.[111] In other words, the forms of cultural and technological outreach associated with 'bringing opera to the masses'. Storey is right to detect 'a certain essentialism – an uncritical residual distinction between art and entertainment' that is not really possible to sustain. 'Perhaps a more productive way to understand what is happening to opera', he argues,

> is not to see it in terms of commodities, but in terms of social practices of consumption. In other words, it is not the 'content' of opera that makes it 'high culture', but how and by whom it is consumed. This is because the difference between what counts as elite and popular culture is never simply a question of the material qualities of particular commodities. What really matters are the forces and relations which sustain the distinction, the difference ... the relations of power which are constantly punctuating and dividing the domain of culture into ... dominant and subordinate formations.[112]

This is a very productive way of parsing the kind of attitudes that predominate around opera cinema.

Barker's qualitative data on opera cinema audiences suggest they feel a sense of 'ownership' over the exhibition space, which occasionally erupts into 'revealing complaints about the wrong kinds of audience spoiling people's enjoyment ... People feel it is theirs, in all senses'.[113] This likely reinforced by the demographic homogeneity of opera cinema screenings, in which an older audience belonging to specific taste culture temporarily 'takes over' the movie house. One can imagine how this might have left my novice subjects feeling like intruders, even in their local cinema. While opera cinema does diminish some of the more formal behaviours of self-policing common to opera houses, it does not appear to overcome associations between opera and 'high style'.[114] This might go some way to explaining opera cinema's limited effect as a means of audience development. In the case of opera cinema, high culture is renegotiated through digital media, rather than negated and overcome.

When formulating the ontology of opera cinema, and especially its associations with elitism, it is necessary to understand its relative position in a broader ecology of cultural experience. There is a tendency by research subjects in comparative studies to draw explicitly negative comparisons between screen media and stage performance. Devotion to one often relies on disavowing the other. For example, the student audience members who participated in Barker's research on screen and stage adaptations of *Crash* justified their love of theatre by expressing disdain for cinema and its audiences. Barker observed that in his audience's discussion, 'theatre's qualities are always best grasped by stating them in opposition to something else: in this case, the cinematic'.[115] This negative comparison was especially evident with regards to sexual and violent content, which was praised as daring and artistic on the stage but vacuous and gratuitous on the screen: 'Theatre is "culture" while cinema is "only at best entertainment"'.[116] Pierre Bourdieu called this dynamic the 'habitus', observing that participation in the 'correct' kinds of culture assists in social distinction.[117] To paraphrase: taste classifies, so it classifies the classifier.[118] In my view, Bourdieu overstated this a bit, or rather got it back to front. The rich might like to give the impression of being cultured, but no matter how many Wagners you attend, it will not make you a leader in industry or grant you a Baronet. Social mobility through culture alone is impossible if you lack the funds to participate in 'high' culture to begin with. Rather, the process of cultural distinction is self-reinforcing. It is certainly true that there are perceived social advantages to embracing 'high' culture and conspicuous rejecting the 'low'. I got the impression that some of my novice respondents' comments evince a degree of overcompensation, reflecting their desire to belong within an esteemed cultural community: perhaps indicating an intuitive understanding of the devotional aspect of opera fandom.

The hybridity of simulcasting has led to it occupying a middle position: possessing some of the cult value and esteem attached to live experience in general and opera in particular, but diminished by the cinematic exhibition context and the material limitations of digital remediation. What is very clear from my research is that opera cinema is broadly seen as transmitting value generated by the co-present performers at Covent Garden, with varying levels of success. However, as demonstrated in Chapter 2, opera cinema has objectively distinctive ontological features that formally and technologically distinguish it from both stage opera and recorded cinema. I contend that the fact of opera cinema's perceived inferiority or ancillary status is a deliberate (or at least inveterate) formal strategy. The objective of opera cinema is to virtually transport audiences to a spectacularized version of a physical opera house, and encourage future attendance. This represents a significant change from the formally experimental screen opera of the post-war period that used the technical features of screen media to their artistic advantage. My subjects' comments (even where they were hostile) evince an impression of the opera house as grand, valuable and - ultimately - the natural home for opera. Relative to this, opera cinema can only ever be a pale, unsatisfactory alternative. In terms of understanding the status of screen and digital media relative to co-present theatre, this is a refutation of postmodern assumptions about the brave new, post-taste world of digital convergence. Clearly, the cult value of live theatre retains an esteem that is (if anything) enhanced by the ubiquity of digital remediation.

Protocols, viewing registers and audience behaviour

While simulcasting possesses technical and experiential features that are objectively distinct from both staged opera and recorded cinema, all available evidence implies that opera cinema remains a secondary product, with an audience dominated by experienced opera attendees.[119] I propose that opera cinema is nevertheless a unique, nascent and maturing cultural experience. It is also in a state of transition: its exhibition conventions are still taking shape, undergoing a process of what Martin Barker describes as 'sedimentation'.[120] Opera cinema has begun to establish a discrete taste culture and a mode of engagement somewhere between the 'theatrical' and 'cinematic'. However, this hybridity is occasionally awkward, which is indicative of growing pains. Moreover, its exhibition practices are consciously borrowed from older media, rather than being a synthesis specifically tied to a singular media phenomenon. In the last part of this chapter, I want to deal with the social dimension of opera cinema as a new cultural experience. I posit that opera cinema hybridizes theatrical protocols with a cinematic viewing context: combining a 'sense of occasion' with the comfort and diminished social risk of the movie house. Moreover, I will address overarching attitudes about opera cinema within a broader field of cultural experience. Throughout the book, I contend that technical specificity is not enough to determine a new medium as such: it also requires audience recognition. Furthermore, an audience's acknowledgement of a medium is not absolutely determined by objective, technical characteristics.

For instance, classical cinematic ontologies predicated on the indexical, celluloid image have been clouded by digitization.[121] Objectively, the cinematic apparatus has not changed much from its pre-history. It remains a recording technology and exhibition system predicated on still frames moving in succession to create the illusion of movement. What have qualitatively changed are cinematic practices and environments in which cinema is generally experienced. There is a world of difference between the saloons, travelling sideshows and Nickelodeons where cinema was accessed 120 years ago and the situation today. I posit that contextual factors of theatrical exhibition are as constitutive of cinematic ontology as anything fundamental about the cinematic image. Cinema's transition from a scientific apparatus, to a novelty attraction, to a theatrical, narrative-driven entertainment medium was not only a development of style and form but also exhibition practice, environment and norms of audience behaviour. Moreover, this process involved the imposition of 'discipline' over cinema audiences.[122] The 'twilight reverie'[123] (as Roland Barthes famously put it) was not automatically adopted, but remediated from theatre (and particularly post-Wagnerian opera), and enforced by the burgeoning cinema industry.[124] Following this logic, audience protocols and exhibition practices must factor into any theorization of opera cinema's ontology.

I accept Gitelman's definition of a medium as not a merely technological apparatus but also a socially realized structure of communication, including 'both technological forms and their associated protocols'.[125] These protocols constitute 'a vast clutter of normative rules and default conditions, which gather and adhere like a nebulous array around a technological nucleus ... [expressing] a huge variety of social, economic, and material relationships'.[126] For cinema, as Chuck Tryon describes, protocols could include 'arriving in time to watch the trailers, sitting quietly during the movie, buying popcorn or other snacks, or other behaviours sanctioned by the theater, as well as the use of a projector to display a movie image on a giant screen'.[127] These protocols are especially significant for media ontology after digitization, in which media content can flow into a variety of exhibition contexts. Barbara Klinger's research indicates that cinema is still treated as a distinctive phenomenon when viewed outside of the cinema.[128] In the case of home viewing for example, the deployment of various ritual behaviours - like acquiring snacks, viewing in a group setting, maintaining relative silence throughout and so on - enact codes of behaviour learned from the movie house. These ritual practices are part of a cultural system: 'a ritualized collection of different people on the same mental map, sharing or engaged with popular ontologies of representation.'[129] When such conventions become generalized, and associated with a particular medium in the popular consciousness, then the 'rules of engagement' for that medium become 'self-evident'.[130] This is the social process by which a mere remediation matures into a medium. As Gitelman points out, these develop out of 'the habits associated with other, related media'.[131] This is clearly the case for opera cinema, where protocols are borrowed primarily from the auditorium and the movie house.

Gitelman describes the different pathways by which media protocols are established: Some emerge at a grassroots level (especially in online cultures, forums, message boards and such). Others 'seem to arrive sui generis, discrete and fully formed,' while others, like the QWERTY keyboard, emerge as complicated engagements among different media'.[132] Furthermore, some media protocols are imposed by exhibition and distribution industries, bodies like the National Institute of Standards and Technology, or corporate monopolies like Microsoft and Apple.[133] As discussed in Chapter 2, *Live from the Met* established the formal default for opera cinema, in turn based on opera telecasts from the 1980s, but its protocols are a combination of imposed practices and autonomous, 'grassroots' behaviours. These are both probably subject to variability for different countries and opera companies, but I only have substantial data on the Royal Opera House.

The Royal Opera House has had little time to establish exhibition conventions for opera cinema. As late as 2010, the Royal Opera House had only been putting content in cinemas for a year, it had no international presence, and had never done live work – instead, it screened recorded material. The Royal Opera House's very first foray into cinema was with was More2Screen: a distributing partner for indie film projects utilizing multipurpose venues. The big challenge at this time was that the Royal Opera House knew nothing about cinema, so they relied on outsourced experts, with More2Screen handling things domestically and Arts Alliance Media on the international side. Today, the Royal Opera House is a lot more integrated in the transmission process, with artists corresponding much more closely with cinema, administrative and media personnel. In terms of selecting repertoire, it would be the 'hits' every time (Mozart, Verdi, Wagner – occasionally – *Carmen*, and the *Nutcracker* every Christmas). There is also plenty of pressure from the opera cinema audience for the shows they 'know and love', which especially given the high up-front outlay for a simulcast tends to mean the productions that make it to screen are canon pieces, though a balance of new productions is also sought.

The technical parameters of simulcasting result in certain protocols being enforced from the vendor's side, creating a number of unique challenges. One of my respondents – an employee of the Hatfield Odeon – discussed the special preparations made by the cinema to accommodate a simulcast. She explained that 'we'll test the screen and then they transmit the signal and we'll test the sound and the image quality and the format.' This process is pre-programmed and mostly automated, 'so you just kind of have to turn it on and communicate from the projector room'. On the night of the transmission, another test is performed fifteen minutes before the audience is allowed in. Issues often arise over quoting running times for cinema operators. Some slack is built into the programme (sent from the opera house) to ensure everyone takes their seats in good time: 'although the programme might say it's at quarter-past seven, the actual show will start at half-past seven.' The live simulcast also demands more work from cinema employees than playing a recorded film:

> We have a person monitoring the screen, just to make sure we have the sound as well, for our guests to enjoy the experience in the same way the live audience would. They want to get it as perfect as possible. In the intermission, because it's a one-off performance, the lights are not programmed so we have a dedicated staff who overlook the screen and then switch off the lights.

To facilitate this heightened level of labour and attention, event cinema is usually transmitted on Mondays and Thursdays: 'it's the best timing because we're not very busy with other performances so we can dedicate more time to the live showings.' Opera cinema's temporality is quite unlike the disciplined scheduling that Charles Acland describes for recorded cinema, in which the predictable regulation of audience behaviour must be sustained over a course of weeks.[134] It is also distinct from stage opera, in which shows run for at least a fortnight, with matinees offering the possibility for different showtimes. Instead, the whole enterprise of simulcasting is focused on a single night – midweek. This is a highly atypical temporality that does not favour certain demographics, particularly families with school-age children, which helps to reinforce opera cinema's strong slant towards mature and experienced attendees. The relative inconvenience and one-off performance also favours devotional rather than casual engagement, which aligns with the existing profile of opera cinema audiences. Ontologically, this temporality does not imply a 'mass' experience, but one bound for niche status. It is also quite out of step with general trends towards participatory, new media cultures characterized by spectatorial empowerment, content sharing and cross-platform 'flow'.[135] The parameters of opera cinema are modernist, rather strict, heavily choreographed from the institutional side, and more in-line with 'old' theatrical media.

From the audience side, there are protocols for simulcasting that I have experienced personally many times and will touch on anecdotally here, before elaborating in Chapter 4. One often arrives to find the bar well-populated prior to 'curtain up', in a manner uncommon for recorded cinema, in which audience members generally grab their snacks, hurry to their seats and sit in the dark. Often, a member of staff gives audiences due warning when the show is about to start, and similarly for the end of intervals. In some venues, like the Courtyard in Hereford, this announcement is made over an intercom. I find there is no social compulsion to remain in one's seat during the documentaries that play during breaks, but getting up to leave during acts is strongly discouraged – even for bathroom visits. At the end of the show, a lack of end credits means the entire cinema tends to leave as one, resulting in the lobby filling up rapidly. This, coupled with the fact that simulcasts generally conclude between 11p.m. and midnight, contributes to a special atmosphere. I have observed that the relative newness of opera cinema means its audiences *consciously* draw on these existing protocols, implying that opera cinema has not yet acquired self-evident exhibition practices of its own. Audiences deliberately enact different codes of dress, buy different refreshments and behave differently than they would during a 'normal' film screening.

From these clusters of behaviours, a distinguishable viewing strategy, to use Barker's term, is beginning to emerge.[136] Barker's concept of viewing strategy was developed 'as an alternative to, in many ways, in opposition to' Stuart Hall's the encoding/decoding approach as a mode of theorizing audience agency in relation to viewing practices. Departing from homogenous conceptions of 'dominant' readings (against which negotiated and oppositional readings are developed), Barker looks at the complex and skilled process by which audiences develop modes of engagement with unfamiliar media – drawing on their existing expertise, and culturally established conventions for media use. For instance, my research subjects drew on existing competences with various forms of cinematic and theatrical experience to negotiate an appropriate viewing register. But the heterogeneity of behaviours across even across this relatively small group suggests that and viewing register for opera cinema has not yet settled.

My findings in Chapter 4 are based on subjects who are quite distinct from the typical profile for opera cinema attendees. This came across very strongly in the data, with numerous subjects describing other attendees as 'older', 'middle-class', 'well-dressed', 'experienced' and so on. The aforementioned subject gave an arresting account of covering the snacks bar during simulcasts: 'They just buy coffees and ice cream! So, we know that if the intermission starts we just put more people on ice cream and coffee. They seem very disappointed if they don't get their rum and raisin ice cream, which we don't sell, we sell Ben & Jerry's.' The choice of refreshment makes a marked contrast to the hotdogs and Coca-Cola cited by respondents across several factors as a heuristic measure for cinema's populism.

Behavioural conventions remain attached to their host medium even when they transition to new exhibition contexts. They are socially negotiated as part of a cultural system, rather than being wholly individuated behaviours. Opera's protocols affect even inexperienced attendees, because opera cinema's associated exhibition practices persist beyond direct experience of the art form itself. They are part of the wider cultural imagination. The stereotype of men in tails and women draped in peals and mink is closely bound up in the mythology of opera, irrespective of how closely it accords with actual patterns of ritual behaviour and dress at auditoria. There is a paucity of empirical data on 'dressing up' and other ritual behaviours associated with opera attendance. Based on my personal experience, donning regalia is a widely observed convention. There are few major opera houses today that enforce dress codes, though most did in the past.[137] Nevertheless, I would feel uncomfortable visiting Covent Garden in a hoodie. However, while protocols have 'remarkable inertia' they are 'far from static'.[138] As Gitelman points out, 'norms and standards can and do change, because they are expressive of changeable social, economic and material relationships'.[139] The very fact that opera has relaxed its etiquette on dress over the years is evidence of this. Moreover, behavioural codes cannot be predicted at the level of the individual, as evidenced by my respondents' varying deliberations over what to wear, with some making more of an effort than others.

While clapping is standard practice for opera (at least in the West) and film festivals, it is only common at commercial cinemas in the United States – and even there, it can meet with disapproval.[140] In the simulcast environment, the convention is clearly carried over from live opera, and somewhat incongruously, given that virtual attendees are congratulating a cast that cannot hear their ovations. This is evidence of the culturally determined nature of media protocols, which exist semi-independently of technologies and media as part of a collective consciousness and are remediated by new exhibition contexts. The resulting middle ground shows the slightly uncomfortable hybridity between two related-but-distinct sets of exhibition practices, and further suggests that opera cinema has yet to acquire a fully stable and consistent viewing strategy.

But even this middle ground points to a contradiction at the heart of Phelan's ontology of the theatrical event, which assumes the aura of live performance cannot survive the process of mechanical remediation.[141] On the contrary, event cinema has clearly eked out a niche for itself by reproducing the aura of live performance, via digital remediation. The status of opera cinema as a theatrical event has important, theoretical implications for our understanding of the 'event' in an era of digitization that warrant explication. Elsaesser describes the significance of the 'event' as a cultural product whose 'commodity value resides in its temporality'.[142] That is to say: it possesses commodity value because it is time limited – it must be experienced in the moment. More specifically, the broadcast event, as Stephanie Marriot describes, implies a very particular concomitance of media communication and temporality, one that is especially salient to opera cinema. Namely, the 'dynamic relationship between centre and periphery' facilitated between spectators and the 'simultaneous elsewhere' during a broadcast event. The 'extraordinary intricacy' of the broadcast event can encompass multiple locales simultaneously via digital remediation.[143] Opera cinema combines multiple locales (Covent Garden and the various locations of the dispersed, virtual audience) into a simultaneous elsewhere that is mediated by the Royal Opera's camera and technical team and relayed via satellite. However, opera cinema is also a theatrical event, owing to the content transmitted and the exhibition context. Willmar Sauter explains that a key source of audiences' pleasure in theatrical events is in the reflexive relationship between the theatrical and the everyday:

> When we speak about a Theatrical Event, we think of someone doing something, ostentatiously enough to be distinguished from everyday life ... The distinction is twofold: on the one hand there is someone who does something in a different way than in regular life; on the other hand, there is also someone who sees and acknowledges this difference. Furthermore, both the doer and the observer have some idea that the possibility of such a distinction indicates that the doings during a theatrical event are different from similar actions outside a theatrical event.[144]

The theatrical event permits an audience to suspend the course of everyday causality in a way that domestic technologies do not. The act of cinema going, for example, necessitates going to a fixed location at a certain time, to watch a film in a collective setting. It necessarily suspends the flow of everyday life. The type of event that opera cinema represents is of particular significance to contemporary media cultures. Opera cinema reflects a larger trend (encompassing live and event cinema) towards finding 'new ways of monetizing content in an era of declining cinema ticket sales and an increase in on-demand, online access to films'.[145] 'Eventising' cinema has been prioritized in recent years. Cinema chains need to promote their product's unique selling point - theatrical exhibition. Audiences are prepared to pay for a film while it is still an 'event'[146] - for instance, the initial run of a major blockbuster. However, older films can also be made *eventful* in various ways, such as by theatricalizing the exhibition space, as in Edible Cinema, Secret Cinema (which also relies heavily on nostalgia), Pillow Cinema and so forth. Opera cinema is eventful at four levels: it is a time-limited commodity, it is a broadcast event, it is theatrical and it stems from a trend towards 'eventful' cinema in a period of competition from new media platforms and changing patterns of audience behaviour towards something more akin to theatrical conventions.

Cultural value, accessibility and democratization

I will conclude this chapter by touching on the issues of cultural value and democratization, which cannot be stated without qualification. These are, first and foremost, a policy buzz terms, favoured by funding bodies like the Arts Council, and rather amorphous. When utilized by policymakers, cultural value generally relates to the social and economic benefits of cultural engagement. In Britain, it was an especially prized subject in the period surrounding the 2012 London Olympics, and the subsequent Olympic legacy project. In 2013, Hasan Bakshi indicated that cultural value was a 'key area of importance for current research in the cultural sector',[147] citing the then Warwick Commission on Cultural Value, which was published in 2014, and the AHRC Cultural Value Project.[148] These definitions of cultural value are a legacy of the 'accountability' culture in the culture sector demanded by the Thatcher administration and expanded under New Labour. The definition of cultural value that I employ, however, refers to audiences' perception of the aesthetic and experiential quality of cultural experience, and the significance of that experience in political, artistic and moral terms in a broader context. In general, findings from other researchers suggest that audiences value opera cinema as an alternative to and support column for stage opera.[149] However, the value described by these studies is often undifferentiated, and lacks deeper analysis.

Regarding democratization, as I have stated, opera cinema does not currently serve to broaden and diversify opera audiences. On the contrary, it caters overwhelmingly to an expert and demographically homogenous cross-section of existing opera fandom.[150] Moreover, despite Gelb's original, express intention to 'bring opera to the masses' through simulcasting, opera houses have begun to withdraw from the objective of democratization.[151] In part, this is due to the medium's shortcomings as a recruiting tool, but it also reflects pressure from existing audiences, who tend to equate democratization with 'dumbing opera down'.[152] In 2002, British baritone Sir Thomas Allen, at a speech delivered at the thirteenth Royal Philharmonic Society Music Awards in London, claimed that opera was becoming increasingly 'money-grabbing' and 'PR-led', underlining his opposition to inclusivity: 'We kowtow more and more to mass appeal ... I am sick and tired of hearing of those performers who talk of it as their life's work to bring culture and the classics to a wider public,' adding hyperbolically, 'We have undoubtedly become a civilisation in rapid cultural decline.'[153] Clearly, the discourse of democratization is politically loaded, and as such one cannot deploy it uncritically. In the UK, the term is a holdover from the Thatcher and Blair governments' attempt to metricize cultural access and engagement.[154] Any capacity for opera cinema to democratize opera is limited by the level of state investment in the arts and broadening the cultural ecology – but is motivated by it as well.

Operatic relays from the Royal Opera House started in the Royal Opera House under Tony Hall. The Arts Council is a major pillar of support for the Royal Opera House, but the public money it provides comes with caveats. Among these is the requirement that arts institutions must do educational work, and must try to bring their products to wider audience. Hall apparently took this to heart and expanded the Royal Opera House's educational department. At the time, audience development took the form of big screens in Covent Garden piazza and Trafalgar Square, but Hall felt it should go further. I've heard whispers that Royal Opera House had the idea of putting live operas into cinemas before the Met, but dragged its feet possibly due to its relationship with the BBC. Up until 2008, the Royal Opera House had an arrangement with the public broadcaster whereby the BBC promised to relay a certain number of productions. But the decline of network TV means that arts institutions felt they were better off finding alternative modes of promoting their product. Given the political and financial pressure from the Arts Council, the stars aligned.

Nevertheless, the subject of democratization emerged organically from my novice subjects, and from other research projects on this subject. This suggests that democratization remains an important social dimension of opera cinema's ontology. The fact that simulcasting has not substantially broadened opera audiences is a repudiation of technological determinist accounts of new media. The technical capacity of opera cinema to extend the reach of opera at reduced cost to the consumer does not overcome opera's historically ingrained reputation as an elite art form. Nor does it bring opera closer to people's lives through integration into education, nor revive the touring and regional opera scene undercut by aggressive centralization of arts funding and audiences from the 1980s onwards.[155]

This is not necessarily through lack of trying. For example, the Royal Opera House routinely invites young people to see opera, targeting deprived areas. For a while, it was investigating cinema school matinees. Apparently, the trial run was unsuccessful. There was limited interest from secondary schools. This is partly because there needs to be a very engaged teacher to make this happen, not to mention the space and the time in teaching schedules, which was a tough sell given the perceived lack of curriculum links. In the case of primary schools, there was more interest, as there were no exam clashes and more freedom in terms of cultural trips: but again, the lack of any clear link to curriculum was a stumbling block. The idea of livestreams to classrooms was touted, but apparently few teachers were willing to sit their class in front of a three-hour opera/ballet. The National Theatre and an organization called Frog Technologies have Digital Rights Management (DRM) protected their broadcasts, and offered select streams offered exclusively to schools that sign on, complete with additional resources. Arguably the products from the NT are an 'easy sell' with clear curriculum cross-over, whereas the Royal Opera House cannot bend its content as easily to fit curricula. The lack of success thus far does not mean these technologies lack potential benefit to the cultural ecology. However, there are clearly bigger, structural barriers involved for opera.

Benzecry's case study of opera fandom in Buenos Aires demonstrates how the socio-economic and demographic composition of opera audiences can be significantly diversified by general access to and acceptance of classical music.[156] In Britain, opera remains a foreign medium and has tended to be reserved for an elite taste culture. In my estimation, based on both my own research and extant data elsewhere, opera cinema has minimal value as a conduit to opera for new layers of audiences insofar as opera remains an unfamiliar and challenging medium for most of the population.[157] Changing this situation would necessitate major shifts in general curricula to make opera attendance a feature of state schooling, and greater financial and geographic availability of opera performances. Moreover, opera must remain a part of a local cultural ecology, ensuring that it is not only visible to more people, but also that there are more opportunities for participation from an amateur to professional level. Royal Academy of Dramatic Arts (RADA) and national opera houses are not sufficient: the survival of global opera depends on a healthy local ecology and a revival of regional opera. Unfortunately, precisely the opposite process is currently underway: local and touring companies are nearly always the first casualties of budgetary reviews.[158] For young people to grow as opera lovers, they must be familiar with the medium from school age and able to imagine themselves onstage. For opera to live, it must be a part of life.

Nevertheless, most of my subjects (even those with a dim view of opera cinema) complemented the simulcast for at least attempting to make opera cinema more 'accessible': that is, cheaper, easier to engage with and more convenient. While this might seem a prosaic issue, it was probably the most widely discussed aspect of the simulcasting experience amongst my subjects. There are two conclusions to draw from this. The first is further confirmation of simulcasting's status as an 'alternative' to stage opera, rather than a distinct art form. The second is that this question of accessibility deserves more serious analysis than it generally receives. It figured heavily in my subjects' impression of simulcasting and is pertinent to its ontology. That such questions are rarely discussed in academic appraisals of media ontology reflects, I believe, an overwhelming focus on technology and apparatus, but also an unconscious disdain for 'mundane' questions that cut rather close to commercial considerations. However, we cannot understand a medium without assessing its social function and use, which naturally invite questions about access. Opera tends to be staged in big cities, especially with touring companies drying up: a process that is only going to accelerate in a post-Covid world.

My data also possibly reflect national specificity. The British public was comparatively late to engage with this effete and emotionally exuberant musical drama form.[159] As such, opera has generally been perceived with suspicion, bar a few significant cultural events like the Proms and the Festival of Britain. The fact that so many subjects said they had never gone to an opera before because of the language barrier, yet did not know about surtitling in the opera house, points to a very straightforward way opera companies might reach out to newcomers: making it clear that this concession is provided. Interestingly, my subjects threw a great deal of emphasis on subtitles at the cinema as a crutch for newcomers, confirming opera cinema's enduring perception as a means of bringing opera 'to the masses', regardless of its actual success in this regard. This is assisted by the fact that many less-experienced attendees the cinema as a relaxed and familiar exhibition context, in which etiquette and behavioural codes were less stringent than the opera house.

In my view, opera cinema is still a long way from stepping out of the shadow of the stage form. In technological and aesthetic terms, it has a lot of novel attractions to offer. However, the social dimension of opera cinema's ontology remains in flux, which is partly evidence of its youth, but also demonstrates it has not yet attained consistent acknowledgement as a medium. Nevertheless, a viewing register for simulcasting is beginning to emerge. Some of opera cinema's unique protocols are dialectically related to its technical parameters and enforced strictly by the exhibitor, while others are in the process of being negotiated by audiences. Opera cinema operates on a unique temporality demanded by the 'one-night-only' transmission; it boasts an audience distinguished by its maturity and knowledge of opera; and it adapts theatrical exhibition practices like physical programmes, dressing-up and occasionally applause to a cinematic exhibition context. These practices are not transmitted wholesale but are remediated by the traditions of cinema attendance. Moreover, the simulcast is eventful on multiple levels, existing as part of a broader trend towards 'theatricalising' the movie house.

Notes

1. Matt Trueman, 'English National Opera Chief Attacks Live Cinema Broadcasts', *Guardian*, 10 May 2012, accessed 16 December 2017, https://www.theguardian.com/music/2012/may/10/eno-director-hits-live-broadcasts.
2. Kate Molleson, 'ENO's Peter Grimes on Screen: A Test of What Opera-in-Cinemas can Deliver', *Guardian*, 24 February 2014, accessed 10 May 2017, https://www.theguardian.com/music/musicblog/2014/feb/24/britten-peter-grimes-eno-opera-in-cinemas.
3. RobKing, 'Laughter in an Ungoverned Space: Actuality Humour in Early Cinema and Web 2.0', *New Silent Cinema*, edited by Katherine Groo and Paul Flaig (Oxford: Taylor and Francis, 2015), 294.
4. Jay David Bolter and Richard Grusin, 'Remediation', *Configurations* 4.3 (Fall 1996): 311–58.
5. WolfgangErnst, *Digital Memory and the Archive*, edited by Jussi Parikka (Minneapolis: University of Minnesota Press, 2013), 25.
6. Jay David Bolter and Richard Grusin, *Remediation: Understanding New Media* (Cambridge, MA: MIT Press, 1999), 29.
7. Emanuele Senici, 'Porn Style? Space and Time in Live Opera Videos', *Opera Quarterly* 26.1 (2010): 70.
8. Theodore Adorno and Thomas Y. Levin, 'Opera and the Long-Playing Record', *October* 55 (1990), 64.
9. David Held, *Introduction to Critical Theory: Horkheimer to Habermas* (California: University of California Press, 1980); Louis Althusser, 'Ideology and Ideological State Apparatuses (Notes towards an Investigation)', in *Lenin and Philosophy and Other Essays* (London: Verso, 1970).
10. Catherine Belsey, 'Shakespeare and Film: A Question of Perspective', *Literature/Film Quarterly* 11.3 (1983): 152–8.
11. Ien Ang, *Watching Dallas: Soap Opera and the Melodramatic Imagination* (London: Routledge, 1985); David Morley and Charlotte Brundson, *The Nationwide Audience* (London: Routledge, 1980).
12. Kim Schrøder, Kristen Drotner, Stephen Kline and Catherine Murray, *Researching Audiences* (New York: Oxford University Press, 2006); Martin Barker, 'I Have Seen the Future and It Is Not Here Yet; or, On Being Ambitious for Audience Research', *Communication Review* 9 (2006): 9.
13. Philip Auslander, *Liveness: Performance in a Mediatized Culture* (London: Routledge, 2008).
14. Senici, 63.
15. Ibid., 64.
16. Peggy Phelan, *Unmarked: The Politics of Performance* (London: Routledge, 1993), 146; Erika Fischer-Lichte, *Ästhetik des Performativen*, edition suhrkamp (Frankfurt am Main: Suhrkamp Verlag, 2004).
17. Ibid.

18 Martin Barker, 'CRASH, Theatre, Audiences, and the Idea of "Liveness"', *Studies in Theatre and Performance* 23.1 (2003): 28.
19 Stephen Prince, 'True Lies: Perceptual Realism, Digital Images, and Film Theory', *Film Quarterly* 49.3 (1996).
20 Ibid., 31.
21 Karen Wise, 'Opera in Cinemas', report for ETO and Guildhall School of Music & Drama (London, 2013).
22 Brent Karpf Reidy, Becky Shutt, Deborah Abramson, Antoni Durski and Laura Castle, 'Live-to-Digital', AEA Consulting for Arts Council England and Society of London Theatre, October 2016, 13–14.
23 Duncan White, 'British Expanded Cinema and the "Live Culture" 1969–79', *Visual Culture in Britain* 11.1 (2010): 93.
24 Christopher Morris, 'Digital Diva: Opera on Video', *Opera Quarterly* 26.1 (2010): 100.
25 Matthew Reason, 'Theatre Audiences and Perceptions of "Liveness" in Performance', *Participations* 1.2 (2004), accessed 22 January 2022, http://www.participations.org/volume%201/issue%202/1_02_reason_article.htm.
26 Barker, 'CRASH', 43–4.
27 Ibid.
28 Ibid., 27–8.
29 Morris, 101.
30 Barbara Klinger, *Beyond the Multiplex: Cinema, New Technologies, and the Home* (Berkeley: University of California Press, 2006).
31 Hans Ulrich Gumbrecht, *Production of Presence: What Meaning Cannot Convey* (California: Stanford University Press, 2004), xiii–iv.
32 Christopher Balme, 'Surrogate Stages: Theatre, Performance and the Challenge of New Media', *Performance Research: A Journal of the Performing Arts* 13.2 (2008): 83.
33 Phelan, 146.
34 Claudio E. Benzecry, *The Opera Fanatic: Ethnography of an Obsession* (Chicago: University of Chicago Press, 2011), 21.
35 Walter Benjamin, 'The Work of Art in the Age of Its Technological Reproducibility, Second Version', in *The Work of Art in the Age of Its Technological Reproducibility, and Other Writings on Media*, edited by. Michael W. Jennings, Brigid Dohert and Thomas Y. Levin (Cambridge, MA: Harvard University Press, 2008); André Bazin, *What Is Cinema? Vol. 1 & 2*, edited and translated by Hugh Gray (Berkeley: University of California Press, 1971).
36 Stephanie Marriott, *Live Television: Time, Space and the Broadcast Event* (London: Sage, 2007), 36.
37 Ibid., 36.
38 Wise, 19.

39 James Steichen, 'HD Opera: A Love/Hate Story Staging the Backstage at Carmen, Live in HD', *Opera Quarterly* 27.4 (2011): 447.
40 Balme, 90; Martin Lister, Jon Dovey, Seth Giddings, Iain Grant and Kieran Kelly, *New Media: A Critical Introduction*, 2nd edn (London: Routledge, 2009), 21.
41 Bolter and Grusin.
42 Henry Jenkins, *Convergence Culture: Where Old and New Media Collide* (New York: New York University Press, 2006).
43 Raymond Williams, *Television. Technology and Cultural Form* (London: Routledge, 1974), 89.
44 Sarah Atkinson, *Beyond the Screen: Emerging Cinema and Engaging Audiences* (London: Bloomsbury, 2014), 47.
45 Ibid., 47.
46 Marie Gillespie, 'Television, Ethnicity and Cultural Change', in *The Audience Studies Reader*, edited by Will Brooker and Deborah Jermyn (London: Routledge, 2003), 322.
47 Jenkins.
48 Stuart Hall, 'The Local and the Global: Globalization and Ethnicity', in *Dangerous Liaisons: Gender, Nation, and Postcolonial Perspectives*, edited by Anne McClintock, Aamir Mufti and Ella Shohan (Minneapolis: University of Minnesota Press, 1997).
49 Daniel Snowman, *The Gilded Stage: A Social History of Opera* (London: Atlantic Books, 2009).
50 Olivia Turnbull, *Bringing Down the House: The Crisis in Britain's Regional Theatres* (London: Intellect Books, 2008).
51 Anne Friedberg, *The Virtual Window: From Alberti to Microsoft* (Cambridge, MA: MIT Press, 2006), 195.
52 Jay David Bolter, 'A Night at the Opera Cinema', paper delivered at 'Opera Cinema: A New Cultural Experience?', Symposium at King's College London, 16 June 2017.
53 Marcia J. Citron, *Opera on Screen* (New Haven, CT: Yale University Press, 2000), 48–9.
54 James Steichen, 'The Metropolitan Opera Goes Public: Peter Gelb and the Institutional Dramaturgy of the Met: "Live in HD"'. *Music and the Moving Image*, 2.2 (2009): 27.
55 Steichen, 'The Metropolitan Opera Goes Public,' 24–5; my emphasis.
56 Fiona Tuck, 'Understanding the Impact of Event Cinema: An Evidence Review', *Arts Council England and British Film Institute* (2016): 7.
57 Ibid., 7.
58 Steichen, 'The Metropolitan Opera Goes Public', 24.
59 Jean Baudrillard, *Simulacra and Simulation* (Ann Arbor: University of Michigan Press, 1981).

60 Thomas Elsaesser, 'Digital Cinema: Convergence or Contradiction?', in *The Oxford Handbook of Sound and Image in Digital Media*, edited by John Richardson (Oxford: Oxford University Press, 2013), 13–14.
61 Philip Auslander, *Liveness: Performance in a Mediatised Culture*, 2nd edn (London: Routledge, 2008); Guy Debord, *Society of the Spectacle, Marxist Internet Archive*, accessed 10 May 2017, https://www.marxists.org/reference/archive/debord/society.htm; Jean Baudrillard, *Simulacra and Simulation: The Body in Theory: Histories of Cultural Materialism* (Michigan: University of Michigan Press, 1994).
62 Steichen, 'The Metropolitan Opera Goes Public', 28.
63 Steichen, 'HD Opera',453.
64 Ibid., 455.
65 Ibid., 453.
66 Ibid.
67 Ibid., 455.
68 Sam Abel, *Opera in the Flesh: Sexuality in Operatic Performance* (Colorado: Westview Press, 1996), 164.
69 Melinda Esse, 'Don't Look Now: Opera, Liveness, and the Televisual', *Opera Quarterly* 26.1 (2010): 82.
70 Morris, 99.
71 Herbert Lindenberger, *Opera: The Extravagant Art* (London: Cornell University Press, 1984), 235.
72 Ibid., 15.
73 Ibid., 234–40.
74 Theodore Adorno and Thomas Y. Levin, 'Opera and the Long-Playing Record', *October* 55 (1990): 64.
75 Ibid., 64.
76 Walter Benjamin, *The Work of Art in the Age of Its Technological Reproducibility* (Berlin: Schocken, 1936): 25.
77 Barker, *Live to Your Local Cinema: The Remarkable Rise of Livecasting* (Basingstoke: Palgrave Macmillan, 2013), 62.
78 Morris, 105–6.
79 Sinéad O'Neill, Joshua Edelman and John Sloboda, 'Opera and Emotion: The Cultural Value of Attendance for the Highly Engaged', *Participations* 13.1: (2016): 34.
80 Lesley Stern, 'The Tales of Hoffman: An Instance of Operality', in *Between Opera and Cinema*, edited by Jeongwon Joe and Rose Theresa (New York: Routledge, 2002), 45.
81 O'Neill, Edelman and Sloboda, 37.
82 John Willett,*Brecht on Theatre: The Development of an Aesthetic* (London: Methuen, 1964).

83   Carolyn Abbate and Roger Parker, *A History of Opera: The Last Four Hundred Years* (London: Penguin Group, 2012), 10–11.
84   Norman King, 'Film-Viewer Relations Before Hollywood', in *Babel and Babylon: Spectatorship in American Silent Film*, edited by Miriam Hansen (Cambridge, MA: Routledge, 1991), 43.
85   John Storey, 'The Social Life of Opera', *European Journal of Cultural Studies* 6.1 (2003): 5.
86   Henry Raynor, *A Social History of Music: From the Middle Ages to Beethoven* (New York: Schocken Books, 1972), 171.
87   Bernard Zelochow, 'The Opera: The Meeting of Popular and Elite Culture in the Nineteenth Century', *History of European Ideas* 16.1–3 (1993): 262.
88   Bruce A. McConachie, 'New York Operagoing, 1825–50: Creating an Elite Social Ritual', *American Music* 6.2 (1988): 182.
89   Lawrence Levine, *Highbrow/Lowbrow: The Emergence of Cultural Hierarchy in America* (Cambridge, MA: Harvard University Press, 1988), 103.
90   Ibid., 229.
91   Irving Kolodin, *The Metropolitan Opera, 1883–1935* (New York: Oxford University Press, 1936), 5.
92   Ibid., 12.
93   Janet Wolff, 'The Ideology of Autonomous Art', in *Music and Society: The Politics of Composition, Performance and Reception*, edited by R. Leppert and S. McClary (Cambridge, MA: Cambridge University Press, 1989), 5–6.
94   Storey, 37.
95   Susan Bennett, *Theatre Audiences: A Theory of Production and Reception*, 2nd edn (London: Routledge, 1997).
96   Abbate and Parker, 19.
97   Otto Erich Deutsch, *Das Freihaustheater auf der Wieden 1787–1801* (Berlin: Deutscher Verlag, 1937); David Buch, 'Mozart and the Theater auf der Wieden: New Attributions and Perspectives', *Cambridge Opera Journal* 9.3 (1997).
98   Ibid.
99   Steven Huebner, 'Opera Audiences in Paris 1830–1870', *Music & Letters* 70. 2 (1989).
100 François R. Velde, 'Economic History of Opera', *Federal Reserve Bank of Chicago* (2015): 20–1.
101 Norman Taylor,*Cinematic Perspectives on Digital Culture: Consorting with the Machine* (London: Palgrave MacMillan, 2012), 14.
102 Henry Jenkins, *Convergence Culture: Where Old and New Media Collide* (New York: New York University Press, 2006); Chuck Tryon, *On-Demand Culture: Digital Delivery and the Future of Movies* (New York: Rutgers University Press, 2013).

103 Benzecry, 7.
104 Ibid., 93–4.
105 Ibid., 93.
106 Ibid., 82.
107 Ibid., 100.
108 Ibid., 127.
109 Ibid., 135–6.
110 Ibid., 27–9.
111 Storey, 24.
112 Ibid.
113 Barker, *The Remarkable Rise of Livecasting*, 32.
114 Lindenberger, 15.
115 Barker, 'CRASH', 34.
116 Ibid., 38.
117 Pierre Bourdieu, *Distinction* (London: Routledge, 1984), 5–6.
118 Ibid.
119 Amanda Fallows, 'Royal Opera House Cinema Research', Royal Opera House research data, October 2014.
120 Barker, *The Remarkable Rise of Livecasting*, 35–6.
121 Martin Lister, Jon Dovey, Seth Giddings, Iain Grant and Kieran Kelly, *New Media: A Critical Introduction*, 2nd edn (Abingdon: Routledge, 2009) .
122 Chuck Tryon, *Reinventing Cinema: Movies in the Age of Media Convergence Tryon* (New Brunswick: Rutgers University Press, 2009).
123 Roland Barthes, 'Leaving the Movie Theatre', *The Rustle of Language* (Toronto: Collins Publishers, 1984), 346.
124 Lindenberger, 223.
125 Lisa Gitelman, *Always Already New: Media, History and the Data of Culture* (Cambridge, MA: MIT Press, 2006), 6.
126 Ibid., 7.
127 Tryon, 5.
128 Barbara Klinger, *Beyond the Multiplex: Cinema, New Technologies, and the Home* (Berkeley: University of California Press, 2006), 195.
129 Gitelman, 7.
130 Ibid., 5.
131 Ibid., 6.
132 Gitelman, 8.
133 Ibid., 8.
134 Tryon, 5–6.
135 Lister et al.

136 Barker, 9.
137 'The History of the Opera Dress Code', English National Opera, accessed 10 May 2020, https://eno.org/discover-opera/the-history-of-the-opera-dress-code/.
138 Gitelman, 7–8.
139 Ibid.
140 Steven Pate, 'Movie Rant: Clapping in a Movie Theater', *Chicagoist*, 14 February 2012, , accessed 1 April 2018, http://chicagoist.com/2012/02/14/movie_rant_clapping_in_a_movie_thea.php.
141 Benjamin, 23.
142 Thomas Elsaesser, *Digital Cinema: Delivery, Event, Time* (Amsterdam: University of Amsterdam Press, 1998), 212.
143 Marriot, 36.
144 Willmar Sauter, 'Introducing the Theatrical Event', in *Theatrical Events: Borders Dynamics Frames* (Amsterdam: Rodopi, 2004), 11.
145 Atkinson, 49.
146 Ibid., 48.
147 Hasan Bakhshi, Ian Hargreaves and Juan Mateos-Garcia, 'A Manifesto for the Creative Economy', NESTA, 71, accessed 17 February 2020, https://www.nesta.org.uk/sites/default/files/a-manifesto-for-the-creative-economy-april13.pdf.
148 Geoffrey Crossick and Patrycja Kaszynska, 'AHRC Cultural Value Project', Arts and Humanities Research Council, 2014, accessed 1 April 2018, http://www.ahrc.ac.uk/documents/publications/cultural-value-project-final-report/.
149 Karen Wise, 'Distinct/Distinctive: What Opera Audiences Take to and from Cinema Simulcasts', paper presented at 'Opera and the Media of the Future' conference, Sussex, 24 October 2014; Fallows, Florin Vladica, 'Value propositions of opera and theater live in cinema' (Thessaloniki: Ryerson University/World Media Economics & Management Conference, 2012), 15.
150 Fallows.
151 Andrew Clark, 'Royal Opera House Head Rejects "Democratising Art"', *Financial Times*, 31 March 2014, accessed 16 December 2017, https://www.ft.com/content/8fc034fe-b8f2-11e3-98c5-00144feabdc0.
152 Snowman, 398.
153 Storey, 18–19.
154 Turnbull, 193.
155 Ibid., 201.
156 Benzecry, 28–9.
157 'Share of Adults who Attended an Opera or Operetta in the Last Year in England from 2005/06 to 2015/16', *Statistica*, accessed 1 April 2018, https://www.statista.com/statistics/556334/adults-opera-attendance-uk-england/.

158 Alex Beard, 'Arts Council England: National Portfolio and Bridge Funding Announced', *Royal Opera House*, 1 July 2014, accessed 13 June 2021, http://www.roh.org.uk/news/arts-council-england-national-portfolio-and-bridge-funding-announced; Jen Harvie, 'Funding, Philanthropy, Structural Inequality and Decline in England's Theatre Ecology', *Cultural Trends* 24.1 (2015): 56.

159 Ibid., 67.

4

The opera virgins project

As noted throughout, a key aspect of my approach to media ontology is talking to real audiences about their actual experiences. The predominantly digital media landscape presents a unity of opposites between multiplicity and convergence. There have never been so many ways to consume media: never so many screens, never greater access to such a variety of experiences. And yet this content is largely delivered in the same digital format, which can migrate easily between large screens and small, public and private exhibition contexts. This 'platform agnosticism' presents certain challenges when it comes to developing taxonomies for new media experiences and art forms.[1] A postmodern approach might see us abandon any attempt to define one media experience against another, dismiss all boundaries as fundamentally arbitrary or a purely subjective matter and embrace an undifferentiated mass of media content. This book takes a different view. If the question of media ontology is more fluid than in the past, then we simply require more flexible models for understanding it. Live opera can be consumed on the stage, at the cinema and on a smartphone via a streaming service, all of which create a different reinterpretation and audience encounter with the original performance. But it is all the same performance. So, at what point do we stop talking about opera cinema as a remediation of opera and start talking about a new art form? In part, and put crudely: you know it when you see it.

The historical and formal aspects described so far are part of the ontological equation, but we can only talk about a medium at the point that audiences embrace and recognize an experience as something new, and adjust their behaviour accordingly. This chapter will present findings from an audience research project I conducted between 2015 and 2016, in which a small number of subjects experienced opera for the first time in a combination of different settings. Their impressions, despite lacking statistical weight, offer a novel insight into what people might regard as distinctive about the experience of opera cinema. In isolation, they tell us little, but together with the historical and formal features of opera cinema in the rest of the book, they offer a more complete picture of this hybrid media experience.

This chapter will demonstrate how my project design aimed to scrutinize my respondents' subjective engagement with opera cinema. My core research tool was Q Methodology, supplemented by traditionally qualitative research methods including focus groups and subject testimonies. I argue that my project design overcomes some limitations of quantitative, demographic-focused, audience research that merely describes general correlations ('social bracket C1 prefers cultural event A') without deeper explanation or context. I contend that, particularly for a nascent cultural phenomenon (whose aesthetic and exhibition conventions are still malleable), data about the peculiarities of audience experience are necessary to give both demographic correlations and audience talk deeper meaning. Such experiential data is therefore necessary to grasp the ontological character of opera cinema.

Additionally, before moving into my audience data, I sketch the timeline of my research from a pilot project conducted in March 2015 through to the final phase of data collection that concluded in September 2016. I relate how my initial intention to compare the responses of novice audiences to existing opera cinema audiences evolved into an exclusive focus on the former. I also discuss how I was forced to adjust and adapt my design in response to unexpected challenges and explain how these challenges are themselves instructive about the public perception of opera cinema. Hopefully, this account will offer something of a cautionary tale to future researchers investigating novice audiences, who in my experience prove more of a logistical challenge than dealing with engaged, experienced subjects.

Q Methodology

My main research tool, Q Methodology, is an epistemological hybrid, designed in the 1930s by psychologist-physicist William Stephenson to 'objectively uncover and analyse similarities and differences in the subjective viewpoints of individuals', which makes it particularly appropriate for assessing the subjective experiences of media audiences.[2] Originally conceived to test subjects' political orientation, this method requires respondents (individually referred to Q sorts, collectively as the P set) to rank-order a series of two to five dozen items, typically on a sliding scale of +4 (entirely agree) to -4 (entirely disagree) – a quasi-normal distribution in the shape of a bell curve. In so doing, the researcher asks subjects to 'operationalize his/her own viewpoint through an ipsative [self-referencing] procedure'.[3] Items traditionally consist of text on cards and are lifted from a concourse: a selected set of stimuli reflecting cultural associations surrounding the phenomenon under scrutiny. This concourse can consist of pre-existing material (e.g. photographs, music, academic and media coverage) or can be generated by the researcher. For instance, the following statement (taken from a *Guardian* article published 2 October 2016)[4] could be used as an item in a Q Methodology study of the 2016 US Presidential election:

> Trump has won over many who feel neglected by what they view as the metropolitan intelligentsia.

Alternatively, the researcher could conduct preliminary focus groups on the election and use statements from his or her transcript as items for a secondary round of participants. For his research on *Live from the Met*, Florin Vladica's concourse included sixteen semi-structured interviews in which respondents were asked to discuss their thoughts and feelings after a variety of cultural performances in numerous locations.[5] These ranged from the Northern Sea Jazz Festival in Rotterdam, a U2 live concert in Barcelona, a *Cirque du Soleil* performance in Las Vegas, a contemporary opera in Innsbruck, *Mary Poppins* on Broadway in New York and *Don Pasquale* live in HD cinema from the Met in New York.[6] Additionally, Vladica obtained statements and phrases 'relating specifically to opera' from the Facebook and Twitter accounts of the National Theatre in London and Metropolitan Opera in New York. He collected further statements from relevant websites including *Madison Opera*, *Well Sung*, *Opera Cast*, *Living at the Opera*, *Opera Today*, *I Hate Opera* and *Opera Critic*.[7]

The selected items are referred to as the Q sample, which is submitted to respondents for sorting. Even with only a few dozen items, the number of possible comparisons is vast, meaning that one's sample rarely exceeds fifty or sixty items. The subjects' chosen configuration during the sorting procedure is taken to represent a 'holistic expression of each person's perspective, such as degree of agreement with, or preference for, the items'.[8] Once the sort is complete, the researcher performs factor analysis on the resultant data, creating a 'matrix of correlations among the set of Q sorts'. Put simply, factor analysis determines the extent to which respondents agree or disagree with one another, grouping subjects with similar results into factors. These groups of similar Q sorts 'typically express a shared and coherent point-of-view [among persons] on the topic addressed by the item set'.[9] While factor analysis used to be conducted via an onerous process of manual statistical modelling, modern software packages (such as PQMethod, which I utilize) now carry out this process. The Q sorts are often coupled with qualitative data – in the form of subject testimonies, focus groups or both – which aid in the final analysis.

Q Methodology is well-suited to inductive research, because it utilizes subjects' own self-reflective engagement with cultural phenomenon to generate new insights. Therefore, the method is especially appropriate for studying relatively nascent cultural experience like opera cinema, for which attitudes and viewing strategies are still formative. For the same reason, Q Methodology struck me as an appropriate tool for studying novice audiences. On the latter point, Charles H. Davis (a proponent of Q Methodology) discusses a tendency in the British Cultural Studies tradition to produce an abundance of mostly anecdotal qualitative case studies, depicting individual encounters between audiences and texts.[10] As a result, audience research ceases to be collaborative project and is relegated to atomized studies on a multitude of frontiers. Q Methodology attempts to overcome this problem by providing the depth of insight into audience subjectivity associated with qualitative methods, while fortifying these impressions with the statistical operation of factor analysis. Therefore, the method boasts a more rigorous analytical framework than interviews, focus groups and ethnography in isolation. Also, following the logic of complexity I discussed in Chapter 1, this approach permits us to create a multi-directional conversation between audiences' immediate experiences and a wider social context.

Q Methodology also has its limitations. It is perhaps unique in deliberately restricting its sample size, downplaying the standard measure of statistical viability. It could be argued that such small data pools make it impossible to produce generalized claims about the future behaviour even of one's research subjects – let alone larger populations. Small groups could easily be dismissed as an aberration. Moreover, the interpretation stage of Q Methodology not only risks but encourages subjective intervention on the part of the researcher, which invites accusations of bias. Finally, it is arguable that the same research subjects, performing the sorting process on different occasions, can produce totally different results. Rather than striving for a big picture view of cultural phenomena, Q Methodology provides a snapshot of an on-going cultural process from the perspective of a selected sample. For my purposes – gathering the experiential impressions of a particular type of audience (opera novices) to determine opera cinema's ontology – it is quite appropriate. However, these findings would be extremely narrow without situating them within a broader historical and social analysis of opera cinema, which I have tried to do in Chapters 2 and 3.

Conducting the project

My initial design was experimental and developed considerably over the course of my fieldwork – as did the emphasis of my research. For instance, it was not my original intention to focus exclusively on opera virgins, but to obtain the impressions of a sample of novice respondents for comparison with an experienced sample, more representative of typical opera cinema audiences. I hypothesized that certain aspects of event cinema, such as relatively inexpensive tickets (and thus reduced risk) and the visual vocabulary of film, might have intrinsic appeal for newcomers that for whatever reason is not translating to attendance at live screenings. I also suspected that experienced opera cinema audiences would be inclined to view broadcast opera in comparison to the staged experience they know and love, rather than viewing it on its own merits.[11] I had planned to make novices the focus of a pilot project of twenty respondents, through which I could also test my methodological design. I would then use the data from this pilot for comparison with a larger sample of opera cinema attendees.

I commenced fieldwork for my pilot study in March 2015. To help my novices make an effective comparison between the cinematic and theatrical incarnations of opera, I felt they would need to experience the same production in both the cinema and Covent Garden. I was aware that insisting that subjects watch the same show twice in quick succession might daunt prospective recruits, but this did not ultimately cause any problems with obtaining participants. I was also concerned that this requirement would impact on my data, perhaps resulting in a less-positive impression of the opera the second time around, and thus skewing respondents' results towards whichever viewing context came first. To accommodate and balance for this, I split my sample in half. The first group viewed their first opera in the Covent Garden auditorium, followed by a cinema and the second group vice versa. Despite taking these precautions, I observed no evidence of a clear pattern of preference in either group.

The opera in question was John Fulljames's English-language production of *The Rise and Fall of the City of Mahagonny*, by composer Kurt Weill and librettist Berthold Brecht. The choice of opera was a matter of practicality: the simulcast date suited my research schedule. *Mahagonny* is less acclaimed than Brecht and Kurt Weill's *The Threepenny Opera* (1928), and certainly not a canon piece. It also has a troubled history on the stage, having previously bombed at both ENO and the Salzburg Festival.[12] Loathed by Adolf Hitler and banned under the Nazi regime,[13] *Mahagonny* satirizes Weimar-era Berlin through its depiction of the titular hyper-capitalistic, gangster utopia. Brecht depicts the exploits of purposeless drifters, prostitutes and strays who become ensnared by the dark delights of Mahagonny like flies caught in a spider's web - for which the city is named. Musically, the opera incorporates several popular idioms from the 1930s, including jazz, ragtime and music hall. In short, the opera is very un-opera-like by the standards of the Wagner, *verismo* and Mozart that dominate modern stages. The Royal Opera House's production was enlivened by Fulljames's visually arresting production, which evoked the sleaze of Mahagonny through a cacophony of neon street signs and shipping crates. The cinema broadcast was filmed with a seven-camera set-up and edited on-the-fly, following a pre-rehearsed shooting script.

Following discussions with the Royal Opera House, it was agreed that I would receive twenty circle tickets for the auditorium, and subjects would be invited to purchase cinema tickets themselves. My first port of call for recruitment were the channels afforded by my university, King's College London, including the regular research subject recruitment circulars sent around to students and staff. I also approached a handful of former colleagues and their partners, resulting in a slightly more demographically varied sample than had I relied exclusively on the subjects provided by King's College London. Even this initial phase of recruitment proved enlightening. The response to my recruitment advertisements was overwhelming. Several of the email exchanges I shared with prospective candidates attested to exceptional levels of enthusiasm, with at least one participant describing the opportunity to see an opera as a 'dream'. Others confessed that despite never having attended an opera they had 'always thought about it' and that taking part in my research would be a 'great opportunity'.

My subjects were issued a questionnaire, through which I obtained basic demographic data. My final sample consisted of thirteen King's College London students, a junior lawyer, an office secretary and her retired husband, a financial data analyst, a freelance journalist and two online content managers. I amassed a relatively broad age-range (from twenty to fifty-two) with an average of twenty-five years. Given that most of the Royal Opera House's cinema attendees are over the age of sixty-five, this is a very atypical sample relative to the existing opera cinema audiences. My sample consisted of thirteen women and seven men.[14] Three-quarters of my sample was of White British descent, with five non-white individuals taking part. Commonalities in age, media competence, frequency of film attendance and general conditions of life skewed my first round of data towards a particular viewpoint on opera cinema: that of young, tech-literate, university educated inhabitants of a culture-saturated metropolitan centre.

When it came to developing a concourse, I sourced statements from eighty different sources from the popular and industry operatic press, interview scripts from meetings with Royal Opera House staff, academic texts, social media chatter and fan blogs. My sources variously focused on livecasting,[15] opera's status as a cultural phenomenon more generally,[16] the nature of 'live experience'[17] and opera as a novelty.[18] I grouped my items under six themes: *accessibility*, *context*, *enjoyment*, *liveness*, *learning and esteem* and *value*. Each of these categories contained separate items for opera cinema and staged opera based on a phrase lifted from the concourse (edited and reinterpreted for clarity). Once my data was analysed, I produced a three-factor solution: three groups of respondents with comparable results. I incorporated a field for 'additional comments', which allowed subjects to provide qualitative, testimonial data concerning their experiences that aided my final analysis. I also hosted a focus group with five participants after the sorting procedure was complete.

I had hoped to represent the entire factor solution in the focus group, but this could not be arranged. Nevertheless, the focus group was still quite instructive. I opted for an unstructured design; given that we were dealing with an unfamiliar experience I wanted to give my subjects the opportunity to explore their feelings about the opera in their own terms. I concluded this phase of the project with a discourse analysis on the focus group discussion transcript, deriving the most pertinent recurring themes, which were (in order of most-to-least commonly raised):

1. The auditorium is the superior viewing context;
2. Opera is an elite, exclusive art form;
3. The cinema is a more accessible viewing context;
4. A live relay is more of an occasion than a typical film screening.

Following the first round of subjects, I was satisfied that Q Methodology was a serviceable means of describing audiences' subjective engagement with opera cinema. For the second round, I decided to focus exclusively on opera novices, rather than expanding my horizons to existing opera cinema audiences as I had originally intended. There were several reasons for this. On a practical level, my research partners at the Royal Opera House were especially interested in this angle for their own commercial reasons. From my own point of view, I felt that focusing on novices would help distinguish my research from the work that Barker, Vladica and others have already performed on opera cinema audiences.[19] Furthermore, I decided to focus my wider phase of data collection exclusively on opera cinema, dispensing with the comparative element of my pilot study. In part, I felt it betrayed the spirit of my project not to allow opera cinema to fully stand on its own merits. On a more mundane level, it would have been prohibitively expensive to pay the travel expenses and tickets to Covent Garden for a larger sample of respondents.

Despite moving to a larger phase of data collection, I was not aiming for numerically representative results: as mentioned, Q Methodology does not excel at this. Instead, I wished to use a larger pool of subjects to explore variables that I suspected would significantly impact on audience engagement. For example, what little research presently exists on opera cinema tends to be London-centric. This seemed counter-intuitive – given that one of the key advantages of livecasting is its potential to extend the audience for live operatic performances beyond the confines of a physical opera house in a major city. I sought to determine whether major metropolitan centres – which offer a plethora of live content from a variety of providers – promote a different interpretive community for opera cinema compared to smaller settlements.

I suspected that different types of cinema would also motivate discrete engagements with live opera. It is notable that art house venues make a higher proportion of their overall profits from event cinema compared to multiplex chains. Where Cineworld has never seen more than 2 per cent of its box office returns come from livecasting, many independent sites depend on event cinema for up to 20 per cent of their revenue (excluding ancillary income from refreshments and so forth).[20] I hypothesized that premium and independent venues may foster a greater sense of occasion, which might befit the one-off, premium-ticketed simulcast event. The acoustic properties and technical apparatus of different cinemas also result in varying visual and sonic qualities, which I thought might be a factor in my subjects' engagement.

Furthermore, I wished to scrutinize the effect of repertoire on audience engagement. Anecdotally, I feel that some productions lend themselves more readily to live broadcast than others. For example, the Royal Opera House's 2014 production of *Andrea Chénier* leapt off the screen thanks to Robert Jones's sumptuous period set design and the movie star looks of lead tenor Jonas Kaufman – with a Hollywood-esque *verismo* score to match. Moreover, the language of cinema can invest performances with additional layers of meaning. As I discuss later in the chapter, the broadcast of *Lucia di Lammermoor*, directed by Katie Mitchell (of *Written on Skin* fame) exploited cinematic imagery to great effect.

When it came to selecting regional case studies, I sought locations that were not metropolitan centres and as distinct as possible from one another in terms of demography. My ambitions were constrained by practicalities. I relied on the Royal Opera House's cinema operations department to pitch my project to cinema managers, offering up some of my data in exchange for complimentary tickets for my participants. For national chains, this was not such an imposition, as opera cinema events rarely sell out. However, for independent venues with seating capacities below 100, putting aside seats represents a serious financial outlay. As such, I needed to choose independent cinemas with whom the Royal Opera House had an especially close relationship, which narrowed my options considerably. I eventually arrived upon four cinemas across the counties of Herefordshire and Hertfordshire: Hereford Odeon, Hatfield Odeon, the Campus West cinema at Welwyn Garden City and the Richard Booth's Bookshop Cinema in Hay-on-Wye.

Both within striking distance of London, Hatfield and Welwyn Garden City are commuter towns in the Welwyn Hatfield borough, which boasts a combined population of 116,000 and somewhat higher ethnic diversity than the larger Hertfordshire country (76.5 per cent White British versus 80.82 per cent).[21] A high proportion of student residents from the University of Hertfordshire results in a predominant age band of twenty to twenty-four, representing 10.5 per cent of the population[22] – 39,202 as of 2016.[23] Meanwhile, Welwyn Garden City is notably more affluent that Hatfield, with a higher proportion of professional London commuters, and a total population of 43,252.²⁴ Herefordshire, a border county on the boundary of Wales and England, has a population of 188,100 and displays a high degree of demographic variability across its urban and rural territories. The county has an older age structure compared to the rest of England and Wales, with 23 per cent of the population being over the age of sixty-five.²⁵ Twelve of Urban Hereford's Lower Layer Super Output Areas (LSOAs) ranked among the twenty-five most deprived in England, including Hereford City (population 58,896), where the Odeon is based. Furthermore, 10 per cent of the locality's working-age population are presently underemployed or in partial employment.²⁶ By contrast, rural Hereford experiences lower-than-average levels of deprivation, containing some of the least-deprived LSOAs in England and Wales.²⁷

Concerning my participating venues: Odeon is the best-known cinema chain in the UK and practically synonymous with commercial cinema in Britain. The Hatfield Oden is a larger venue than Hereford, at nine screens versus six. Both cinemas seat around 200 per screen, offer 3D and IMAX, and have been equipped for digital streaming since 2008. By contrast, the Campus West Cinema has three screens that seat around 100 viewers apiece. Hosted by the Campus West cultural centre in Welwyn Garden City, the venue doubles as a performance space for community theatre companies.²⁸ Campus West places a special emphasis on independent films and event cinema, which are displayed prominently under separate genre tabs on its website. Richard Booth's Bookshop is literally a bookstore, fitted with a projector and around thirty armchairs to accommodate small audiences for special film screenings.²⁹

When it came to selecting repertoire, I was fortunate that the Royal Opera's 2016 summer season offered a variety of productions, making for apt comparison between different musical traditions and dramaturgical styles. The first opera in my research schedule, *Boris Godunov*, depicts the rise, reign and fall of the titular Tsar, who ruled Russia during the so-called Time of Troubles between the end of the Rurik Dynasty in 1598 and the rise of the Romanovs in 1613.³⁰ This period saw the country afflicted by famine, civil uprisings, court intrigues and war, which collectively eradicated over a third of Russia's population.³¹ This calamitous period inspired Modest Mussorgsky's only completed opera: a work whose creative history is almost as fraught as the era it depicts. There is no definitive version of *Boris Godunov*. Mussorgsky's original was rejected by the Imperial Theatres in 1869 – allegedly for lacking a decent female role.³² Mussorgsky's second and much-expanded attempt, which contained an additional act, eventually premiered in Saint Petersburg in 1874. The 1874 version is most familiar to opera audiences. While Pytor Tchaikovsky's *Eugene Onegin* is perhaps the most famous Russian-language opera internationally, *Boris Godunov* is the most-recorded and thus perhaps the most widely consumed. The Royal Opera House's 2016 production (starring Bryn Terfel, one of the best-known opera singers in Britain) was directed by Richard Jones and returned to the 1869 version – a first-time move for the Royal Opera House. The lack of female performers was picked up on by two of my novice participants (both women). Richard Jones's creative production was roughly period appropriate, but added a psychedelic edge with a Mucha-esque palate of golds, pinks and purples, fostering a dreamlike quality to foreground Godunov's insanity. Most strikingly, in a 'golden room' raised above the stage, the assassination of Ivan the Terrible's young heir, Tsarevich Dmitriy Ivanovich, played out over and over, visually displaying Godunov's nagging guilt for his role in the murder.

Although it could scarcely be less similar in terms of music, language and subject, *Lucia di Lammermoor* shares one thing in common with *Boris Godunov*: a tortured and idiosyncratic composer. While Mussorgsky eventually drank himself into oblivion, Gaetano Donizetti's struggles with physical and mental illness saw him institutionalized and limited his activities throughout his life.[33] Unlike Mussorgsky, however, Donizetti was tutored in music from a young age and was a leading composer in the *bel canto* style during the nineteenth century – a tradition later eclipsed by *verismo*.[34] His 1835 operatic adaptation of Sir Walter Scott's historical novel, *The Bride of Lammermoor*, focuses on Lucia of Lammermoor and the object of her affections, Edgardo of the rival Ravenswood clan, who are caught in a family feud – with inevitably tragic results.[35] Much was made during the simulcast of the composer's use of the glass harmonica, whose mournful, keening beauty offers a perfect sonic accompaniment to Lucia's eventual descent into madness.

It was not Donizetti but director Katie Mitchell who dominated discussion on the run-up to opening night. The Royal Opera House is no stranger to controversy (e.g. shortly before I began my research, a 2015 production of *Guillaume Tell* was nearly booed off the stage during its premiere for its opening rape scene),[36] but its decision to employ a feminist auteur to handle a delicate, *bel canto* tragedy drew media interest. Or more accurately, presumptions of a shocking, violent and sexually liberated interpretation were deliberately cultivated by Royal Opera House publicity, which paired posters that hinted at nudity with Mitchell's 'feminist agenda'.[37] As it happened, the production contained no nudity (although it did feature a fully clothed, simulated sex scene) and aged Lucia up from a tragic, gothic teenager to a confident adult woman, driven by rational ambitions and desires rather than adolescent impulsiveness. The most interesting aspect of the production was a split-stage, which allowed Mitchell to incorporate additional dramatic action that was only hinted at (or non-existent) in the original *libretto*. While some of the principals were performing, others could simultaneously enact an entirely different scene in dumb show. For instance, Mitchell chose to explicitly show Lucia's murder of her bridegroom Arturo, which occurs off-stage in the original. This approach drew some criticism from the press, with reviewers complaining that having to divide their attention between two scenes at once was jarring.[38] However, the split-staging married so well with the filming process during the broadcast that I was led to wonder whether Mitchell had the camera in mind all along.

With my case studies all in place, I developed my project design in collaboration with my research partners, aiming for the best balance between representativeness and financial/practical expediency. Ultimately, we opted for an eighty-participant design, with eight groups of ten subjects split across four cinemas. I recruited participants through several channels, first-and-foremost via on-site invitations on the streets of Hereford and Hertfordshire, both of which I visited multiple times throughout 2016. Additionally, both Odeon branches circulated an advertisement to their staff inviting them to take part, and Campus West shared information about the project on their social media channels. Moreover, I placed inserts promoting the project in a number of local papers and rang around schools, colleges, sheltered accommodation facilities, amateur dramatics companies and Women's Institutes asking after potential respondents.

At this stage, I began encountering difficulties. Given the overwhelming enthusiasm for my pilot project, I assumed that recruitment would be straightforward, particularly given that I was only asking subjects to attend one performance. In fact, my original intention was to over-recruit and select a demographically balanced sample of respondents. During the planning stages, my research partners at the Royal Opera House had expressed a particular interest in balancing for a range of age groups and socio-economic backgrounds, given data on these key demographic variables is rather narrow for existing opera cinema audiences. However, willing respondents were notably thin on the ground.

There are many possible explanations for why I struggled. In London, scarcely a day goes by in which there is not something worth seeing taking place within a mile's radius. It is possible that my London-based subjects were primed for engagement with an unfamiliar, cultural phenomenon. By contrast, the rest of the UK has been gradually starved of arts funding by an increasing centralization of the culture sector, particularly in the past twenty years, making the simulcast seem more alien.[39] Also, for much of the British public, it seems opera remains an esoteric, elitist and expensive art form - although this alone does not square with the discrepancy in levels of interest between my pilot and the main bulk of data collection. Another explanation for this discrepancy is that the students who made up the bulk of my first round of data had more free time. But I suspect the main issue was that I was not offering a free ticket to Covent Garden - the simulcast was evidently less tempting.

Regardless of the explanation, I redoubled my efforts to fill the gaps in my recruitment with further visits to Hereford and Hertfordshire. Ultimately, the arduous process of recruiting in-person proved the only effective method.

This did however have the advantage of allowing me to immediately collect demographic data with physical sign-up sheets and questionnaires. Despite the initial set-back, I was ultimately able to fill all my allocated spaces for the *Boris Godunov* broadcast. However, following the relay, a representative from Richard Booth's Bookshop informed me that none of the respondents allocated to that cinema had turned up on the night – while people were lined up outside in the hopes of getting a seat. As a result, the cinema pulled out of the project, which left my entire design unbalanced. A major problem was that respondents would generally ask to reserve several tickets for themselves and their partners, spouses and/or children. Such a request was difficult to deny but involved a greater risk to the project. In one instance, a family of six signed up and none of them showed.

Because of this poor turnout, I was forced to adapt. Following an emergency discussion with the Royal Opera House we determined that, in order to balance the project, we needed to incorporate an additional opera and cinema into the data collection process. This concession weakened the comparison between *Boris* and *Lucia*, but that could no longer be helped. As we approached the end of the Royal Opera's summer season, the only viable candidate was Benoît Jacquot's production of *Werther*. Composed by Jules Massenet and based on a romantic novel by Johann Goethe, the opera depicts the calamitous arrival of passionate young artist, Werther, to the simple, peasant town of Wetzlar. Tragedy ensues after Werther falls for the beautiful Charlotte, who is already betrothed to another man. Jacquot is better known as a film director and the show marked a revival of his 2003 production – his debut as an operatic director. I was curious as to how a live broadcast with two cinematic minds behind it would translate to the screen. Jacquot's painterly backdrops were somewhat reminiscent of *Lucia*'s moody, gothic tones: composed of sombre blues, blacks and greys. However, there was nothing about Benoît's direction that formally interacted with the filming process to unconventional effect.

Fortunately, finding a new cinema was easily accomplished. The Courtyard Arts Centre in Hereford (just outside of the town centre) was already on my long list of potential independent venues. The Courtyard is something of a cultural hub in urban Hereford, having opened in 1998 on the site of the outdated New Hereford Theatre following a £3.75 million contribution from the Lottery Commission.[40] The venue contains a bar, dining area, children's play facilities and two studios that are frequently utilized by local theatre companies but also double as cinemas, seating 400 attendees between them.

The unexpected change of plan impinged on my recruitment efforts, as I had little time for further visits to Hereford. Ultimately, I was only able to recruit a further three subjects to view *Werther* in the Courtyard. In all, this left me with a sample size of forty-one, against my original goal of eighty. This was far from an ideal outcome. However, eighty respondents would still not have resulted in a statistically viable sample – the intention was simply to facilitate a decent level of comparison between my eight groups. In the end, I accomplished this. On the plus side, I managed to obtain a fairly diverse sample that was significantly more demographically balanced than existing opera cinema audiences on a national level. Most subjects held some form of academic or professional degree (twenty-three) and were in full-time employment (twenty-six), but nearly half earned below £20,000 a year (twenty) – a figure skewed by a significant minority in full or part-time education and a handful of retirees. Only a slim majority (twenty-four) were over the age of fort-five, which brings the average age of participants for this project significantly below the national average for opera cinema audience members. Ethnic diversity in the sample was of apiece with that of national opera cinema audiences: the overwhelming majority of subjects identified as 'White' (thirty-five) and women made up a narrow majority (twenty-seven). This profile was roughly reflected in each regional, repertoire and venue group. Two anomalies are the *Boris Godunov* group, which was on average older, more formally educated and wealthier than the rest of the sample; and the *Werther* group, which at three participants was too small to carry any real weight. Finally, I ran a single focus group with three participants at the Hereford Odeon and three separate interviews in Hatfield (two individuals and one mother–daughter pairing), lasting between thirty and forty minutes each.

I sourced items for my Q Methodology concourse from my pilot project, adapting comments from subjects' testimonies and my interview transcript. Subjects' feedback from the pilot project suggested some of the items were confusing and repetitive, so I opted for a leaner selection of twenty-nine items. For the interviews, I used the subject testimonies entered during the Q sorting phase as the basis for guiding discussion. For instance, one subject who viewed *Lucia* at the Hereford Odeon made a revealing additional comment about the sense of 'privilege' she felt during the broadcast – a loaded term that I invited her to develop during our interview. Once my interviews were transcribed, I collated them with the testimonial data and performed a content analysis to identify recurring themes. I then cross-referenced these themes with the three factors that emerged from the Q sorts, ordering them according to the number of participants that raised the same subject unprompted and secondarily by the overall number of mentions.

On reflection, the difficulties encountered during my second round of data collection are revealing in and of themselves, especially in comparison to the relative ease of my pilot project. That a young, metropolitan, student audience showed such enthusiasm about viewing their first opera, while a more varied population displayed lack of interest, evinces variable attitudes not just towards opera, but engagement with unfamiliar cultural experiences in general. Also, these setbacks suggest that live cinema ranks below physical attendance at Covent Garden in terms of cultural esteem. I was left with the impression that participants were far more willing to experiment with opera at an opera house, despite the relative convenience of the cinema. At least for now, the opera house remains the default entry point for curious newcomers. Opera cinema is faced with two separate hurdles: only a small cross-section of the public is actively curious about opera and within that cross-section the majority are saving themselves for the auditorium. It is beyond the remit of this book to deal fully with these questions, which deserve books of their own. When one is tackling a nascent cultural experience, snags are only to be expected – it is only fortunate if they happen to be instructive. Furthermore, despite these issues I was able to obtain a viable sample of respondents, offering insight about the opera cinema experience.

Meeting the opera virgins

Before introducing my data proper, I will make some a few general observations. Most of my respondents, even those who had never seen an opera on stage, valued stage opera more highly than the simulcast. Some stated categorically they did not believe it constituted watching an opera, describing various aspects of the simulcast experience as deficient. Also, while it would be very simplistic to define opera as an inherently elite art form, my subjects clearly regarded it as such to varying degrees. Many admitted to feeling intimidated by opera; and several subjects from the pilot study attested to feelings of alienation and exclusion at both Covent Garden and the cinema. These data demonstrate the extent to which opera cinema has not distinguished itself as an art form in its own right, and remains subject to attitudes and protocols surrounding its source medium.

That being said, while my subjects' assessment of opera cinema's cultural value varied significantly across the sample, very few felt that it had *no* value. Many respondents made comments that highlighted the sense of occasion fostered by the simulcast. These data subdivide into two main strands. The first pertains to protocols that emphasize the liveness or theatricality of simulcasting, particularly the distribution of printed programmes and the celebrity talking-head interviews during intervals. These 'theatrical' protocols were seen to prime audiences for an eventful experience – distinguished from 'normal' cinema. The second strand concerns the temporality of opera cinema, and the exclusivity associated with a media experience that, by its very nature, can only occur once. William Eversmann defines this quality as the 'transitive nature of the performing arts'.[41] My subjects were in general agreement that the 'one-night-only' simulcast fostered a sense of exclusivity, and that this was a positive aspect of their experience.

There was a more personal dimension to my subjects' perception of opera cinema's cultural value. This is based on what Pierre Bourdieu might have described as 'cultural capital'.[42] Bourdieu made the argument that 'high culture' operates as a means of exclusion and subordination, because engaging in the 'correct' forms of culture endows one with esteem, status and class distinction compared to others.[43] While I disagree with Bourdieu's view of culture defining economic class relationships, rather than merely reflecting them, it is fair to say that 'knowing opera' is often taken as evidence of elevated standing. As described in Chapter 3, several respondents started out feeling alienated from and intimidated by opera and its audiences. For some, the simulcast did little to disabuse them of this assumption. For others, opera's hauteur was a source of enjoyment. But most interestingly of all, a cross-section of respondents across multiple factors felt that their satisfaction derived from their ability to appreciate an art form they expected to find challenging served as confirmation of their pre-existing acculturation. Being able to enjoy opera proved how smart they were – which was a source of appeal in and of itself, and simulcasting provided a route to acquiring this sense of self-satisfaction at reduced economic and social risk.

Additionally, most of my subjects still attested to feeling more comfortable overall in the cinema than in Covent Garden, due to the former being a more 'relaxed' space, whereas subjects felt 'a lot more conscious of not fitting in at the opera house'. Many respondents spoke positively of the greater comfort afforded by the cinema, with one commenting: 'it's always comfy and there's air con – the temperature's maintained nicely'. However, many did not regard the heightened comfort at the cinema to be an adequate trade-off, for instance: 'It was comfortable in the cinema, but I'd still forego that to go to the theatre. I didn't feel uncomfortable in the theatre it just wasn't an issue as far as I'm concerned.' Also, subjects from both rounds of data collection were critical of the cinema as relatively mundane, as compared to Covent Garden. Despite likely being even-less-in-line demographically with the opera cinema audience than the auditorium crowd, any sense of hierarchy was de-emphasized during the simulcast, and there was less evidence of collective connoisseurship. My subjects reported that cinema attendees were less-formally dressed ('they were all old people but at least they were wearing casual clothes'), while the familiarity and conviviality of the cinema as an exhibition context ameliorated my subjects' feelings of isolation. Subjects were not blind to the genteel composition of opera cinema audiences – although not all of them construed this negatively. More devotional subjects craved access to the cultural esteem afforded by opera, and felt that simulcasting dilutes the medium's inherent aesthetic and what might be termed its cultural value.

Limited though they are, my data do not support assumptions that opera cinema is a direct detriment to the operatic ecology by wooing audiences away from the stage. On the contrary, several respondents discussed opera cinema as a 'gateway' to physical auditorium attendance, stating that the simulcast experience 'encouraged' them to attend staged opera in the future. These respondents cited the financial accessibility and convenience of opera cinema as an effective bridge for newcomers, or as one subject succinctly put it in a Q-sort testimony: 'This medium is affordable, accessible and desirable.' Participants across multiple factors also made statements to the effect that opera cinema presents less of a time and financial risk to the consumer. Subjects from every factor spoke about opera cinema subtitles, which, combined with double-direction, were generally seen as promoting intellectual accessibility. None of the respondents who attended my focus groups and interviews seemed to be aware that opera houses routinely surtitle productions. Interestingly, this also applied to subjects with a sophisticated knowledge of music and cultural performances. Even musically trained and culturally engaged subjects did not realize that the Royal Opera House performances are surtitled and picked out subtitling as a specific advantage of opera cinema. Subjects from the round one were a bit more divided when it came to comparing the surtitles in the opera house to the subtitles in the cinema. Some praised the simulcast for putting subtitles at the bottom of the screen where they were 'easier to follow', while others criticized them for being distracting, with one complaining: 'it irritated me having the subtitles there so I preferred not having them in my line of sight.' It should be noted that *Mahagonny* was staged in English, although opera is a challenge to understand even in one's native tongue. This diversity of opinion is especially curious given that the introduction of surtitling at opera performances was initially resisted by purists as a populist concession.[44] The fact that none of my subjects knew about surtitling casts doubt on the extent to which this concession has had much 'cut through' with the wider public.

A number of subjects from round two (and who therefore only went to the cinema), who were broadly positive about the simulcasting experience, admitted to feeling 'jealous' (or similar) of the auditorium audience depicted on the screen. Such comments reflect the negative dimension of institutional dramaturgy – the virtual audience being reminded they are not actually present at the physical auditorium – and were particularly strongly attached to codes of dress. This was one of the most frequently discussed protocols across my sample, and one of the most variable. Several respondents made a conscious effort to ritualize and 'elevate' the simulcast by dressing up. This decision that was specifically parsed as an attempt to 'get the full experience' despite not having gone to Covent Garden in person. That being said, some subjects claimed to always 'dress up smart for going to the cinema', irrespective of the type of show. It would be interesting to explore the intersections of generation and gender in subjects' decisions of what to wear, but I lack sufficient data for this. Codes of dress were not the only operatic exhibition practice that carried partially into the cinema. From both my data and personal experience I can confirm that applause does occur after simulcasts, but is usually hesitant, and occasionally awkward. In the *Mahagonny* focus group, subjects reported that 'some people' clapped 'at the end', but none of my respondents took part, except for Fred, who applauded 'when everybody else did'. June simply said she 'couldn't remember' whether people clapped – implying any applause that occurred was hardly unanimous. This, again, is evidence that the behavioural conventions for opera cinema are still negotiable, which suggests we are not dealing with an art form with a clear identity.

I will now introduce my focus group participants, and establish their unique perspectives on opera cinema. Hopefully, these deeper impressions will inform the more general conclusions derived from my Q Methodology data. While most of my subjects were strangers to myself and one another, several were romantic partners, colleagues or relatives, which naturally affected group dynamics and thus my results. The first round of the project included a single focus group, with five participants. Three were King's College London students and two were young professionals, and all were in their twenties. The youthful sample meant that the conversation particularly lingered on the disparity in age and experience between my subjects and the existing opera cinema and Covent Garden audiences. When it came to the opera house, this disparity was associated with perception of being judged and alienation of other attendees. For instance, Andrew (twenty-two, and a student nurse from King's College London) commented:

> In front of us at the theatre were a lot of tourists by the looks of it, who'd just come in shorts. This lady who was sat in front of us, her phone went off even though she'd been told not to [have it switched on] and a really old man and a really old woman, both turned to her at the same time and said something like: 'This is the Royal Opera House, you know!' It made me feel really self-conscious, because I'd not gone black tie and I thought: I'm now being stereotyped [as the] people who are going around and like not following the rules … I look more like this sort of younger generation.

Throughout my focus group discussions, a sense of generational alienation came across very strongly. Andrew, being notably distinct from the veteran contingent in the auditorium and conspicuously 'underdressed', felt judged by association during the above altercation, and so especially at pains to conform to the behavioural conventions of the auditorium. Other subjects made comments about 'snooty [audience members] commenting on people being on their phones', which made them feel 'like [they] needed to be on [their] best behaviour'.

There are grounds to suggest this impression could be even stronger during the simulcast. As I have noted elsewhere, opera cinema audiences tend to be even older than auditorium crowds on average. But Andrew put a more positive slant on the elderly audience at the cinema, perhaps owing to his medical discipline. He commented on simulcasting's greater accessibility for older, less-mobile operaphiles: 'I did see a lot of wheelchair-bound people ... I think that if I got too old and frail to make the trip I'd definitely go to the cinema.' This is an important, positive contribution by opera cinema, which should not be overlooked in the future-orientated conversation about new media and audience acquisition. Aside from wheelchair accessibility and restrictions on travel, the additional physical strain incurred by auditoria can pose a challenge to older operagoers. This helps to explain opera cinema's popularity within an older cross-section of opera's existing audience base. Physical accessibility is not a decisive aspect of opera cinema's ontology, and seemed to be of limited importance to novice audiences. However, it plays a very key role in opera cinema's current social function and is a major influence over its present audience composition.

Andrew introduced an aspect of the live transmission that came up several times across my interviews: the value of failure. He was particularly enthusiastic about evidence of mistakes that foregrounded the liveness of the experience, citing a particular mishap in the *Mahagonny* simulcast as a highlight of his opera cinema experience:

> In the cinema showing, Jenny [the leading lady] was taking her knickers off ... in the cinema showing she couldn't get out of them. But I liked that, because I felt like 'Oh, then you know it was live', so then that makes it better ... That there is a possibility of it failing is what makes it pay off when it does succeed.

Another goof occurred when Trinity Moses fell down a set of stairs in the second half - an incident that Andrew also enjoyed. I asked him to expound on these 'pay-offs' and he replied by mode of comparison, arguing that, had he watched a recording of the performance, it would have been 'edited and watered down [to] the best, perfect example', which would have diminished the value of the experience. Along with a number other subjects, Andrew's impressions of liveness expressed the implicit exclusivity of witnessing an event that most people never will. For Andrew, this dimension of live experience overlapped with the importance of risk: 'It's the potential for failure that makes it brilliant, because then you know that it's something that no-one else is going to see, because ... the fact that they did manage to succeed throughout the whole performance, that was what made it so special. When you knew it was live.' On the more negative side, he described the sound in the cinema as relatively 'flat'. By contrast, he stated that the music in the auditorium was 'overwhelming', to the point that 'at the opera the sound ... went beyond what you could hear' – meaning it exceeded his capacity to fully absorb. Again, inferior sound was a common complaint about opera cinema, interestingly enough raised by subjects from both rounds, that is, even those who at the time of the project had never experienced the real thing. This suggests subjects drawing on comparable experiences of live music, combined with an imagined sense of what operatic music must sound like close-to.

Andrew's aforementioned self-consciousness at Covent Garden was shared by a newly married couple, Samantha and Jeff (both twenty-six): a freelance journalist and software developer respectively. Samantha described other members of the audience tutting at the use of phones prior to curtain-up, complained that refreshments were not allowed inside the auditorium and conveyed a sense that she and her husband judged for having 'rocked up off the street' rather than appearing in formal attire. Jeff also highlighted his sense of discomfort amongst the Covent Garden audience by describing a minor confrontation during the stage performance of *Mahagonny*:

> [Another member of the audience] had his hands full, so it just looked like he was trying to push his seat down to sit in it. So, I courteously just tried to hold his seat down to try and help, he just stared at me and went: 'I'd rather you didn't.'

These subjects' comments support Barker's characterization of opera cinema attendees as 'self-aware, knowledgeable ... aware of each other'.[45] Several respondents, including Samantha, made comments about experienced attendees interacting enthusiastically prior to the show: 'there was this group of old people chatting about it and reading the programmes.' On a related point, both Samantha and Jeff were notably interested in the capacity of simulcasting to diversify opera's audience (or lack thereof) – a concern which reflected their hostility towards opera's 'elitism' (a term they both used in discussion). Samantha pointed out that opera cinema was potentially 'a really brilliant way of making [opera] accessible', but she was sceptical that this was being achieved: '[the simulcast] still felt like there was a very specific audience demographic.' Indeed, Jeff and Samantha made a game of identifying this demographic prior to the simulcast:

> Samantha: One of the things that I thought was quite interesting ... we went for dinner before ... we went to the Pizza Express just downstairs ... And we were kind of looking around while we were eating going, 'do you think they're going to the opera? Do you think they're going to the opera?' and trying to guess which of the other dinners were going to the opera.
> Jeff: They were all old. None of the people in Pizza Express went, incidentally.

The cinema in question was the Stratford Picturehouse, situated close to the Olympic Village and the site of one of London's most rapid and dramatic social gentrification projects, but nevertheless with a high proportion of low-income and non-white residents.[46] Samantha noted these residents were not drawn into the operatic fold by the mere presence of *Mahagonny* at the movies: 'there wasn't a sense that, because it was in the cinema that it was attracting like ... the youths of Stratford. It was definitely middle-class, white, old people ... I guess it was the kind of demographic that you would've expected.' It is likely that pilot project's focus on novice, student respondents threw this demographic tendency into even-sharper relief. For Samantha and Jeff, opera remains the domain of the elderly and well-heeled – and simulcasting has done little to change this. Their characterization of opera as 'quite exclusive – sort of inaccessible' applied to both Covent Garden and the cinema. This demonstrates the extent to which opera cinema remains tethered to general attitudes surrounding the source medium.

It should be noted that I threw my novice subjects in at the deep end by sending them to the most prestigious and expensive opera house in Britain. A multitude of regional and touring companies in Britain, such as Opera North and the English Touring Opera, perform at smaller, less-formal venues throughout the country, meaning my subjects' negative impressions might have less to do with opera in general than with Covent Garden in particular. Furthermore, despite feeling more self-conscious at Covent Garden, some of my subjects argued that this contributed somewhat to the mystique of their experience. For instance, Samantha commented: 'I guess, there was a part of me that kind of expected the snootiness and the elitism, and the formal dress as just something you inevitably get, that goes with the territory. So I guess it did in a weird sort of way add to the experience.' It seems the novelty of being 'the odd one out' within an elite taste culture contains a masochistic appeal for some.

On the technical front, Samantha was of the opinion that liveness constitutes nothing short of co-presence, stating of the simulcast: 'It's like watching a football match on telly as opposed to going to the stadium or something. Like, you know that it's not quite the same, but ... it's the convenience.' Despite her negative comments on the behaviour of some audience members and the exclusionary atmosphere at Covent Garden, it was apparent that she valued the auditorium experience more highly than the cinema. She reported that the simulcast actively detracted from her immersion and perception of realism:

> I felt like the cinema version was a lot more flat than being in the opera house. Because in the opera house it felt a lot more intense and a lot more ... *real*. Which I guess is different from seeing a play where there wasn't that kind of ... disconnect.

The 'realism' Samantha references has little to do with perspectival or indexical realism: the simulcast was generally felt to convey a less authentic, emotionally engaging and affective experience. These comments are in line with prior research on opera cinema.[47] Relevant to this point, and echoing Andrew, Samantha and Jeff's assessments of the simulcast's 'live' sound were rather negative, particularly regarding the live singing, the potency of which Samantha felt was 'missing' at the cinema. Jeff concurred with her, stating that the 'feeling of live, pure vocals really is incredible and I think it's kind of lost once it's through the speakers'. Indeed, the visceral materiality of live operatic vocals, which must be felt reverberating in one's eardrums to be fully understood, is an aspect of live performance that does not readily translate through digital remediation, despite the sophistication of modern surround sound. The co-presence of live music was an important experiential aspect of subjects' engagement during the staged performance of *Mahagonny*, which constituted one of the primary pleasures afforded by the auditorium. This point was made evident in the following comparison Samantha drew between the staged and screened versions of *Mahagonny*:

> It's quite difficult to compare because, I felt like what I felt was missing from the cinema version was more the kind of the feel of the music that you had when you were in the opera house. So the whole kind of musical experience just felt a lot more kind of vivid and 3D and close to you. It was a lot more kind of overwhelming and surround sound-esque than in the cinema.

Furthermore, Samantha's phrasing of 'surround sound-esque' speaks to the experiential distinction between viewing and listening. Where the former is unilateral – with a line of sight drawn between the subject and the object viewed (except in the recent case of VR and 360-degree filming) – sound is dependent on the physical interaction of sound waves with a three-dimensional space. Unlike images, sounds fill the exhibition space and in a sense, become the space, communicating the scale of one's surroundings and the material quality and positioning of their source through timbre and directionality. Digital sound, by contrast, is compressed – resulting in a clear but detectably artificial facsimile of analogue acoustics. Samantha described the cinema experience as insipid, both emotionally and aesthetically, as opposed to the 'intense' staged performance, owing in part to the artificiality of the digitally compressed music. For her, it seemed the simulcast's remediated sound exerted a greater distancing effect than its remediated visuals.

That being said, she did attribute some significance to the simulcast's 'sense of occasion', which demonstrates the various possible interpretations of liveness:

> I didn't feel that kind of connection the others have talked about, of it being particularly special because there were mistakes and you knew it was live and it was authentic and you were part of this big experience.

But I guess the fact that it was the *only* screening that there was, so you couldn't just go back the next night and watch the next night's performance – that, for me, is what made it a one-off. The fact that there was only one screening of it rather than something you could just do whenever you fancied. That had more of an impact on the kind of sense of occasion for me, rather than the knowing that it was live. So I think if there had been one showing of a pre-recorded version but there was only one showing of it, I would've experienced it in the same way.

Jeff, who was similarly unmoved by the simultaneity of opera cinema, shared his wife's appreciation of this element of the show, stating that 'with [the simulcast] just being the one off … people are maybe still going be sort of captivated by the uniqueness of it'. Furthermore, the insight films and celebrity host distinguished opera cinema from 'regular' (that is to say, recorded) cinema in Samantha's mind. For example, she associated these aspects with the theatrical elements introduced into the exhibition space:

It did feel different [from recorded cinema]. Partly because we had to wait outside before we could go in and there was this group of old people kind of chatting about it and reading the programmes and you had the whole introduction; the behind-the-scenes guy with the kind of interviews and everything … and then obviously having an interval, made it feel different than just going to see *The Avengers*.

Although Samantha was generally sceptical of the simulcast's 'liveness', the multi-mediality of the show distinguished the simulcast from a normal film screening, elevating the simulcast event beyond cinema. Both these periphery features are overtly televisual, and indeed the simulcast programme in many respects resembles the 'flow', or multiplicity of content (both live and recorded) that Williams theorizes as intrinsic to television broadcast schedules.[48] Moreover, Jeff specifically identified the clarifying effect of double-direction as a boon to newcomers. He noted that, while he was more struck by the 'technical skill' showcased by the full cast of performers visible in the opera house, he found the cinema simulcast 'much easier to follow'. The enhanced legibility assisted his interpretation of symbolism and subtext, such as during protagonist Jimmy Mahoney's execution in *The Rise and Fall of the City Mahagonny*'s final act:

The close-up when Jimmy has the 'electric chair headpiece' fixed onto his head allowed me to instantly see the allusions to him being a Christ-like figure well before the other symbols were put into play. I appreciated that a lot as I felt like I may have missed it otherwise and was able to notice it much more readily during the auditorium performance.

Note the connection between legibility and the use of close-ups. From the earliest history of screen opera, this shot choice has been subject to (usually negative) interest: from throwing an unfair emphasis on opera singers' looks (sometimes necessitating overdubbing) to the 'tongue-and-teeth' problem that has allegedly hampered the medium on screen. Close-ups are prominent in subjects' impressions across the small number of prior audience research projects on opera cinema, and typically cited as a source of frustration.[49] A number of my opera virgins emphasized opera cinema's extensive use of close-ups, which were praised for forging a deeper emotional connection with the principal performers, and criticized for cutting out other aspects of the staging.[50] However, the clarifying effect of close-ups only arises through discussion with novice audiences. Experienced attendees do not need this crutch, and are perhaps more likely to see this shot choice as overbearing.

Despite the demographic homogeneity of opera audiences, the two non-white respondents in my first focus group during the comparative study made little comment on audience composition. One of these subjects, Frank (a film studies postgraduate, aged twenty-four, who identified as white/Asian) concurred with Samantha and Jeff's assessment about the demography of the simulcast audience, but did not raise the question independently. Interestingly, he was the only participant who attested to a sense of 'national pride' at the thought of a global audience turning its attention towards London, as evident from the following exchange with Andrew:

Andrew:	When the tweets were running along the bottom, that's when I was thinking, 'oh there's people in like, Portugal, watching it!' And I was like, oh yeah, there actually *are people around the world watching it, so that did make me feel like it was some kind of big experience of everyone pulling together to watch it.* [My emphasis]
Frank:	Yeah, I agree, especially hearing that it was being broadcast internationally. I felt a small amount of national pride as well at that … It was the London Royal Opera House and that would be something that other people would be watching from abroad.

All my other subjects flatly and specifically denied feeling any sense of nationalism. Andrew and Frank were the only ones who explicitly attached the appeal of the global event to national identity, although several other respondents highlighted this sense of international participation as a source of appeal. Frank was also the most overawed by the esteem imparted by opera, making several comments to the effect that he felt more 'cultured' having taken part in the project: 'There is something kind of exciting and sort of almost mystical about [opera] ... there's definitely a prestige surrounding the opera. And that's true today. It's thought of as highbrow but whether people were impressed and they might have thought I would be spending a lot of money going – or they thought "oh, you must be intelligent."' On a separate point, he shared Andrew's appreciation for failure, commenting that: 'the fact that it was happening and kind of unfolding in real time really did bring out the edge ... I wouldn't want to watch the DVD at home or something.' Again, recorded media was drawn on as shorthand for 'low' culture. In fact, Frank's comments were more focused on their individual cultural competencies. Perhaps owing to his background as a film student, Frank was the only subject in his focus group to comment extensively on the technical and multimedia aspects of opera cinema, particularly the Twitter stream and the simultaneous transmission, without which he said the simulcast would have felt 'like any other occasion at the cinema'. He was also especially complimentary about the double-direction, which he described as 'kind of what you're used to in a cinema' and that a less remediated image would have looked 'really strange'.

Meanwhile, June (twenty-three), who identified as Black Caribbean, made no remarks at all about the racial makeup of the Royal Opera House or cinema audience. Given her experience in classical music, having performed as a concert pianist, she seemed far more interested in the technical aspects of the opera itself than the simulcast. For instance, she complimented the quality of the orchestra, noted that watching a more 'modern' piece helped broaden her perspective on classical music. Where she did discuss the simulcast directly, she tended to be critical. For instance, she felt overwhelmed by the cinematic remediation and tight framing, which detracted from her enjoyment of the performance:

> The whole thing it felt very ... right in your face. Sometimes I'd be kind of turning away from it because it was just like too much. So, you just sort of got disinterested after a while.

June also clearly stated that the simulcast 'didn't feel like [the simulcast] was live'. For her, the digitally remediated sound robbed the music of its authenticity. But like Samantha, she attributed significance to the fact that simultaneous performances represent a discrete, ephemeral event. She also tended to perceive the value of this ephemerality in relation to recorded media: 'Even if you see a different show of it, it's always going to be just a little bit different. Because they might make a mistake for another performance, or they might make it perfectly through, so it's always going to be different. But in the cinema, the movie's going to be exactly the same.' Like Samantha and Jeff, her interpretation of liveness depended less on simultaneity than ephemerality, while she shared Andrew's view that the possibility of failure validates the value of the live performance. These data hopefully urge against a simplistic interpretation of 'live versus recorded' media experiences, and demonstrate the value of experiential impressions in elucidating media ontology.

The second round of focus groups and interviews involved a greater diversity of age groups, ethnicities and socio-economic profiles, with the youngest subject being twelve and the oldest in her fifties; two people of colour and an income range from under £20,000 annually to over £50,000. Larry and Mandy (a married couple in their thirties) described their experience of opera as a relationship milestone:

> Having known each other since school, and we've been married two years now, been together 10, every time we do something new it's like something new for us, it's like, 'Oh, done another first!' So that was why this was so special.

Both participants expressed exceptionally high levels of enthusiasm for all aspects of the simulcast experience: from the performance itself, to the double-directed screen action and multimedia aspects like the insight documentaries and social media interaction, as described by Larry:

> The whole experience was great, everything from seeing everyone going in at the beginning of the opera to the whole hustle and bustle of what was going on in the theatre, and then people tweeting their experiences onto the screen that was coming up – I thought that was brilliant ... It made it feel a bit more real, like you were there rather than just watching an opera on a screen.

Larry and Mandy also lavished fulsome praise on the performance of *Lucia di Lammermoor*:

> I absolutely loved it. It was very long, but that didn't matter, I was really drawn into the whole show and I had goose bumps at one point. The tragic scenes, you could see the relationship building between her [Lucia] and her fella ... [Edgardo] and then the brother [Lord Ashton] found out and you could see the pain in her heart, she was never going to see her fella again. The whole story ... I was just completely drawn in.

After the show, Larry was inspired to begin following *prima donna* Diana Damrau on social media: 'I'm actually following her on Twitter now! Because, as soon as I got on Twitter I just messaged her like, "Oh you're fantastic!"' The Twitter feed served another function for Larry - one that was picked up on by several my respondents - it displayed the global audience engaged in the simulcast event:

Larry: Watching the Royal Opera House, all their tweets and people tweeting and seeing all these people from all around the country and all around the world saying they enjoyed it, that was a really nice little twist. Even though you weren't there with these people, hearing everyone else having such great experiences was brilliant.

Mandy: Yeah the fact that we could see it and it was also broadcast through other cinemas in the country as well. Brilliant. Really good.

This is in contrast to other subjects (like June), who did not experience this sense of global participation, and explicitly stated that she felt no affinity whatsoever with the global crowd. Furthermore, Samantha and Jeff stated they felt more connected to 'the live audience that were actually there in the opera house, because we were actually seeing them [on screen]'. Nevertheless, Larry and Mandy tell us something very significant about the institutional dramaturgy of opera cinema, as compared to live opera on television, for example. Television relays remediate the visual dimension of opera; simulcasting does the same for its theatrical dimension, as is evident from Larry's comments:

> Just knowing that other people were getting up, getting ready and going up, it gave you a sense that you were really going to see a real opera ... the fact that you heard the audience clapping and everyone going quiet, like, 'Shush!' and you heard the music starting, you feel that sense of everyone really enjoying this experience.

Moreover, because of opera cinema's hybrid status, subjects tended to position it between theatre and film in terms of cultural value - inferior to the former, but superior to the latter. Subjects were almost unanimous in their criticism of cinema. Larry underlined this point during the Hereford focus group: 'I think, when you're watching a film, you're there to watch a film. You get up, you go and it's entertainment, bang in your face. Whereas with *Lucia*, I felt more involved in it.' For Larry, opera cinema facilitated a sense of immersion and collective participation that elevated it beyond 'normal', recorded cinema. Larry went on to describe how his unfamiliarity with the cast, compared with the pantheon of Hollywood stars ('there were no Johnny Depps!'), enhanced his capacity to identify and empathize with the characters.

The extent to which subjects' positive comments applied to opera cinema per se or opera more generally was not always clear. But Larry identified specific aspects of the experience of simulcasting and highlighted their unique value. For example, regarding the double-direction and its interaction with the staging, he said the following: 'the way it was set up, almost like a split-screen, so you always had two things going on – I thought it was a cracking idea … I think if it was just a pre-recorded show and if you were just watching it on a big screen, it would be just like you were watching it on TV.' These comments distinguish the cultural value of opera cinema from both stage opera and pre-recorded opera.

Even very enthusiastic subjects tended to identify a degree of social stratification implicit in opera. Larry described attendees as 'a certain class of people that wouldn't listen to Radio One' (a UK radio station associated with pop music and a young audience). But notably, he appeared to enjoy the opportunity for virtual class tourism provided by the simulcast. Mandy corroborated this assessment, but was more interested in the class composition of the Covent Garden audience depicted on screen:

> I liked the fact that I've never seen inside an opera house. I've seen one on a television but to some of us the idea [is] that the opera is only for certain people. So to see the sort of people who were going – that was interesting as well.

For Mandy, the simulcast provided access to an unfamiliar, elite cultural formation. However, it is notable that Mandy still employed the language of 'us and them', implying a distinction between the average citizen and 'certain people' who go to the opera. Her experience was not of cultural democratization as much as virtual class tourism – seeing how the other half live, via satellite. Larry and Mandy also appreciated the cultural capital the event conferred to them, with the latter stating that she had not been to a theatrical performance since secondary school and noted that her 'sixteen-year-old, fourteen-year-old' self probably would not have derived much enjoyment from opera. The pleasure that *Lucia* afforded to her thus charted the development of her taste from girlhood to adulthood. Larry concurred that the experience made him 'all grown up'. He was clear that opera cinema was seen as a point of initiation, with Larry commenting: 'I think that for people who've never been to an opera before, like us, the fact that it was almost filmed in a cinematic way sort of broke you in a bit more gently.' He further noted that journeying to a metropolitan centre would have been a tall order for him and Mandy, both in terms of financial outlay and the hassle of having to travel and potentially book accommodation:

> It's definitely the monetary issue for me, because to go to London, get a hotel, buy opera tickets and then get there and absolutely hate it would be … an expensive risk. And you just can't really justify spending that much money on something you've never seen before.

Based on this comment, one potential way in which opera cinema might complement rather than - as is sometimes feared[51] - cannibalize auditoria is by lowering the economic and functional risk associated with opera for newcomers. Furthermore, both subjects strove to elevate their experience further by dressing for the occasion – donning their 'finery'. Though Larry admitted he erred on the side of caution because 'the first time you don't know what everybody else is going to be wearing'. He confirmed that, having attended a simulcast, he would 'definitely' dress up for opera cinema in future. Enacting these codes of behaviour, which for lack of a better term we might call theatrical, proves Gitelman's point that media consist not only of technologies but the constellations of behaviours and assumptions that surround them.[52] These are routinely imported into new contexts, albeit rarely unanimously and seldom unchanged.

There is evidence from these subjects' impressions that the institutional dramaturgy of opera cinema is both ethically and aesthetically complex. The effect was powerful, but imperfect. My respondents did *not* forget they were sitting in a cinema. Indeed, several respondents complained of a lack of 'atmosphere' in the movie house; an issue that was exacerbated for Odeon attendees given the higher number of empty seats compared to the independent venues. As Larry pointed out, 'There were only about ten of us ... that was the only negative thing about it for me, the cinema was so empty.' He further said of watching *Lucia di Lammermoor* in the Hereford Odeon that 'you don't get the true atmosphere and excitement of being at the opera house'. This initially seemed an odd statement given Larry's operatic virginity prior to taking part in the project, but on further questioning proved congruent on two levels. First, he *had* been inside a converted opera house in Bournemouth – 'which is now a night club'. He related his sense of awe on entering this venue and explained that he 'wanted to have the same feeling going to see this show', but was left wanting by the simulcast. Furthermore, he found the barren cinema a let-down compared to the hustle and bustle at Covent Garden depicted on the screen. Here lies the corollary of opera cinema's institutional dramaturgy, which at the same time as inviting audiences to watch a performance 'live from the Royal Opera House', reminds them that they are *not present* at Covent Garden: you are *there*, watching us *here*. Even where my respondents had no direct experience of staged opera, they regarded the Covent Garden performance as a more valuable cultural experience than remote viewing. Larry admitted to feeling 'quite jealous' of the auditorium audience, 'all there in their finery, swanning around talking to all their friends!' These data reinforce Steichen's perspective on the stratifying and exclusionary undercurrent of institutional dramaturgy.

Furthermore, Larry deigned the sound quality at the Hereford Odeon as merely 'alright', stating: 'it was the same quality you would get if you went to see a film.' He also lamented the lack of visceral engagement with the 'loud music when the orchestra was playing'. Several subjects from the first round also spoke of feeling less 'drawn in' to the cinema simulcast than the staged performance of *Mahagonny*, stating that the physical sound production and reception in the auditorium made the experience more 'real', evincing its sonic immediacy. True immediacy - sonic, visual or otherwise - is of course inconceivable: light and sound waves are both inevitably mediated by the material world. In the case of opera auditoria, the physical properties of the space are specifically tailored to convey sound all the way up to the gods, a very clear instance of deliberate, technological mediation.

One of my research subjects, Ellie (in her fifties), was actually an employee at Hereford Odeon. Like some other subjects, she was unsure of how to tackle the problem of attire, admitting that she 'didn't know what to wear!' In other words, despite the special insight one would expect (having observed audiences attending simulcasts before), her novice status and the hybridity of opera cinema made it harder for her to establish an appropriate viewing register. In general, she expressed a dim view of the simulcast. For instance, she criticized the cinematic double-direction, which she felt robbed her of agency to observe the stage action:

> When I go to the theatre, I don't just like to look at the main actors I like to look at other things on the stage, and I found, because it was filmed, not all the time but sometimes it focused just on the main singer, and I wanted to look at other things. And if I was at the opera I wouldn't be just having a big close-up of the main singer.

Like Larry, she also noted that the low turn-out at the Odeon diminished the sense of occasion: 'I was rather hoping there was going to be more, I was rather sad on your behalf that more people hadn't come.' Although she was complimentary about the production of *Boris Godunov* - praising the set design, costuming and quality of the singers - she nevertheless criticized opera's male-dominated cast ('I think mine was mainly male singers'), as well as the amount of recitatives ('the way it was, they could almost have spoken the lines because it was almost like a play'). Regarding the lack of female singers, the Royal Opera House production in question was based on Mussorgsky's original version, rejected by the Imperial Theatres in 1869 for lacking a substantial female role.[53] Perhaps Ellie would have viewed Mussorgsky's 1874 revision (with its additional 'Polish act', featuring augmented female roles) more favourably. I was left with the impression that - for Ellie - this was simply the wrong production, experienced in the wrong context.

I interviewed Sandy and Trisha, a mother and daughter who watched *Lucia di Lammermoor* in the Hatfield Odeon, together. This resulted in an interesting dynamic, in which Sandy's assessment of opera cinema seemed to be influenced by her motherhood. She convinced Trisha to take part in the project after acknowledging the educational value of opera, and further commented on the broader potential of opera cinema to nurture new generations of operagoers, arguing that schools ought to bring their classes to simulcasts. Sandy was one of the most vocally class conscious of my respondents. She admitted to being intimidated by the prospect of opera, but she tended to frame the issues of class and elitism positively, claiming to feel culturally elevated and 'privileged' at having participated in the project. This sense of privilege operated at multiple levels. In the first instance, Sandy cited the exclusivity of simulcasting (as opposed to a recording that 'everybody else' could watch) as a major source of its appeal. Moreover, she enjoyed flaunting her newly acquired cultural esteem to her colleagues: 'The next day I was at work and I was like: "Oh I went to the opera! I saw the opera!"' Finally, she explicitly associated opera attendance with class privilege, owing to its (presumed) high price of admission, introducing an additional layer of exclusivity: 'I don't think that it's something we all get to see because it's so expensive.'

Indeed, most of my novice subjects were enthusiastic about the democratizing capacity of simulcasting. They aligned to varying degrees with the 'grateful' audience orientation identified by Vladica's 2013 study of *Live from the Met* audiences, which was also conducted using Q Methodology.[54] My subjects praised the philanthropic, 'democratising' aspect of simulcasting, despite typically judging the experience itself as aesthetically lesser than stage opera. These data pose the question of why opera cinema has thus far failed to capture the imagination of new operaphiles. One particular focus group conversation proved instructive. I questioned Sandy about the democratizing potential of opera cinema, and she pointed out that, for simulcasting to become a bridge to opera, it must be allowed to penetrate a new generation of potential opera audiences. She offered some practical suggestions in this regard:

> I also think it should be in the schools. I think like with Trisha, I wouldn't necessarily have taken her to go and see it, but the fact that this was advertised in the school I was like, you know what, Trisha, you, you should, experience this. Even though she was like, '*eh*', I was like, 'Look I'll go with you, try it: you should experience this'. Schools, maybe instead of them going to see whatever it is they watch in the cinema, should have a trip to the local cinema and watch a livestream of opera.

Trisha (at twelve years old, my youngest participant) was clearly influenced by Sandy's presence, as she tended to be led by and agree with her mother's assessments. Nevertheless, she was firm enough in her opinions to disagree with Sandy on occasion. For instance, she stated that she did not feel the same degree of sympathy for Lucia, despite her mother's urging:

Sandy: But the part when she was upset, you felt upset? Because you said, 'Oh I feel so sad'.

Trisha: I felt sad for her ... but not as much. I don't know why. I enjoyed it a lot and I'd love to go again but I wasn't emotional.

Most of my respondents from the second phase were emotionally engaged with opera cinema to greater or lesser extents. Both Larry and Mandy attested to feeling 'goosebumps' on witnessing Lucia's descent into madness, for example. However, for Trisha at least, the physical and psychological wall of the cinema screen dampened her capacity to identify with the physical performers. She stated that in the cinema 'you have a screen that separates you from the actors and the opera singers. If you're actually [at the opera house] *you can reach out and touch them*' [my emphasis]. The latter point evokes Gumbrecht's conception of presence as the potential for a viewed object to enjoy a spatial relationship with human hands – to be literally 'tangible'.[55] He described a reciprocity of presence, one that implies the capacity for physical interaction between the viewer and the object viewed.[56] However, there are limits to this model of theatrical presence. Playing devil's advocate, I put to Trisha that the kind of physical interaction and closeness she described is not possible in an auditorium. Most attendees are so far from the stage that they can only vaguely see the performers, and none are permitted to physically touch them. With this in mind, Trisha admitted that the cinema provided its own advantages:

> I feel like the cinema is good [in] part too, because you can feel you can see the close-ups, but if you were [at the auditorium] you'd be far away, you wouldn't be able to do anything about it. You couldn't move forward or see anything closer.

These comments relate back to the question of audience agency and evince possibility of overstating one's control over viewing the staged performance relative to the simulcast. This exchanged moved our conversation in a different direction and demonstrated that Trisha's engagement was inhibited by some aspects of the cinema, but enhanced by others. Barker's research on attendees at a live, theatrical adaptation of the novel *Crash* highlights empathy between performers and spectators as a central, affective dimension of live performance.[57] This kind of empathy was an important feature of several of my respondents' liveness contracts. For instance, Sandy and Trisha both pointed out that the language of cinema (particularly the close-up) could enhanced the empathy that was central to their sense of the performance happening in the moment:

Sandy: What stood out was the fact I could see every angle, whereas with normal theatre there are pillars or it's not that clear. But here I could see all angles, which I appreciated as I could see

	the persons' expressions and get more of a feel for what was going on.
Trisha:	You could see them clearly; there was no barrier – it was like they were actually there.

Despite theorists like Erika Fischer-Lichte, for example, claiming empathetic connection between spectators and performers (in addition to the simultaneity of production and reception) as the exclusive ontological property of co-present theatrical performance,[58] opera cinema fulfilled this criterion of liveness for these respondents at least. For Sandy, the visual language of cinema facilitated greater intimacy than a physical theatre, in which the singers are too distant to perceive the detail of their facial expressions. For Trisha, the cinema moved the performers further away, but the cinematic editing brought them closer. This goes to show the limitations of asking research subjects to rate their impressions of liveness without qualification or nuance. There are multiple layers to this concept, which subjects often need to parse out to fully understand themselves. In contrast to Auslander's thesis about a stark, binary antagonism between live performance and mediation, my subjects deemed the process of cinematic remediation as 'more live than live', in some respects.

Trisha's youth arguably imparted a special level of personal accomplishment compared to other subjects. She described her positive experience of opera as making her feel 'older' (more mature and culturally competent): 'Because everyone there may have been there already and knows how to follow it a bit more and understand the language and analyse [the show]. But I *could* understand it. I could follow it even though I didn't understand the language ... I could understand it and handle it' [subject's emphasis]. Trisha's capacity to both engage with and enjoy *Lucia* rewarded her with confirmation of her existing cultural sophistication and maturity, hence enjoying the opera made her feel more distinguished and intellectual. Her enjoyment of opera thus served as confirmation of her own cultural competence. Based on her other comments, it seems improbable she would have sought to obtain this confirmation via an opera house, because it would have been intimidating. As such, this 'short cut' to acculturation constitutes a distinctive element of opera cinema's ontology.

This reminds me of Tambling's point about the policing of certain forms of art, wherein there is an assumption that 'a certain education is necessary to understand it at all: which is a convenient way of policing culture, and making sure it is kept as the property of an elite'.[59] This affect was heightened because, prior to the project, she imagined she would feel like 'the odd one out' at the simulcast. This is a potentially significant choice of words. As noted, I recruited to this small-scale project based on availability and goodwill, rather than demographic sampling. Therefore, I lack the means to scrutinize the effect of race, class, gender and so forth on my subjects' impressions. However, Sandy and Trisha were the only Black focus group participants in the second round of field work, and this comment – coupled with Sandy's emphasis on opera's elitism – led me to question the extent to which such comments were racially coded. Given the emphasis on audience democratization in the wider conversation around opera cinema, the issue of demography and opera cinema audiences would be a productive avenue for future researchers to explore.

Trisha and Sandy both felt that the simulcast overcame one problem of stage performance: namely, that if you are sat far away from the stage in an opera house 'you wouldn't be able to do anything about it'. In general, *Lucia*'s double-direction enjoyed the most positive reception of any of my case studies. Trisha and Sandy both complimented the simulcast for permitting simultaneous appreciation of the concurrent narrative threads displayed on stage, pointing out that their attention would have been divided in the auditorium:

Trisha: [The] split screen ... on one level you could enjoy the singing and on a second level you could enjoy the acting.
Sandy: Yeah because ... in the cinema you've got one screen and you're looking at certain angles, but in the theatre, you're looking at two screens, so there's more angles to look at and if you were actually there. I think it would be better – the split screen – in the cinema.

During the simulcast, the visual language of cinema takes over the role of theatre glasses, presenting everyone with a clear and equal view of the stage – an advantage that was also acknowledged by some of Karen Wise's respondents in her research for the English Touring Opera.[60] This implies a certain levelling effect. Although this should perhaps not be overstated, given that the price of entry is double the cost of a normal cinema ticket, and that opera cinema largely caters to experienced opera audiences.

More negatively, Sandy concurred with Larry that depictions of excited attendees mingling during intervals fostered a palpable atmosphere that was immediately undercut when she looked around the sparsely occupied Hatfield Odeon to find that 'everyone was just there with their popcorn, and whatever'. Multiple respondents reported this cognitive dissonance during the simulcast, when the prosaic surroundings of the cinema undercut their sense of live participation and dragged them unceremoniously back to reality. Andrew made this comparison most stark. Having attended the simulcast first, he recalled 'looking around and seeing how splendid it looked compared to the cinema, which just sort of ... *happens*' [my emphasis]. This is a telling statement: the opera house is (to use Matt Hills' term) a cult geography:[61] a resplendent beacon of high society and history – whereas the cinema was seen as utilitarian, underwhelming and mundane. These comments imply that opera cinema's relative lack of success at multiplex venues is something of a self-fulfilling prophecy. The lack of attendance created a rather barren setting that failed to match the energy of the Royal Opera House audience. This had the effect of undercutting subjects' sense of live participation. Relatedly, Sandy made no effort to dress up for the cinema, although the particular cinema she attended played a role in this decision. The only significant contextual deviation visible in the Q data was between the independent and multiplex cinema groups, and Sandy clearly perceived the Hatfield Odeon as unworthy of special etiquette or dress ('I ain't dressing up for Hatfield!'). When I asked whether she would make a greater effort for the Royal Opera House, her answer was immediate and specific, stating that she would 'wear a black dress', and that doing so would 'be part of the fun'.

In her written testimony during the Q-sorting process, Sandy noted that the simulcast would have been improved by the addition of a wine bar. I was struck by the specificity of this idea, and I brought it up in our focus group. Apparently, the suggestion was based on a live cinema screening of *50 Shades of Grey* that Sandy had previously attended: 'It was a late night showing. We were all adults and there was a bar there you could also bring your own drinks and everybody had dainty wine glasses. It was a very grown-up atmosphere.' Sandy equated the maturity of alcoholic refreshments (that are, in fairness, usually available even at the lowly multiplex) with the mature subject matter of *50 Shades of Grey*, and in turn with an audience sufficiently mature to appreciate both. In fact, food and drink were used across the sample as a metonymical device for adjudicating the puerility of cinema and its audiences, with hot dogs, popcorn and Coca-Cola used as shorthand for a juvenile cultural form. This clearly demonstrates how ritual practices like refreshment choices are intimately bound up in media ontology. Many respondents made an association between certain types of refreshments and a different class of audience.

Emma (twenty-seven), originally from Lithuania, was an employee at the Hatfield Odeon. She was also musically trained – having gone to music school and played acoustic guitar for seven years. Additionally, she belonged to a musical family, with her sister playing piano and guitar and her parents 'traditional percussion instruments'. I was curious about how these two sources of privileged knowledge would impact her impressions. During our interview, she spoke about the special esteem afforded to music and theatre in her home country: 'We would go to see ballets and theatre but because there is this stereotype that you have to educate yourself in all areas to be just like a more well-rounded individual.' As such, Emma regarded participating in opera as an important step in her personal development. However, she stated categorically that she did not consider watching the simulcast to constitute opera attendance:

I still feel like, because the surroundings and you don't really sit in an opera house as such, so, I've seen an opera performance but not in an opera [house], *so I still feel like I haven't been to an opera*, if you like. [subject's emphasis]

For Emma, being in an opera house is an intrinsic aspect of opera as an art form. Emma's sense of liveness overlapped with June, Sandy and Trisha's immediate, empathetic connection to the human labour involved in live performance. For her, this appreciation was explicitly based on a sense of peril: 'With *Lucia* in particular there is a part with her singing a solo where she hits the highest notes, and not everyone had been successful in hitting the note, so there's that aspect to that as well ... There is a challenge for the singers.' Emma's contract of liveness was thus predicated primarily on her empathetic engagement with a skilful cast engaged in feats of physical and technical mastery, faced with the ever-present possibility of calamity. Emma emphasized the salient point that, for liveness to function affectively in opera cinema, one must either know in advance that the performance is live or discover as much at some point during the show. If the performance runs smoothly, it should be indiscernible from an edited recording. However, the marketing material surrounding opera cinema clearly delineates liveness as a source of added value, and throughout the simulcast the presenter repeatedly reminds the international audience that what they are watching is beamed 'live from the Royal Opera House'. As such, a paradox emerges: liveness is specifically emphasized prior and during the show, but overt evidence of liveness is suppressed. Only mess ups can absolutely confirm liveness: the 'immediate' event is confirmed as such - and the contract of liveness validated - through transmission of 'undesirable' content.

Furthermore, Emma directly discussed the 'exclusivity' of opera cinema attendance at Hatfield: 'It's not like we're showing every week in nine screens, it's a one-off. So, people would come in just for that performance.' This exclusionary aspect of live performance is key to a 'cult of liveness' in popular and academic criticism that constitutes an idealist obsession with the self-evident superiority of live experience over recorded media. Overall, she characterized opera cinema as an alternative for established opera fans who are 'all delighted to come to the cinema because the opera house might be sold out', or for reasons related to accessibility:

I think [opera cinema] attracts the audience from the price perspective. The audience that would typically come to these kind of performances [are] not always mobile because of their age restrictions and the price! ... It's a very good alternative I think.

Her profession gave her a special level of insight into these attendees, and she claimed she could 'spot them a mile away' - owing to their 'grey heads' and preference for rum and raisin ice cream. She further commented on their impressive knowledge of opera and conveying a sense of having 'achieved something in life'. Additionally, Emma considered the simulcast to be a more valid experience than the simulcast and pre-recorded, 'encore' screenings of Royal Opera House performances. She related that the atmosphere is appreciably dampened during these screenings: 'it becomes more like a film.' Alternatively, opera cinema offered a way for people to experience opera for the first time at lower risk: 'If someone had said to me, "Would you like to go and see an opera" and you'd have to pay a lot of money, I'm not sure I would've gone, so this was a perfect opportunity to go and see whether I'd enjoy it or not.'

This psychological dimension of liveness was underlined by my final focus group participant, Jen (self-employed and in her fifties). Halfway through our interview, Jen revealed that she did not realize that the simulcast was live – she believed that she had watched an encore recording. Up to that point, her comments had been rather critical. Despite having completed a secondary school qualification in Russian language, she apparently found the foreign-language performance challenging. She also admitted to finding the sung-through performance of *Boris Godunov* 'difficult', despite singling out the vocal gymnastics of Bryn Terfel for praise. In her consent form for taking part in the project, Jen mentioned she regularly attends dramatic theatre, which I assumed would put her at more ease with opera. In fact, she was rather nonplussed by the Royal Opera House auditorium depicted on screen: 'I suppose I had no idea that if you go to the opera everyone gets dressed up – it's all a bit formal.' When I corrected her mistake about attending the simulcast, it had an immediate impact on her retrospective appreciation of the experience:

> You do appreciate that they're performing and you're watching and it wasn't being cut and rehearsed and re-taken lots of times. To see a performance live is much more exciting. Much more interesting.

This was a fascinating revelation, which demonstrated psychological and experiential value of liveness – even when it has no perceptible impact at a formal level, it contains a cultural and subjective cache. This contradicts canonical, pure theory definitions of liveness from the likes of Peggy Phelan and Fischer-Lichte, based on co-presence and simultaneity of production and reception.[62] Like several other respondents, Jen felt the cinematic direction enhanced their engagement with the drama by intimately illustrating characters' emotional states, as she explained in our interview: 'You can see their faces and you can see the emotion. I like that because sometimes if you're in a theatre you can't see their faces close. Even though it's good you're missing out a little bit there I think.' This in turn permitted an additional layer of interpretation – enhancing rather than diminishing the intellectual value of the performance. Moreover, in a large, physical theatre, one's capacity to engage with the drama depends on physical proximity, which is dependent on the cost of one's seat. There is a potential class reading of double-direction that bears consideration here, concerning what Barker describes as opera cinema's 'front-of-house-feel'.[63]

Jen later backtracked on her comments about the relative merits of live versus pre-recorded shows, contending that she had once 'seen a theatre [simulcast] that was also an encore, where it wasn't the live one, it was a recording of the live one, and I still got the same enjoyment'. On exploring the matter further, it transpired that Jen valued the fact that event encore performances have not been retouched, and thus capture a raw, comparatively unmediated live performance. Like other respondents, failure was the only yardstick by which the simulcast could be judged 'live'. As Jen noted, she would not have realized the screening was simultaneous, 'unless there'd been some awful disaster in it'. Obviously, there are contradictions in Jen's comments (which is the nature of qualitative audience data), but in general her conception of liveness depended on her knowledge of the risk and human labour involved in an unscripted performance. Curiously, whether the *actual* media event was simultaneous was less important to her.

The experienced audience, made up of people who are not regular cinemagoers,[64] predominates at simulcast events, introducing a new set of contextual parameters for my respondents. As reported, some subjects were alienated by the presence of older, opera-literate attendees. However, others were more positive. Jen, for example, complimented the simulcast's 'grown-up audience', and contrasted it with typical cinema crowds, which she characterized as youthful and unruly. To make the point, Jen drew a comparison with a cinema club in Letchworth that she frequents, which screens foreign and art house films. She explained that 'everybody's there because they want to be there. It's adults and it's quiet ... I wouldn't go and watch a blockbuster where there's gonna be lots of children. I suppose the opera has got the nice, well-behaved audience!'

Two things bear consideration here. First, Jen's comments support Gitelman and Barker's contention that new media protocols are always repurposed from established media, which serve as touchstones for engagement with new cultural experiences. Second, the presence of a 'mature' and invested audience constitutes one of opera cinema's distinguishing features – as confirmed by similar accounts across my sample. There is undeniably a socially recognized hierarchy of the arts, and within them, a corresponding social hierarchy of consumers: 'This predisposes tastes to function as markers of "class."'[65] A couple of subjects made the conceptual link between maturity and class explicit. As noted, cinema and opera were deemed to have a patrician and plebeian character, respectively. Opera cinema clearly aligned more closely with the former. As Jen stated, making the comparison with 'normal' cinema crowds: 'There was nobody scruffy. They all looked sort of middle-class.' Associating themselves with a taste culture of a high social rank during the simulcast permitted some of my opera virgins to elevate themselves above the cinema mob. There was a clear generational divide here: younger respondents tended to acknowledge the class composition of the audience, but parse it more negatively than older subjects, distancing themselves from fellow attendees. Respondents from the comparative study drew a direct contrast between the dressed-up opera house audience and attendees at the simulcast for *Mahagonny*, in which 'they were wearing casual clothes'. Conversely, Jen described the audience for the *Boris Godunov* simulcast as 'well presented' – particularly the women. So, it seems that sartorial conventions from the opera house have dialectically interacted with the casual attire typical of cinema attendance, resulting in a rather visually mismatched audience.

Interestingly, this experienced audience in the cinema made no attempts to initiate my novice subjects into the operatic fandom, nor police their viewing stratagem. Subjects simply made comments to the effect that the cinema was 'casual' and 'relaxed'. This made for a marked contrast with feedback from the comparative study, in which respondents who attended Covent Garden reported having their behaviour rigorously policed by experienced opera fans – enacting the collective connoisseurship described by Claudio Benzecry and educating neophytes in the 'correct' form of operatic appreciation.[66] This could imply that opera cinema audiences feel less of a sense of ownership over the cinema compared to the auditorium, less of an investment in creating 'proper' conditions for viewing, or less of a burden of duty to physically co-present performers. In any event, my respondents seemed to experience greater freedom to develop their personal viewing strategies without external interference.

Q Methodology results

Having introduced the qualitative impressions from my focus groups and interviews, I move to the results that emerged from Q Methodology analysis. During the first round of data collection, the twenty participants fell into three factors that I characterize (in order of largest to smallest) as New Purists, Awed Initiates and Opera Cinephiles. Before profiling these factors, I would like to re-emphasise that, due to the size of my sample, none of my data, impressions or conclusions carry quantitative, statistical weight. I am not in any way suggesting these groupings are generalizable across the millions of people who watch opera cinema. My research project was small-scale and inductive, and its purpose was to contribute to an understanding of the experiential contours of opera cinema, and thus inform my ontological analysis.

The New Purists

The largest factor, New Purists, were instinctual traditionalists who were new to opera, but felt that it can only be experienced to its full potential in an opera house. These subjects also expressed feelings of responsibility towards the future of opera, evidenced by their most agreed-upon statement: 'I feel like people make a greater contribution to the art form by seeing an opera in the opera house [as] compared to going to the cinema. It's important to keep this medium alive.' Conversely, these subjects were rather disparaging about the simulcast, which at least one respondent likened to 'watching play productions of *Romeo and Juliet* on a widescreen TV in GCSE [high school] English Literature class'. However, these subjects were cognizant of the potential 'worthiness' of opera simulcasting insofar as it serves to broaden opera audiences and so sustain the medium: 'I think the screening of opera in a cinema should definitely continue and reach greater audiences.' Thus, they considered opera cinema to be an aesthetically inferior experience that is valuable only to the extent that it develops and consolidates opera house audiences.

These subjects often parsed their negative comparisons between the staged and simulcast versions of *Mahagonny* in terms of emotional engagement, which appeared to rely on physically co-present performers: 'You don't feel the raw passion and emotion conveyed by the cast and orchestra [in the cinema].' The subjects associated this heightened emotional engagement in the cinema with authenticity and immersion, with many respondents commenting to the effect that the opera was more emotive and thus more 'real' in the auditorium. Sinéad O'Neill, Joshua Edelman and John Sloboda obtained revealing results from research on 'highly-engaged' (expert) opera attendees, whose descriptive language about their experience of opera equated authenticity with emotionality.[67] This research also compared results between experienced respondents' emotional engagement with opera in a physical auditorium versus other formats, concluding: 'In most cases, our interviewees were more engaged by opera performed live in a theatre than by other available options. They were stimulated by the risk of live performance, and felt excited and privileged to be in the same space as the performers.'[68] This negative correlation between engagement and remediation bore out for the New Purists, which in turn precluded them from perceiving opera cinema as a medium in its own right - for them, it was merely a mode of transmission.

Furthermore, these subjects always described the aesthetic superiority of opera by denigrating traditional cinema and its audiences, both of which the New Purists associated with populism, mundanity and unsophistication, given testimonies like the following: 'In my opinion, people who go to watch opera shows in the cinema instead of the latest blockbuster do so for a reason.' Barker obtained similar results by comparing audience engagement with stage and screen adaptations of *Crash*. He writes, 'Theatre *by contrast with cinema* is valuable. The very cultural scaling of values which has put theatre and drama in its unstable, ambiguous position is being appropriated – at the expense of another medium's reputation' [original emphasis].[69] Similarly, opera cannot simply be great – cinema must be inferior and opera cinema somewhere there in between. It is possible that the New Purists' comments evince overcompensation, reflecting their desire to fit in with the 'opera people' by distancing themselves from the cinematic rabble. This in turn suggests an already-formed understanding of opera audiences as an elite cultural community that precedes direct experience. Aside from permitting that opera cinema might serve as a viable gateway to the real thing, the New Purists' love-at-first sight encounter with staged opera precluded any appreciation they might have had for simulcasting. Many of the New Purists went further, and not only qualified their positive comments about the auditorium with reflexive denigration of cinema, but also of *cinema audiences*. For instance, consider the following subject testimony:

> In my opinion, people who go to watch Opera shows in the cinema ... are likely to be more cultured and aware of Opera and what it entails, and so with this in mind, their behaviour wasn't really too different to how you'd expect in the auditorium.

Here, the aesthetic superiority of staged opera is paired with contempt for cinematic taste cultures, which are associated with populism and childishness. It is not surprising that the only advantages New Purists identified from the simulcast were its relative affordability and convenience, and its potential appeal to the uninitiated. Even then, praise was offered grudgingly, Consider the two following testimonies:

> Yes it's cheaper and (much) more convenient, but this comes at the expense of the experience only found in the auditorium.
>
> I think the screening of opera in a cinema should definitely continue and reach greater audiences.

These comments suggest that opera cinema is valuable only insofar as it provides a last resort for opera lovers or – better yet – permits novices to graduate to the 'proper' exhibition context for operatic appreciation.

The Awed Initiates

Subjects in the second-largest factor were torn about their experience of staged and simulcast opera. They broadly concurred with the New Purists that opera cinema is inferior to staged performance ('[The simulcast] lacked the incredible atmosphere that a live performance has, there is only so much sound that can be digitally reproduced'), but they expressed a significant degree of discomfort with the opera house as an exhibition space compared with the cinema ('I felt underdressed [at Covent Garden], and encountered a number of snooty audience members'). Not only did these subjects reach a looser consensus, but their two most-agreed-upon statements were apparently contradictory: 'The operatic voice is incredible in person. Hearing a human voice fill a huge space without amplification is something the cinema can never recreate' versus 'I felt totally out of place in the Covent Garden auditorium. Seeing my first opera was hard enough, but the whole setting just made me self-conscious and uncomfortable.' The focus group I held with five of these subjects helped to unpick this paradox.

The respondents were generally more complimentary than the New Purists about the simulcasting experience, which they predominantly praised for being cheaper and more convenient than staged opera attendance. Moreover, they concurred that opera cinema represents a valuable cultural experience than 'normal' cinema and other recorded media. Subjects also praised the cinematic remediation for making the stage action and subtext more legible, for instance, during Jimmy Mahoney's execution in *Mahagonny*'s climax. The Christian illusions were plain to see, whereas Jeff, for example, admitted 'may have missed [them] during the auditorium performance'. These data resonate with Emanuele Senici's analyses of live opera videos, a format with similar formal conventions to opera cinema. Senici talks about opera on video being 'rhythmized', resulting in a 'quadruple *mise-en-rythme*, so to speak: verbal text, music, *mise-en-scène*, and video'.[70] The redirected screen action is both a distinctive formal element of opera cinema and a specific advantage for newcomers, given that the screen direction offers novices additional visual guidance.

Despite filmic technique exerting a relatively minor influence on opera cinema, most of my subjects described the simulcasting experience as 'cinematic'. The contradiction indicates the extent to which engagement with media is informed by exhibition context. Although opera cinema (to my eyes) *looks* televisual; because it took place on a large screen, in a movie theatre, it *felt* cinematic to my respondents. This perceived hybridity was received variously across the sample. Several respondents praised the simulcast for taking cues from cinema; with Fred commenting in the *Mahagonny* focus group that in the cinema '[you] expect your view to be directed'. Samantha added that the double-direction 'made it feel more like a film, rather than just having a really static, wide angle shot of the stage. That would've been *more* unnatural than having the shots selected for you'. Some of these subjects' statements were cognate with these classic critiques of screen media spectatorship. For instance, Samantha said that the auditorium experience 'felt a lot more like you were being immersed into it rather than just passively watching [the opera]'. Other criticisms focused on the simulcast's insistence upon a preferred reading, as June explained:

> Obviously, the film director chose what you saw at any given time. *I certainly felt that I lost some of the stage.* Certainly, when we were in the theatre, the stage is amazing and, y'know, massive, and there's stuff going on all over the place. It certainly gives you the freedom to look at whatever you want, to *see* whatever you want. Whereas when you're watching the cinema, obviously you see what the director wants you to see. [subject's emphasis]

Contradicting his previous comments, Jeff cited an instance in *Mahagonny* in which 'four guys are on the plane - it's just like a cut out of the side of a plane - there's two dancers on the far right, sort of stage left with batons like they're on a runway'. These dancers were removed from the simulcast, keeping the focus on the principal characters, resulting in the loss of a 'nice feature'. However, the fact that Samantha and June recognized (and critiqued) the coercive nature of the simulcast experience is evidence of their active *resistance* to this coercion. This critical and conscious engagement cannot be considered passive.

Moreover, the Awed Initiates were very sensitive to opera's elitism - particularly in the opera house. Some subjects felt their behaviour was scrutinized by other attendees - one subject was apparently scolded for fiddling with his phone before the show. This intrusive behaviour by experienced attendees resembles the 'formal process of initiation' described in Claudio Benzecry's ethnographic research on opera fans in Buenos Aires. Benzecry describes how veterans police inappropriate intrusions (clapping at inopportune moments, whispering during the performance, crinkling sweet wrappers and so on) to 'socialise the rest of the house into their understanding of opera'. This results in a 'complex system whereby rules of civility both constrain and enable emotion and allow for its proper public display'.[71] This kind of unsolicited policing was absent from the cinema, resulting in a less-stressful encounter with opera:

> It is a good start for people who haven't gone to an opera before. People might not know the etiquette or be nervous because people might be snooty, so this is kind of a good gateway, because they're like more relaxed environment ... '[t]here was that kind of, like discomfort of feeling like 'I'm not supposed to be here' ... I think we've all said we all felt more comfortable in the cinema, felt like we were more at home with the other people in the cinema.

It is conceivable that, because cinema is a more familiar exhibition context to a larger cross section of the public, it fosters greater comfort than an opera house, which tended to provoke feelings of inadequacy and alienation from these subjects.

Nevertheless, despite their evident discomfort with aspects of the Covent Garden experience, the focus group participants all made comments to the effect that they would prefer to see an opera in an opera house over a cinema, with Samantha concluding: 'I'd go to the opera house. If, like, money was no object.' The 'awe' of this factor refers to their simultaneous respect for and trepidation towards opera. In general, the Awed Initiates' attitude to opera's elitism was bifurcated. Subjects described opera's status as an 'elite' art form positively as a source of cultural esteem (for instance, 'My friends definitely were impressed when I mentioned I was going to an opera'), but negatively in relation to their perceived inadequacies and the allegedly judgemental attitude of other auditorium attendees. Thus, subjects perceived the mystique of the opera house as a crucial aspect of the medium's appeal; even where it provoked feelings of inadequacy, this was also part of the occasion: 'Even though [going to the opera house] can be a sort of elitist and snooty experience, the fact of that somehow makes it more special? Or, you expect it to be special because it's so sort of intimidating?' Therefore, even one of simulcasting's main advantages – making opera more approachable – was somewhat to its detriment. Furthermore, these data strongly imply that subjects regarded opera in the auditorium as the *true* medium – challenging though it was.

In general, the Awed Initiates were more context-sensitive than other factors. Their qualitative impressions de-emphasised the screen and stage content and focused instead on the environmental parameters of their experience: on how the cinema and opera house made them *feel*. They were thus especially attuned to opera's elitism, a response that was most pronounced in their descriptions of the Covent Garden auditorium. Many of the Awed Initiates were of the view that they did not 'belong' in the opera house. Indeed, this issue occupied much of our focus group discussion, and was regarded as a major impediment to general appreciation for opera. Regarding the relevance of opera to contemporary audiences, Samantha contended that the 'elitism and exclusivity makes it difficult for it to *be* relevant to modern consumers and thus have value, not the other way around' [subject's emphasis].

As described, many respondents commented positively on the affordability and convenience of the simulcast relative to staged opera, given that it permitted them to enjoy live opera without necessitating a trip to London. Moreover, they equated this advantage to the potential for widening access across society. Focus group participants from my pilot project also praised simulcasting for opening opera to a wider audience, even as they expressed scepticism towards its aesthetic merits: 'I don't think there's anything wrong with trying to make opera more accessible to a wider audience. The experience might be different, but at least an effort is being made.'

However, lowering the financial barrier for entry was not the only levelling effect of simulcasting identified by my subjects. The Awed Initiates described opera cinema as a viable point of entry for novices who are intimidated by opera's exclusivity, with one testimony concluding: 'Opera is seen as very exclusive, and I think the cinema is a good start, if not the most immediate or impressive.' June put the matter more squarely: 'Usually if you're going to the cinema, it's like an almost regular everyday thing. It's accessible to everybody, so that's why it's a positive sign of having the livestream in the cinema.'

The Opera Cinephiles

The third and final factor in my pilot study was small enough, arguably, to be dismissed as an aberration. However, they reached a very close and emphatic consensus, so bear mentioning. Some of the Opera Cinephiles' testimonial statements were quite negative, indicating that subjects 'did not like parts of the experience very much' and were not 'emotionally moved'. One participant clarified that her lack of appreciation did not stem from limited comprehension, indicating that she 'did understand everything' but was unmoved nevertheless. Where subjects offered more positive impressions, it was clear that they preferred the simulcast. The Opera Cinephiles were the only factor that expressed this preference: 'I'd admit I found quite a lot of it difficult to get into in the opera house but [it was easier] in the more familiar environment of the cinema'. Moreover, the Opera Cinephiles' their top-scoring items evincing a strong preference for opera cinema over staged opera:

1. Being in the auditorium was less enjoyable than the cinema. Three hours is a long time to sit in a small seat and I couldn't see the stage as clearly;
2. Watching an opera in the cinema was far less tiring than spending three hours cooped up in the auditorium;
3. Being in the opera house is different to watching a relay at the cinema, but not necessarily better. I think people get just as much out of going to the cinema;
4. It was much harder to follow the story in the opera house compared to the cinema. I feel like the cinema helps communicate the drama.

It is debatable (given the limited data available) whether these subjects expressed a genuine appreciation for opera cinema on its own terms, or a general lack of enthusiasm for opera, which was at least mollified by a more familiar and comfortable viewing environment. However, some evidence points towards the former. Firstly, the Opera Cinephiles commented that the simulcast of *Mahagonny* was more comprehensible: 'the music, voices and interplay between the two were clearer in the cinema than where I was sat in the auditorium.' Secondly, the Opera Cinephiles appreciated the educational value of the making of documentaries interspersed between acts, as well as patter between the live host (Paterson Joseph in this case) and some of the principal performers: 'With the interviews etc. I came away feeling I'd got more out of it' / 'The background information and interviews at the start and during the interval were interesting.' Despite Steichen's criticisms of these embellishments as a transparent attempt to wring extra money out of backstage material,[72] these multimedia elements discernibly enhanced the experience for my novice subjects. Because these features are unique to opera cinema, these data provide further evidence of formal specificity, supporting my characterization of opera cinema as a new cultural experience – if not a new medium.

As noted, in the second phase of researched I developed a smaller, more focused list of statements based on data obtained during the pilot project. I discarded the comparative aspect of the pilot to focus exclusively on the experience of opera cinema. I also sought to test the influence of repertoire, region and venue on forty-one subjects' experiential engagement with opera cinema. My subjects attended screenings of one of three operas: Boris Godunov, Lucia di Lammermoor and Werther. I selected regional case studies, focusing on two cinemas in Hereford, near the Welsh border (the Odeon megaplex and the Courtyard Cinema), and two in Hertfordshire, north of London (the Odeon megaplex, Hatfield, and the Campus West Cinema in Welwyn Garden City). Once again, I identified three factors. Surprisingly, I found the data were quite consistent across different locations and all three operas. My small pool of data prevents any definitive explanations for this. The only contextual factor that exerted an effect over subjects' engagement was the type of cinema, with comments from subjects in the Hatfield and Hereford Odeons tending to skew to a more negative view.

The Immersed Inductees

Participants in the first and joint-largest factor placed a special emphasis on their sense of absorption. Uniquely, these subjects picked out the remediated aspects of the simulcast as specifically enhancing immersion. For instance, this factor expressed a powerful sense of collective engagement in the live, globalized performance event: 'The whole evening was magical. It felt like being there seeing the hustle and bustle beforehand.' Subjects' top-scoring statement also emphasized their participation in a networked audience: 'I felt connected to the other audience members … I felt like it was some big experience of everyone pulling together to watch it.' Furthermore, the

Immersed Inductees credited the formal characteristics of the simulcast – particularly its double-directed screen action – with facilitating their immersion. Several subjects commented on the 'intimacy' of the camerawork, which they felt brought them closer to the performers and conveyed the authenticity of the live performance: 'I really enjoyed being so close to the action on the stage, seeing the expressions and emotions portrayed made the performance so real.' The relationship between cinematic direction and authenticity was a recurring subject across the focus group discussion. These data contradict the negative correlation between engagement/authenticity and mediation identified by O'Neill, Edelman and Sloboda, and indicate how simulcasting can complement stage opera to unique effect, rather than simply transmitting a diminished version of it.[73]

These subjects concurred with other factors (specifically the Awed Initiates and the Opera Cinephiles) about opera cinema's value to novices. The most popular topic across subjects' testimonial and focus group data concerned the greater legibility facilitated the cinematic direction (which was what subjects were used to at the cinema), and its specific utility as a crutch for inexperienced audiences – 'breaking them in' more gently. The Immersed Inductees also complemented the documentaries on the simulcast programme: 'I thought it was a very impressive production/event. I liked the live simulcast from the Royal Opera House/pre-recorded interviews at the start, which gave the background storyline – for an opera newcomer this made it much easier to follow.' These attributes were connected in turn to opera cinema's perceived value as a gateway to appreciating the art form, with most subjects expressing an enhanced desire to attend a staged performance: 'A very unique viewing of opera, I would have never really bothered before. However, I am now intrigued and want more!' Although these data do not address Peter Gelb's concern that opera cinema might cannibalize opera's existing, experienced audience, [74] they at least suggest that they enhance rather than diminish newcomers' desire for the stage.

However, some subjects (particularly those who visited an Odeon) were critical of the cinema environment for breaking the spell of absorption: 'The cinema style seating was a bit off-putting … I think if you were at the real venue you would dress up a bit more and be in a more sumptuous surrounding.' To compensate for this shortfall, several Immersed Inductees engaged in ritualistic behaviours adapted from theatre attendance that were intended to elevate the experience, like dressing-up. These data resonate with Barker's conception of how media audiences develop viewing strategies:

> The concept conceives viewing (or, by natural extension, reading, listening, participating in other ways) as a motivated activity. It therefore focuses on, first, why people go to see a film – with what hopes, fears, expectations, based on what prior knowledge, with what sense of (and what kind of) importance attached to the event, in what company and why

(and 'company' here includes real, possible, and imaginary companions). The reason for inquiring into all of these is because they are seen as providing the conditions from which a person goes about 'making sense' of a film. [75]

The emergence of a stable viewing strategy is a marker of maturity for a cultural experience, which reveals the social dimension of media ontology. When ritual practices settle into a coherent viewing register, which audiences enact without thinking, it assists them in making sense of a medium, priming them for a particular mode of engagement. Viewing strategies are encoded at a cultural level, constituting a cluster of 'protocols' – behaviours and attitudes – that surround a medium's technological nucleus, as Gitelman puts it.[76] Because opera cinema is not an established medium, my subjects enacted behaviour protocols based on preconceived notions about opera, and their interpretations of the 'correct' way to engage with opera cinema showed a lot of variability.

The Curious Traditionalists

If the Immersed Inductees highlighted opera cinema's uniqueness, the Curious Traditionalists regarded it as the 'next best thing' to the auditorium: 'It's a very good *alternative*, I think' [subject's emphasis]. Unlike other factors whose consensus and preferences were clear from the Q Methodology results, the Curious Traditionalists' results were less instructive in isolation from qualitative data. The subjects' top-scoring statements did complement specific technical and experiential characteristics of the simulcast: 'The cinema relay was easier to follow as you had close-ups of the action. / The view is excellent and much better than a theatre seat.' But their bottom-scoring statements were almost directly contradictory: 'I felt connected to the other audience members who were there at the time. I felt like it was some big experience of everyone pulling together to watch it.' / 'For me it just didn't feel like it was live. For me it just felt like going to a regular cinema.' These ambiguous results reveal some of the limitations of Q Methodology, which relies on small groups of subjects and involves a lot of interpretive work on the part of participants and the researcher. Things became clearer when I looked at the focus group transcripts and testimonies. Members of this factor affirmed a staunch belief in the aesthetic superiority of the auditorium over the simulcast ('I would pick what I wanted to see [in the cinema] whereas with the opera house I would see anything *just to experience it*' [my emphasis]). Nevertheless, they praised opera cinema as a stepping stone to the auditorium, and particularly complemented the clarity and educative value provided by the double-direction and insight films. This was articulated very neatly by one respondent, who stated: 'I would definitely go for a live [performance] rather than for the cinema. But I would go, say, if I was going at a young age and I wanted to educate myself.' So, opera cinema is a worthy and viable enterprise *insofar* as it educates newcomers in opera. It has distinct advantages in terms of communicating the drama, but is ultimately no replacement for the auditorium.

Like the New Purists, these subjects criticized cinema as a populist medium relative to opera, thus relegating opera cinema to a lower cultural status than the stage form. They bemoaned the presence of junk food as breaking the spell of virtual attendance, for example. These data emphasize how protocols like refreshment choices are bound up in a medium's cultural perception. Subjects equated cinema's sweet, fatty and overpriced snacks with children, whereas quality 'mature' cultural experiences (like theatre) were associated with 'dainty wine glasses'. Interestingly, when *Live from the Met* was launched in 2006, Philip Kennicott of the *Washington Post* similarly commented on the novelty of eating ice cream during Tchaikovsky.[77] The juxtaposition of movie house junk food with opera reveals more about the *perception* of opera and cinema's respective reputations as elite and popular art forms than anything essential to either medium. As Barker points out, 'ice cream has been part of the opera experience since at least as early as the 1800s, with this activity even lending its name to a genre, the *aria di sorbetto*'.[78] The data nevertheless demonstrates the cognitive dissonance experienced by the Curious Traditionalists, whose expectations of opera's grandeur were undermined by the cinematic exhibition environment.

Interestingly, this was not the case for the cinematic direction, which subjects praised for providing an optimal vantage point on the action. However, this was still a case of transmission rather than reinterpretation:

> In terms of what [the simulcast] brings differently from the live experience, I guess it *doesn't* really. I mean, at the end of the day it's the same service or product. At the core you have the same plot and you have the same actors, just filmed from different perspective. [subject's emphasis]

Like the Awed Initiates, these subjects were sensitive to opera's 'elitism', which came across very strongly in focus group discussions. However, unlike the Awed Initiates, these subjects regarded opera cinema as a form of cultural evangelism, that would serve to educate the public in high culture: 'It becomes more affordable for the masses.' This has been the motive behind screen opera since at least the 1940s. Early advocates of television opera, such as director of productions at the Met, Herbert Graf, hoped home media could be used to elevate public tastes, and introduce 'the masses' to opera.[79] Peter Gelb hoped that *Live from the Met* would do the same.[80] For now, that ambition has not been realized – opera cinema mostly caters to an even-older cross section of the existing opera audience rather than recruiting newcomers. However, the fact that my novice respondents picked up simulcasting's capacity to bring opera 'to the masses' further highlights that the primary value of opera cinema is as a mode of audience outreach – not as a separate art form. Gelb's comments remind us that this was probably always the idea. In any event, these subjects clearly regarded opera cinema as superior to 'normal' cinema – a fact reflected in both the Q Methodology results and qualitative data sets.

A smaller (but still significant) number of comments were directed towards the formal elitism of opera itself. Jen was the only respondent from Curious Traditionalists who did not watch the simulcast of *Lucia di Lammermoor*, instead attending the screening of *Boris Godunov*. Like Trisha, she approached the project with trepidation, but unlike Trisha (and most other subjects) her scepticism was not overturned. She admitted to finding the sung-through performance 'difficult', although she singled out the costuming and Bryn Terfel's singing for special praise. However, despite having completed a Russian O-level and voicing approval at the presence of insight films to help penetrate the drama, she also found the foreign-language performance challenging. I noted in the qualitative data Jen logged during the Q-sorting phase that she regularly attended dramatic theatre, which I assumed would put her at ease with opera. In fact, she was rather critical of the pomp and circumstance involved in the performance. In sum, opera cinema was only partially effective in mitigating the social alienation associated with opera. While respondents felt more at ease in the cinema than Covent Garden (on average), they were still conscious of the demographic composition of the auditorium crowd.

The Opera Cinema Sceptics

This small factor of subjects (five out of forty-one) was generally hostile towards the cinema simulcast. Furthermore, only one of these subjects attended a focus group, furnishing me with a very limited data set. As a result, any conclusions must be tentatively put and speculative. Furthermore, I was faced with the same problem as the Opera Cinephiles in that the data are sparse enough that it is unclear whether these subjects simply disliked opera altogether. I was not able to conduct an interview with an Opera Cinema Sceptic, and testimonial data are scant. Insofar as I can make an overall assessment from these data, I believe this factor viewed simulcasting as a very distant second to physical auditorium attendance: more a last resort than next-best-thing.

The Opera Cinema Sceptics' highest-scoring item ('It's like watching a football match on telly as opposed to going to the stadium') equates with the negative correlation between mediation and emotional engagement articulated by the New Purists. Furthermore, the second-highest-scoring item ('For me it just didn't feel like it was live. For me it just felt like going to a regular cinema') implies a particular interpretation of liveness as *only* meaning physical co-presence. O'Neill, Edelman and Sloboda also found – when comparing responses to stage and remediated opera – that 'physical co-presence was a more important aspect of liveness than simultaneity'.[81] However, other factors subjects and subjects presented different definitions of liveness, encompassing simultaneity, physical co-presence and a sense of belonging to a 'live', virtual audience. Although the Opera Cinema Sceptics expressed a binary view of liveness, my dataset collectively implies a sliding scale, with the simulcast deemed 'more live' than recorded cinema by most of my subjects – but less so than the stage. Matthew Reason arrives at a similar conclusion, arguing that there are gradations of liveness based on audience interpretation of multitude of cultural experiences that profess their liveness under the digital epoch.[82]

The same but different

A small-scale research project of this kind can offer only a modest impression of the experiential dimension of live opera at the movies. However, the feedback from my opera virgins offers a snapshot of a unique – and developing – cultural experience, and it hopefully does so without many of the biases that colour the impressions of experienced opera audiences. Opera cinema inspired a range of responses; evidence of its hybrid character but also of its nascent state. The range of my subjects' opinions and engagement strategies shows that opera cinema's protocols, and its position in the broader cultural field, are only just beginning to settle. Some subjects dressed for the occasion, others made no special effort. Some thought simulcasting was a more valuable experience than recorded cinema, others felt they were on par. Some had their appetites for opera whetted, others made it clear that opera – on or off the stage – is not for them.

In general, my respondents regarded opera cinema as a lesser experience than staged opera – ancillary rather than a discrete art form. Nevertheless, they mostly claimed to have enjoyed the experience, and a minority were inspired with a genuine love of opera. Moreover, my respondents identified unique formal and experiential features of the simulcast that offered specific advantages for newcomers. These include the greater legibility of dramatic action (facilitated by the visual language of cinema), the convenience and comfort provided by the cinema as an exhibition context, a sense of globalized collective engagement in a virtually networked audience, and the educational value of the recorded documentaries on the simulcast programme.

Many of my novice respondents associated opera cinema with a broader project of audience democratization, despite its limited effect in this regard. I conclude that opera cinema's inability to accrue new audiences has more to do with opera's enduring reputation as an elite, esoteric art form than the merits of the hybrid experience itself. This elite status was not roundly perceived as detrimental: many subjects attained personal satisfaction at having their personal acculturation confirmed by their capacity to 'appreciate' the simulcast, in a context of reduced social threat. Furthermore, most subjects identified experimental elements of opera cinema that were culturally valuable in their own terms. Finally, respondents described the simulcast as fostering greater accessibility on a financial, physical, social and intellectual level. These data which further confirm opera cinema's subordinate status to stage opera, but are nevertheless instructive for theorizing its ontology. At present, I describe opera cinema as a cultural experience rather than a medium. Instead, it is a unique, hybrid phenomenon that has yet to retain sufficient, social recognition as an art form with attendant protocols ingrained and performed instinctually by audiences.

Notes

1. Sarah Atkinson, *Beyond the Screen: Emerging Cinema and Engaging Audiences* (London: Bloomsbury, 2014), 5.
2. Charles H. Davis, 'Q Methodology in Audience Research: Bridging the Qualitative/Quantitative "Divide"?', *Participations* 8.2 (2011): 561.
3. Ibid., 562.
4. David Smith, 'Hidden Faultline: How Trump v Clinton Is Laying Bare America's Class Divide', *Guardian*, 2 October 2016, accessed 8 October 2016, https://www.theguardian.com/us-news/2016/oct/02/trump-clinton-election-class-socioeconomic-divide.
5. Florin Vladica, 'Value Propositions of Opera and Theater Live in Cinema', from monograph collection of papers presented at World Media Economics & Management Conference (Thessaloniki, Greece, 23–7 May 2012), 4.
6. Ibid., 4.
7. Ibid., 4.
8. Davis, 562.
9. Ibid., 563.
10. Ibid., 560–1.
11. Sinéad O'Neill, Joshua Edelman and John Sloboda, 'Opera and Emotion: The Cultural Value of Attendance for the Highly Engaged', *Participations* 13.1 (2016): 24–50.
12. Rupert Christiansen, 'Mahagonny: The Opera that Hitler Hated', *Telegraph*, 10 March 2015, accessed 8 November 2017, http://www.telegraph.co.uk/culture/music/opera/11460804/Mahagonny-the-opera-that-Hitler-hated.html.
13. Ibid.

14 Amanda Fallows, 'Royal Opera House Cinema Research,', Royal Opera House research data, October 2014.
15 Vladica, 4.
16 Carolyn Abbate and Roger Parker, *A History of Opera: The Last Four Hundred Years* (London: Penguin Group, 2012).
17 Jennifer Radbourne, Hilary Glow and Katya Johnson, 'Hidden Stories: Listening to the Audience at the Live Performance', *Double Dialogues* 13 (2010).
18 Sameer Rahim, 'The Opera Novice', *Telegraph*, 26 January 2012, accessed 20 Jun 2015, http://www.telegraph.co.uk/culture/music/opera/9036780/The-opera-novice.html.
19 Martin Barker, *Live to Your Local Cinema: The Remarkable Rise of Livecasting* (Basingstoke: Palgrave Macmillan, 2013).
20 'Exploring the Market for Live to Digital Arts', *MTM* (March 2015): 31.
21 Demographic Profile of Welwyn Hatfield, *Policy and Communication* (2016), accessed 8 October 2021, http://www.welhat.gov.uk/CHttpHandler.ashx?id=9345&p=0.
22 Ibid.
23 Hatfield's Population, *Hatfield Town Council Website*, 29 July 2013, accessed 8 October 2016, http://www.hatfield-herts.gov.uk/hatfields-population/.
24 'Demographic Profile of Welwyn Hatfield'.
25 'Facts and Figures about Herefordshire', *Gov.uk*, accessed 8 October 2016, https://factsandfigures.herefordshire.gov.uk/about-a-topic/population-and-demographics.
26 'Facts and Figures about Herefordshire'.
27 Ibid.
28 'About Us', *CW Entertainment*, accessed 7 June 2018, https://tickets.cwentertainment.co.uk/screenloader.aspx?page=usercontent/documents/aboutus.html&type=include.
29 'Richard Booth's Bookshop Cinema', *Richard Booth's Bookshop*, accessed 7 June 2018, https://tickets.boothbooks.co.uk/m-1-cinema.aspx.
30 Chester S. L. Dunning, *Russia's First Civil War: The Time of Troubles and the Founding of the Romanov Dynasty* (Pennsylvania: Pennsylvania State University Press, 2001), 471.
31 K. L. Verosub and J. Lippman, 'Global Impacts of the 1600 Eruption of Peru's Huaynaputina Volcano', *Eos, Transactions American Geophysical Union* 89.15 (2008): 141.
32 Richard Taruskin, *Musorgsky: Eight Essays and an Epilogue* (Princeton, NJ: Princeton University Press, 1993), 250–1.
33 Herbert Weinstock, *Donizetti and the World of Opera in Italy, Paris and Vienna in the First Half of the Nineteenth Century* (New York: Random House, 1963), 256–71.

34 James P. Cassaro, *Gaetano Donizetti: A Research and Information Guide* (New York: Routledge, 2000), 70.
35 William Ashbrook, *Donizetti and His Operas* (London: Cambridge University Press, 1982), 375.
36 Staff and agencies, 'William Tell: Nudity and Rape Scene Greeted with Boos at Royal Opera House', *Guardian*, 30 June 2015, accessed 8 October 2016, https://www.theguardian.com/music/2015/jun/30/william-tell-nudity-and-scene-greeted-with-boos-at-royal-opera-house.
37 Ottilie Thornhill, 'Watch: Katie Mitchell on Lucia di Lammermoor "My Focus Is 100% on the Female Characters"', *Royal Opera House Website*, 11 March 2016, accessed 8 October 2016, http://www.roh.org.uk/news/watch-katie-mitchell-on-lucia-di-lammermoor-my-focus-is-100-on-the-female-characters.
38 Fiona Maddocks, 'Lucia di Lammermoor Review – Flawed but Full of Provocative Thought', *Observer*, 10 April 2016, accessed 8 October 2016, https://www.theguardian.com/music/2016/apr/10/lucia-di-lammermoor-review-royal-opera-katie-mitchell-diana-damrau.
39 Olivia Turnbull, *Bringing Down the House: The Crisis in Britain's Regional Theatres* (Bristol: Intellect Books, 2008), 48.
40 'About Us', *Courtyard Arts*, accessed 7 June 2018, https://www.courtyardarts.org.uk/about-us/.
41 Peter Eversmann, Brent Karpf Reidy, Becky Shutt, Deborah Abramson, Antoni Durski and Laura Castle, 'From Live-to-Digital', AEA Consulting for Arts Council England and Society of London Theatre, October 2016; John Holmes, 'Opera in Cinemas – Audiences Outside London', *English Touring Opera*, 2014; Hasan Bakhshi, Juan Mateos-Garcia and David Throsby, 'Beyond Live: Digital Innovation in the Performing Arts' (London: NESTA [National Endowment for Science, Technology and the Arts], research briefing, 2010).
42 Karl Marx, *The German Ideology*,Marxist Internet Archive, accessed 1 April 2018, https://www.marxists.org/archive/marx/works/1845/german-ideology/ch01b.htm.
43 Pierre Bourdieu, *Distinction* (London: Routledge, 1984), 1–2.
44 Daniel Snowman, *The Gilded Stage: A Social History of Opera* (London: Atlantic Books, 2009), 398–409.
45 Barker, *Remarkable Rise of Livecasting*, 36.
46 'Stratford and New Town Demographics (Newham, England)', *QPZM Localstats*, accessed 12 May 2018, http://stratford-and-new-town.localstats.co.uk/census-demographics/england/london/newham/stratford-and-new-town.
47 Amanda Fallows, 'Royal Opera House Cinema Research', Royal Opera House research data, October 2014; Karpf Reidy, et al. ; John Holmes.
48 Raymond Williams, *Television: Technology and Cultural Form* (London: Collins, 1974).
49 E.g. Karen Wise, 'Opera in Cinemas', report for ETO and Guildhall School of Music & Drama (London, 2013).

50 Ibid.
51 Tom Service, 'Opera in Cinemas: Is It Creating New Audiences?', *Guardian*, 30 May 2014, https://www.theguardian.com/music/tomserviceblog/2014/may/30/opera-in-cinemas-creating-new-audiences.
52 Lisa Gitelman, *Always Already New: Media, History and the Data of Culture* (Cambridge, MA: MIT Press, 2006), 6.
53 Richard Taruskin, *Musorgsky: Eight Essays and an Epilogue* (Princeton, NJ: Princeton University Press, 1993), 250–1.
54 Vladica.
55 Gumbrecht, xiii–iv.
56 Ibid.
57 Martin Barker, 'CRASH, Theatre, Audiences, and the Idea of "Liveness"', *Studies in Theatre and Performance* 23.1 (2003).
58 Erika Fischer-Lichte, *Ästhetik des Performativen*, edition suhrkamp (Frankfurt am Main: Suhrkamp Verlag, 2004).
59 Jeremy Tambling, *Opera, Ideology, and Film* (London: Palgrave McMillan, 1987), 108.
60 Wise, 19.
61 Matt Hills, *Fan Cultures* (London: Routledge, 2002), 110.
62 Peggy Phelan, *Unmarked: The Politics of Performance* (London: Routledge, 1993); Erika Fischer-Lichte, *The Transformative Power of Performance: A New Aesthetics* (London: Routledge, 2008).
63 Barker, *The Remarkable Rise of Livecasting*, 3.
64 Ibid., 14.
65 Pierre Bourdieu, *Distinction: A Social Critique of the Judgement of Taste*, translated by Richard Nice (Massachusetts: Harvard University Press Cambridge, 1996), 1–2.
66 Benzecry.
67 Sinéad O'Neill, Joshua Edelman and John Sloboda, 'Opera and Emotion: The Cultural Value of Attendance for the Highly Engaged', *Participations* 13.1 (2016): 34.
68 Ibid., 37.
69 Barker, 'CRASH', 37–8.
70 Emanuele Senici, 'Porn Style? Space and Time in Live Opera Videos', *Opera Quarterly* 26.1 (2010): 68.
71 Benzecry, 93.
72 James Steichen, 'HD Opera: A Love/Hate Story Staging the Backstage at Carmen, Live in HD', *Opera Quarterly* 27.4 (2011): 447.
73 Sinéad O'Neill, Joshua Edelman and John Sloboda, 37.

74 Daniel J. Walken, 'The Met Will Lower Ticket Prices', *New York Times*, 26 February 2013, accessed 13 June 2021, https://www.nytimes.com/2013/02/27/arts/music/metropolitan-opera-to-reduce-ticket-prices-next-season.html.
75 Martin Barker, 'I Have Seen the Future and It Is Not Here Yet; or, On Being Ambitious for Audience Research', *Communication Review* 9 (2006): 9.
76 Gitelman, 7.
77 Philip Kennicott, 'Tchaikovsky Goes to the Cineplex', *Washington Post*, 24 February 2007, http://www.washingtonpost.com/wp-dyn/content/article/2007/02/23/AR2007022301846.html.
78 Barker, *The Remarkable Rise of Livecasting*, 24.
79 Citron, *Opera on Screen*, 41–2.
80 Barker, *The Remarkable Rise of Livecasting*, 2.
81 O'Neill, Edelman and Sloboda, 37.
82 Matthew Reason, 'Theatre Audiences and Perceptions of "Liveness" in Performance', *Participations* 1.2 (2004), accessed 22 January 2022, http://www.participations.org/volume%201/issue%202/1_02_reason_article.htm.

5

A night at the opera cinema?

This book has sought to determine the ontological character of opera cinema. I contend that ontology is not simply a matter of analysing technological apparatuses. It must encompass contextual information about a medium's historical development, its social conditions and the kind of experience it facilitates. Opera cinema is still a nascent entity. The small corpus of historiographies and theoretical treatments that exist tend to lump it together with other forms of event cinema. However, opera has unique formal aspects and its own history, as well as a demographically peculiar[1] and extremely dedicated audience.[2] It facilitates a very different type of experience compared to – for example – spoken-word theatre or sporting events, which are also transmitted to cinemas using the same technology. As such, opera simulcasting must be researched as a discrete phenomenon. Furthermore, opera cinema is still treated with hostility and suspicion from some quarters due to its presumed (but unproven) deleterious effect over the operatic ecology, and the belief that it somehow cheapens the art form.[3] Similar charges have been directed to television opera in the past,[4] as well as the introduction of surtitling.[5] These anxieties have undermined objective analysis of opera cinema. There is also a severe lack of qualitative data on the kind of experience opera cinema facilitates. That which does exist focuses exclusively on experienced attendees,[6] which means it tells us less about how opera cinema is different and more of how it is *inferior* to the stage (Martin Barker's research being a notable exception).[7] The book has sought to address some of these gaps in the field.

I have also used opera cinema as a case study for interrogating broader questions around media ontology. The main research questions were: What is opera cinema? Is it a medium? And what does it mean – today – to be a medium? In every epoch (and particularly following digitization), a multitude of media phenomena, attractions and distractions compete for audiences' attention. I contend that a medium must be acknowledged as such by audiences, who associate them with particular formal characteristics and enact viewing strategies that are collectively established at a societal level, before they can attain this status. By this measure – despite catering to an audience of millions and representing the most successful convergence of opera and cinema to date (at least in terms of viewing figures)[8] – I suggest that opera cinema is not a new medium. Aside from the central inquiry, the book argues that media studies must place greater emphasis on audience experience, because digitization means that media content is no longer tied to specific delivery systems. As such, ontologies based on technological apparatus alone are increasingly deficient. The chapter offers an executive summary of my conclusions, explaining how they contribute to a broader field of knowledge, and suggesting avenues for future researchers, whom I hope will continue to interrogate this fascinating phenomenon, and factor and social/historical context audience experience into media ontologies.

History, technology and audience

The book posed the following key inquiries: How is opera cinema distinct from stage opera? Is it a new medium – or does it have the potential to become one? What kind of subjective activity is involved in engaging with a new cultural experience? What sort of viewing practices do new audiences bring to opera cinema? And what insight do these novice respondents offer for theoretical debates on media ontology, digitization, new media and liveness? To answer these questions, I performed three separate interventions. Firstly, I established a historiographical lineage, running from radio broadcasts of opera in the early 1900s, through television opera in the post-war period, to contemporary simulcasting. Inspired by the New Film History,[9] I have sought to illustrate that the emergence of opera cinema – rather than an isolated process – involved many interrelated media experiences and technologies, all contributing to a shared history. This history was shaped by external economic and political pressures. Separate historiographies already exist for opera cinema's forebears, but by illustrating the connection between these phenomena and situating them in a political and economic context, I demonstrated the objective factors that contributed to the development of opera cinema's formal characteristics. Without this historical materialist conception, the technological and aesthetic dimensions of media ontology are simply arbitrary.

I argue that modern event cinema has fulfilled a longstanding, institutional objective to bring live content to the cinema – evident from at least the 1920s. Earlier attempts failed due to technological limitations.[10] Meanwhile, the aesthetic characteristics of remediated opera reflect underlying economic forces. During the post-war consensus, television opera in particular was driven by a paternalistic drive to 'bring opera to the masses'[11] and ambitions to transform the medium with daring, formal experimentation.[12] Privatization of arts funding from the late-1970s onwards, coupled with technological developments, meant brand promotion became the main objective of operatic remediation, alongside providing established audiences with a 'virtual ticket' to the opera house.[13] This resulted in the live television relay (characterized by limited artistic reinterpretation of the source performance, and celebration of the opera house) emerging as the dominant form of remediated opera.[14] These relays provided the visual blueprint for modern opera cinema. Simulcasting is also closely linked to justification of state expenditure by demonstrating opera companies' commitment to 'digital innovation'.[15] Opera cinema's formal conservatism and its idealized simulacrum of national opera houses is no accident - it is the culmination of a historical process. Therefore, in contrast to the McLuhanite, formalist view of media ontology preceding society,[16] the development of opera cinema was motivated by the forces of political economy.

My second intervention is based on a theoretical analysis of the distinctive formal and aesthetic qualities of opera cinema. I posit that, although ontology cannot be solely derived from a medium's apparatus, there are nevertheless unique technical and formal aspects of opera cinema that demonstrate its status as a new cultural experience. Even where these unique elements provoke a negative reaction, they are still evidence of formal specificity. For instance, the likes of Alexander Coghlan, James Steichen and others[17] contend that that opera cinema's 'double-directed' screen action results in a dumbed-down, emotionally stunted experience that forced them to accept the director's preferred reading of the dramaturgy. However, at least some audience members consider the cinematic vocabulary more intellectually stimulating than stage drama alone, because it clarifies the action and illustrates thematic subtext. And in any event, it is undoubtedly a distinctive hybrid of various media experiences, which has evolved to provide the most seamless possible 'reportage' (rather than reinterpretation) of the stage action whose lineage is distinctly televisual. Opera cinema also challenges existing academic models of liveness from the likes of Ulrich Gumbrecht, based on a strict binary of live/mediated or present/absent.[18] Aside from the general blurring of lines between 'live' and 'mediatised' phenomena presented by digitization, opera cinema's hypermediacy (combining multiple media into a single frame) exists as part of a general trend towards hybridity and convergence in contemporary media, with interesting effects and institutional motivations behind them. The tweets praising the performance flooding in from around the world during the event are evidence of the Royal Opera House's privileged position in the global cultural sector, and visibility to an international audience, in addition to the 'local' connection between the cinema attendees and the auditorium crowd depicted on screen.

Despite these unique formal elements, it is clear that opera cinema is constructed and received as an alternative to stage opera. This is written into the formal characteristics of simulcasting, which constitute an effect that Steichen describes as 'institutional dramaturgy'.[19] These include shots of the auditorium interior, footage of the Covent Garden audience filing in, sounds of the orchestra tuning up and so on. The idea is to create an idealized sense of virtual attendance: a night at the opera from one's cinema seat. Due to a combination of historical development, commercial and political pressures opera cinema's present, primary objectives are to advertise the opera house and provide a dispersed, experienced audience with a virtual simulation of a familiar experience. Moreover, in the same way that simulcasting hybridizes and remediates formal and technical characteristics from a range of other media, it also adopts behavioural protocols from other sources. The variability of attitudes and behaviours on the part of its audience is further evidence that opera cinema is not yet a medium, because it has not acquired a stable viewing strategy. However, there is evidence to indicate that it *could* develop hybrid strategies, combining conventions learned from the cinema and imparted by stage opera.

My third intervention involved an audience research project, in which I invited sixty-one opera virgins to experience the art form for the very first time (mostly in the cinema). Data from this (relatively) naive population permits us to understand the kind of experience opera cinema facilitates without the kind of bias one would expect from existing simulcast audiences – who tend to be veteran operagoers. By employing a combination of Q Methodology, which divided my subjects into factors (groups with comparable attitudes) and focus groups, I illustrated clusters of experience within my sample. This permitted some initial insights about opera cinema. Firstly, it was clear that the majority of my respondents did not consider it a new art form. Furthermore, they mostly saw it as inferior to stage opera. However, they confirmed a number of formal and experiential characteristics that were unique to opera cinema – and of specific benefit to newcomers – such as the greater legibility of stage action fostered by the cinematic narration, for example. Moreover, my novice subjects did not approach opera cinema as though from an echo chamber. Instead, they drew on familiar cultural experiences to structure and make sense of simulcasting, revealing the interpretive work involved in encountering and making sense of a new cultural experience.

My subjects displayed a range of attitudes to concepts like liveness: for some, opera cinema is truly live, for others it was 'not live' and for some it was 'more live' than a recording but 'less live' than stage performance. Despite Barker's assertion that the possibility of live performance to fail is of limited importance to audiences,[20] for a cross-section of attendees, the threat of catastrophe was a key source of appeal. Furthermore, the effect of institutional dramaturgy was not perfect. Many of my subjects experienced cognitive dissonance resulting from the disconnect between the images on-screen and their surroundings. The presence of the cinema 'dragged them back to reality'. This emphasizes the double-edge of institutional dramaturgy – permitting virtual access to the live performance, while emphasizing the exclusivity of the 'real thing'. The chapter also dealt with subjects' attitude towards opera's elitism. In contrast to more utopian new media narratives that focus on the cultural levelling of digitization by the likes of Norman Taylor, for example,[21] my subjects clearly regarded opera as an elite art form even in its digital incarnation. They also reported that opera cinema audiences were primarily comprised of mature, experienced attendees (aligning with Barker's characterization).[22] For some, opera's perceived elitism was alienating, but it was embraced by others as simply 'part of the experience'. In some cases, opera's grandeur and elite reputation was seen as central to its appeal. In any event, subjects felt the simulcast merely transmitted opera's cultural value to a new context – at best leaving it unchanged and at worst detracting from it.

While in the main subjects described opera cinema as feeling more-or-less like going to the cinema (and thus more casual and relaxed than theatre attendance), they identified several 'theatrical' dimensions of the experience. Some were enforced on the institutional side, either owing to the technical requirements of opera cinema (the fixed, one-off performance, the inclusion of intervals and so on) or to deliberately create a facsimile of opera attendance (by providing programmes and discouraging departure during the performance). On the audience side, protocols showed a great deal of variation. Some subjects clapped, some did not – and others applauded hesitantly, following the example of fellow attendees. A handful of my respondents ritualistically dressed for the occasion – consciously enhancing the experience – while others made no special effort. Many subjects commented on the appearance and behaviour of the existing audience – who were generally identified as mature and knowledgeable operagoers. While a cross-section of (particularly younger) subjects felt intimidated and alienated by this crowd, others praised the opera cinema audience as respectful, 'grown-up' and cultured. Again, this variety of viewing strategies suggests (within the limits of my small group of subjects) the range of possibilities and directions that opera cinema could develop. These audience data inform the historical and technological arguments that proceed them, ensuring that the ontology of opera cinema presented here does not fall back on abstract schema, but takes audience experience into account.

Significance

Aside from issues directly pertinent to opera cinema (discussed in the next section), the book has also touched on more general questions for media scholarship. It proposes a new framework for ontology, inspired in part by Lisa Gitelman's definition of media as both technological apparatuses and socially realized structures of communication - 'protocols'.[23] By contrast, classical, technologically determinist schools of ontology (McLuhanite and Bazinian, for instance) determine media specificity based on the technological characteristics of different apparatuses. In so doing, they also treat media as abstract frameworks without demonstrating concretely how they are used and experienced. As Raymond Williams pointed out in the 1970s, 'the initial appeal of McLuhan's work was his apparent attention to the specificity of media: the differences in quality between speech, print, radio, television and so on' but the limitation of this formalist tradition was its failure to see media as both technologies and social practices.[24] To understand medium specificity, it is necessary to investigate how media phenomena are used differently by audiences, and embedded in everyday life. The question of audience also cannot be rendered in the abstract - audiences are not monolithic, and adopt negotiated viewing strategies to structure their media engagement, as Martin Barker argues, with regards to film.[25]

Even within a small sample, my research subjects expressed a variety of complex attitudes and behaviours about opera cinema - imported from wider cultural attitudes and formations - that could never have been anticipated by theoretical models alone. I argue that such data - which depict media use as a 'motivated activity' - can be put in service of ontology, because media are *both* technologies and their associated practices. I urge future researchers to apply this ontological framework to all media phenomena, even those that are well-established, but *especially* those that are new. For the latter, we have to get in on the ground floor, as it were, and theorize how audiences make sense of new cultural experiences, in order to equip ourselves with robust theoretical models for understanding them.

The experiential dimension of media use is especially significant given the effect of digitization, which has seen media forms increasingly divorced from specific delivery systems. For instance, what does it mean to watch a film in an era where 'films have become files'[26] - more often consumed on tablets than in a 'traditional', cinematic exhibition context? Furthermore, digitization has dissolved tangible, technological barriers between different forms of media phenomena - resulting in more and more hybridity and cross-pollination between them. If we can no longer rely on technology to define medium specificity, then the media academe must increasingly depend on the distinctive experience that media facilitate. Without this experiential perspective, opera cinema is nothing but a digital transmission of a live performance - my data hopefully demonstrate it is far more than that. Some might identify a danger in connecting audience experience to ontology. Experience is subjective and liable to change - whereas ontology implies an objective, concrete understanding of a medium's characteristics. However, the emphasis on audience also takes account of the fact that media are themselves subject to change. As Sarah Atkinson points out: 'Cinema is and always has been in a perpetual state of becoming. Cinema as a concept, construct and social activity is in need of constant revision, as are its frameworks for understanding, analysis and study.'[27] This same logic applies to all forms of media. By focusing on audience experience, we obtain a concrete measure of the way media change, diverge, combine and transform over time. Digitization has not negated the technological aspect of media - apparatus remains a central aspect of ontology - but it should encourage media theorists to take better account of its social and experiential dimensions.

Digitization has also resulted in a proliferation of media 'attractions',[28] which might be discrete experiences but are not necessarily true art forms. Just as cinema underwent a transitional period, in which it existed alongside and competed with a range of moving-image phenomena (many of which died out),[29] the current mediascape is replete with digital novelties that are unlikely to be widely embraced and endure as media in their own right - it is possible that opera cinema will be one of these. In order to establish a clearer framework for demarcating between attractions, experiences, novelties and media, I contend that a medium must be acknowledged as such by audiences. I have demonstrated that opera cinema is not regarded as a medium but is instead seen by audiences (both expert and novice) as an ancillary to stage opera. This is evident in a lack of a stable viewing register and scepticism about its independent, aesthetic validity relative to stage opera. Opera cinema's formal characteristics (as a relatively unobtrusive remediation of stage performance) dialectically reflect this ancillary role. When investigating the new multitude of digital attractions, it is important for media researchers to begin from the premise that medium status is bestowed and confirmed by the audience – it cannot be imposed on them from without.

My objections about abstract, theoretical schema also extend to theorizations of liveness. Researchers like Barker[30] and Matthew Reason have made significant progress by investigating live media through audience research.[31] This research demonstrates that liveness is a complex phenomenon - especially in the present content, with networked and simultaneous media communication so ubiquitous. My data also imply a range of interpretations of liveness, which cannot be reduced to either an essential, ontological feature of certain media like television or stage performance, or strictly a question of physical co-presence. This variability is only visible at the level of audience experience. Moreover - despite exemplifying the new media tropes of hybridity, virtual experience and networked communication - opera cinema also leverages the cult appeal of 'old media' in the form of a one-off, time-limited theatrical experience.[32] Subjects perceived opera cinema as an event - a 'special occasion' - and even those who were critical of the simulcast - or did not regard it as live - attributed value to this aspect of simulcasting. These data undercut both Peggy Phelan and Phillip Auslander's theorizations of liveness. Rather than a progressive act of resistance to the machinery of capitalist production,[33] the appeal of the live event is predicated on exclusivity. And rather than mediated experiences replacing the live,[34] opera cinema reasserts the cult value of live performance. Instead of placing live and 'mediatised' phenomena in opposition, it would be productive to explore the way in which new media experiences are troubling the conceptual boundaries of live events. The rise of live and event cinema, for example,[35] shows that – far from displacing live experience – digital media experiences are foregrounding liveness in new ways. As Barbara Klinger points out, these phenomena also draw attention to the fact that liveness has always been a part of the cinematic experience - despite the fact that 'recorded' cinema is often presented as the ontological other 'live' theatre and television - which further underscores the limitations of restricting liveness to certain media:

> At the very least, each film screening in movie theatres, film festivals, the home, or other locales is a distinct performative event. As such, it involves different audiences, conditions of viewing and levels of interactivity, while drawing on our senses, including eating, drinking, conversation, physical comfort or discomfort and other variables that might appear to be banal, but are nonetheless among requisite features of cinematic experience. Although cinema as an apparatus – camera, projector, screen, theatre – is not live, to capture its full specificity as a medium we thus need to enlarge our conception of media to include such considerations.[36]

Finally, it is important to stress that media ontology cannot be restricted to audience experience *in isolation* – any more than it is reducible to technology. My objective across this book has been to synthesize audience experience with social and historical context. I have sought to demonstrate – through an archaeological method – that opera cinema developed out of a complex and interlocking series of attractions, experiences and technologies. This process was underpinned and (complexly) directed by the forces of political economy. In different historical periods, similar economic and political conditions have motivated the emergence of new forms of remediated opera – such as in the 1940s, when declining ticket sales and ageing audiences at the Met led Herbert Graf to invest in television opera.[37] The end of the post-war consensus saw a creative retreat from reinterpretation to reportage, resulting in live television relays becoming the dominant form of screen opera.[38] More recently, opera cinema has helped to justify the Royal Opera House's obligations to the Arts Council in a period of massive cuts to arts funding.[39] The aesthetic and formal aspects of opera cinema are explicable with a historical materialist perspective. If opera cinema is aesthetically conservative and reaches for established audiences, it is because concrete historical and economic factors have made it so. Ontology is a product of history. Future researchers should therefore combine audience data with a historical materialist perspective, to determine how and why media phenomena take shape.

Questions for future researchers

The book opens several avenues for future research to opera cinema and associated phenomena. While opera cinema is certainly the most successful form of remediated opera in recent years, other forms exist - and deserve full theorization. For instance, Arts Council research on Live-to-Digital, domestic streaming suggests they cater to a vastly different demographic than opera simulcasting: younger, and more ethnically and socio-economically diverse.[40] It is arguable that these streaming services are more successful at democratizing opera than any other form of remediation. Meanwhile, there is no research on the big screen, outdoor relays, conducted by several major opera houses - including the Royal Opera House. This seems like a rather large oversight, given the potential points of comparison with the extensive corpus of research on public screen cultures,[41] and historical precedents like the drive-in.[42] There are also comparisons to be drawn between these public events and touring opera, Glyndebourne and the legendary Festival of Britain in 1951, which possibly represent the closest opera has approached to becoming a popular medium in the last century.[43] Anecdotally, these 'big screen' events seem to draw on average a far younger crowd: with a high number of families and young couples. A large-scale audience research project with robust demographic sampling could prove very enlightening. It is also notable that these events (among others) are sponsored and bear the name of British Petroleum - a company that has been at the centre of many ecological catastrophes and political scandals.[44] This kind of sponsorship demonstrates that arts companies are seeking to maximize sponsorship from the private sector, in turn reflecting diminished income from the state. These developments deserve academic scrutiny.

There are many aspects of opera cinema's ontology that could still be expanded with new data. For instance, subjects commented extensively on their feelings of immersion during the simulcast. This complex term did not have a single meaning across the sample, and variously related to a sense of being 'really there' at Covent Garden, subjects' emotional engagement with the performance and their perception of artistic authenticity/validity. Across these interpretations, subjects tended to draw comparisons between cinema and live performance, with the former associated with entertainment, populism and inauthenticity; and the latter with art, elitism and authenticity. This accords with Barker's belief that audiences at live theatre tend to affirm their appreciation for one medium by denigrating another.[45] Because of its hybrid status, subjects *generally* positioned opera cinema between cinema and live performance in terms of its cultural value and the sense of immersion it inspired. I say generally, because for some the simulcast actually *promoted* immersion. For example, they credited close-ups for forging a closer emotional relationship with the principal performers. However, my sample was unanimous in its disapproval for the remediated sound, which they regarded as a mere shadow of live music. Unfortunately, this important aspect of opera cinema remains undertheorized and receives only passing treatment in the book - it certainly deserves attention from future researchers.

While I discerned no obvious pattern in respondents' engagement based on the contextual factors of region and repertoire, a larger study - with a wider geographical spread, incorporating more case studies - might derive different insights. It would also be productive to investigate how attitudes and practices around remediated cinema change in different national contexts. Opera has always been a foreign art form in Great Britain.[46] In Continental Europe, opera is more integrated into public life. For instance, the Vienna State Opera follows a tradition of 'opera for all' – screening performances for free outside its walls on a large screen during the holiday periods, allowing members of the public to sit on Karajan-Platz and admire the cream of their nation's musical tradition in the open air.[47] It would be interesting to see if opera cinema (and other forms of remediated opera) are received differently in this national context. Meanwhile, there have been curious developments in countries where differences in time zones make evening screenings impossible without a significant tape-delay. In America, audiences have begun taking coffee and croissants to 'breakfast screenings' from the Royal Opera House.[48] These peculiarities deserve attention.

It is also important to compare opera cinema with other forms of event cinema. A lot more work remains to be done on differentiating between opera cinema, theatre cinema, sports cinema and so on. While separate research exists on simulcasts from the Met, Royal Opera House, Royal Ballet, National Theatre and Royal Shakespeare Company, there are no comparative analyses available of the respective experiences they facilitate. For instance, does the greater shot vocabulary afforded to the National Theatre by the cranes and dollies placed on stage during simulcasts result in a cultural experience that is further along the road to becoming a medium? Are these simulcasts having better luck than opera cinema at diversifying audiences for Shakespearian drama and ballet, for example - and if so, why is this? Certainly, theatre cinema eclipses opera cinema in terms of sheer box office revenue.[49] Secondarily, the book is heavily focused on the Royal Opera House - it would be useful to investigate the extent to which aesthetic strategies for simulcasting vary between opera companies, and the considerations that inform them.

I write at a time where the future of opera cinema is unresolved, and as such a critical lens must remain on simulcasting as it continues to mature. Will it develop a discrete viewing strategy? Will it achieve recognition and status as a cultural experience, or will it remain subordinate? During my research, a number of subjects commented that the split-screen staging of *Lucia di Lammermoor* uniquely complemented the filming process, permitting cuts between locations that would have been impossible for standard dramaturgy. I do not know if Katie Mitchell had this in mind, but *Lucia* nevertheless provided a rare glimpse of the true artistic potential of opera cinema as a genuine hybrid medium. Furthermore, former associate director of the Royal Opera House, John Fulljames, claimed at a conference at King's College London in 2017 that the opera company is striving for a closer creative partnership between the film and stage teams.[50] This would also be a step towards opera cinema developing into a true art form. Future research could perhaps employ institutional ethnography, focusing on the working relationship between film and stage crews to determine whether genuine collaboration is beginning to emerge.

The main problem for simulcasting is that opera was faced with an historical impasse, even before the coronavirus pandemic. The delicate balance of public and private support needed to sustain this extravagant art form is drying up rapidly, with a resultant impact on repertoire and audience development. That is not to say no new or experimental work is being produced - it certainly is. In the Royal Opera House alone, *Written on Skin*, *Anna Nicole* and *Cave* have demonstrated that there is space for new repertoire, which has pushed opera in fresh, new directions. This is not to mention radical work produced by smaller companies. However, the fact remains that the canon continues to dominate stages - and the smaller companies are suffering most of all. Moreover, new repertoire is rarely simulcast. Opera cinema is trapped by its need to support stage opera, which in turn is forced to fall back on the low-hanging fruit of experienced audiences, whom it cannot risk alienating with challenging or unfamiliar repertoire or dramaturgy - especially given the high up-front cost of simulcasting. The demands of opera performance also preclude the injections of star-power that have assisted simulcasts from the Royal Shakespeare Company and National Theatre. While popular actors like Chris Addison can take on a background role in *L'étoile*,[51] Benedict Cumberbatch cannot be reasonably expected to deliver *nessun dorma*. Furthermore, objections from established audiences rules out the additional apparatuses that allow for the greater shot vocabulary of NT Live - with cranes and tracks being out of the question.[52] For opera cinema to truly develop into a new medium it must accomplish two tasks: develop artistically, utilizing its unique advantages over the stage and develop an audience of its own that appreciates its unique characteristics on their own terms.

But of course, the biggest open question left by this book is what impact the Covid-19 pandemic, and the economic catastrophe it triggered, will exert on this fledgling media experience. When I started on my first draft in 2019, I had my entire year planned out in terms of the operas I intended to watch in the cinema. I wanted to get the best possible sense of how much opera cinema has changed and developed artistically since I began researching this subject back in 2014. By 2021, following various states of lockdown, I was unable to watch a single new production.

Cinema has been one of the most severely impacted industries by the pandemic. For the last year before I wrote these lines, streaming has definitively taken over simulcasting as the dominant form of operatic consumption. While I was writing this manuscript, the Royal Opera House released its first live event in eleven weeks, with a programme in June 2020 including performances by Louise Alder, Toby Spence and Gerald Finley, along with a world premiere of a work by choreographer Wayne McGregor. The first of these was made available for free, hosted by the BBC's Anita Rani and the Royal Opera House's director of music, Antonio Pappano. Two further concerts were offered live and on-demand for £4.99. Tony Hall, BBC director-general and former Royal Opera House executive, acknowledged the gravity of the situation: 'The pandemic has had a severe impact on the UK's creative industries, which prior to lockdown were worth £100bn per year. The BBC wants to do all it can to bring British creativity to the widest possible audience. We are working with cultural organizations and artists to make that happen.'[53] Opera was also prominently featured in the BBC's 'virtual festival of the arts: Culture in Quarantine', intended as a holdover while the entire sector convalesced. Other opera houses, including the Met, took similar measures: streaming performances for free, with a summer line up including works by Philip Glass, Verdi, Rossini and Gluck, most of which were recorded for cinematic release in the Met's Live in HD series and later repurposed.

Alongside their greater reliance on digital distribution, it raises the question of whether opera houses' priorities will shift away from the big screen towards an even greater multitude of small ones. The National Theatre has sought to move with the times by setting up its own streaming services for its plays, an innovation motivated by the need to close its doors during the pandemic. If this takes off, will opera follow suit and move emphasis away from cinema as a distribution channel? I was left with the haunting possibility that I am writing about a media phenomenon already approaching the verge of dormancy. Then again, it is perfectly possible that the relief of being allowed back through cinema doors will result in an immediate, post-pandemic boom for the movies that will see the big opera houses investing considerably in riding the wave. I was pleased to see the Royal Opera House announce the resumption of cinema shows in December 2021. It is possible (we hope) that things will settle back into something resembling normality. However things turn out, I hope that the approach to ontology I have outlined here will continue to prove valuable to researchers tackling this and any other nascent media experience to emerge in this brave new world. If the best should happen, and opera cinema not only survives, but thrives, then others will continue to chart its progress, as I genuinely believe it contains a huge amount of unrealized artistic promise.

The future of opera cinema

The book has demonstrated how opera cinema fits in broader debates around new media, digitization, ontology and cultural value. Opera cinema's ontology constitutes more than the act of pointing a camera at a stage and beaming the signal to cinemas. Media ontology in general must encompass social and experiential dimensions. In this case, we have a cultural experience that represents the culmination of a century-long evolutionary process, in which the objectives of remediated opera have transitioned from cultural uplift and artistic reinterpretation to brand promotion. As such, opera cinema's formal attributes strive towards creating an idealized simulation of opera house attendance. Partly for this reason, simulcasting is not regarded by audiences as a new medium, and I do not think it is appropriate to label it as such. It is perceived as (and remains) an ancillary product to stage opera. However, it possesses many unique formal and experiential elements - including double-directed stage action, multi-mediality, globally networked participation and hybridized behavioural protocols - that demarcate it as a new cultural experience. It is less than opera, and yet more than simply a transmission of opera. Whether it will be opera's salvation - as Gelb hoped in 2006 - is an open question.

When I began work on this book, I was firm in my opinion that opera cinema is not going away soon. However, it is clear from my and others' research that there is an appetite for opera amongst novices that is not translating into attendance at either the cinema or the opera house. There are many possible reasons for this. Possibly opera's elitist reputation and hesitance over foreign singing serve as a barrier to entry. It could be that opera companies could and should do more to reach out to newcomers by adapting to new media technologies and distribution/advertisement channels - some have begun to take the initiative.[54] One recent example of online marketing (from the Royal Opera House) that I particularly enjoyed involved several singers with different vocal ranges showing off their abilities in turn.[55] The video was shared on platforms like YouTube and Facebook. The superhuman feat of opera singing is surely sufficient to capture even the most distractible content-snacker. Regarding my project, some of my respondents commented explicitly that they simply did not know that such events existed. 'Particularly because it is a one-off experience it's very easy to miss', Samantha pointed out, 'unless you know it's happening.' It is possible that even prosaic adjustments, like advertising in a wider range of publications, would bring simulcasting to a wider cross-section of the public.

And now, with the artistic and cultural landscape changed so drastically, there is really no telling what form or direction opera cinema will take even in the very immediate future. In a sense, this book is a capstone on one period in the life of this fascinating media experience, which will now be forced to compete and adapt where, on the one hand, audiences are more comfortable with and aware than ever about digital consumption. But on the other hand, they are also more comfortable staying at home. This is not to mention the apocalyptic impact of the coronavirus pandemic on opera more generally, within thousands of artists, technicians and production personnel thrown onto the scrap heap, and dozens of houses are hanging by a thread. The situation is the same elsewhere. For instance, Opera Australia, which boasted an operating surplus in 2019, in 2020 announced an organizational restructure, which the industry union claimed could result in up to 25 per cent of permanent staff losing their jobs. These are undoubtably dark times, with the victims including performers, industry workers and opera-going public alike. But if there is one thing the history of opera teaches us, it is that this art form – which has survived wars, revolutions, technological and economic shifts, and all manner of chaos and calamities – always seems to find a way to make itself known, and to find new audiences. To adapt and survive.

In 2018, as a final experiment, I reached out to all the subjects who had taken part in focus groups to see if taking part in the project had affected their view on opera. For my pilot project participants, three years had elapsed since they lost their operatic virginities. I asked them three questions:

1. Have you watched any more operas since the project?
2. Have you been to any more like relays at the cinema?
3. Has your attitude to opera changed?

I received five replies. Of these, four subjects stated that their opinions on opera had improved, but admitted they had not seen another simulcast, nor visited an opera house. While this was, in one respect, a confirmation of my suspicion that opera cinema is a means of selling opera to the converted, rather than audience democratization, I was nevertheless a little disheartened. However, the fifth reply came from Jen: a 'Curious Traditionalist' whom I would characterized as one of the least-enthused focus group participants. She stated that, while she had not yet been to a stage performance, she had seen an 'Opera Up Close performance of *La Boheme* at Hertford Theatre', which she described as 'brilliant'. She subsequently watched a television relay of *La Boheme* from the Royal Opera House, which was also 'superb'. She concluded that her attitude had changed in that she was 'much more open to giving it a try now whereas before I almost certainly thought it would be of no interest to me'.

Intrigued, I asked if she would provide more information about the Opera Up Close event – as I had never heard of the company before. I quickly received a lengthy email, containing the following description:

> It was a modern version including laptops and mention of 'strong and stable' and Theresa May [referencing the much-mocked slogan of the Conservative Party's 2017 election campaign]! The first part was only 35 mins long and we all trooped out to the bar for our drinks. Then, what a surprise, the opera continued in the bar! It really was 'up close'! This did make me feel much more engaged with the characters and the humour of this part with Musetta and her male friend was very funny. When the second part started back in the theatre I felt that I was getting into the singing much more. I think I am getting more open to opera now and would love to see *Madame Butterfly* sometime, although last time it was performed near me the tickets were sold out in an instant!

If Jen's conversion is anything to go by, there are operaphiles-in-waiting out there. However, they have yet to be convinced by opera cinema in its current guise: an idealized, dreamlike version of a familiar art form, targeted at an experienced audience. Still, the short, experimental, immersive event described in June's email reveals that sceptics could be won around by doing away with the straightjacket of institutional dramaturgy, and being more playful and creative with the source text.

Media technologies have the capacity to transform opera in all manner of ways. In the past, technological remediation was seen as a new frontier for pushing opera's creative limits.[56] There have been daring experiments in recent years, but they remain on the fringes. For example, in 2014 – when I was just beginning my research – I attended a preliminary workshop for a new opera about climate change by British composer, Jonathan Dove, at King's College London.[57] The concept was to divide the cast and orchestra over three countries: the UK, Brazil and South Africa, each with a live audience, and all connected via a virtual network. The singers and instrumentalists would interact with the performers in the other two countries, who would appear on screens, resulting in a show that appeared to be situated in a single, large space, but was actually separated by thousands of miles and vast oceans. Responding to the shared, global threat of climate change, the opera specifically required three sets of performers to sing to one other, as well as three sets of audiences, across borders and continents. The score was written in the form of textures and 'pulses', to permit the performers to synchronize despite latency lag. This bold endeavour never saw the light of day – perhaps a victim of its own ambition – but it reveals the creative potential afforded by digital remediation.[58]

As far as opera cinema goes (which is relatively mainstream by comparison), it seems creativity is still being hampered by the bottom line. However, through *Lucia*, and other productions like the Met's daring simulcast of *The Exterminating Angel*, we get a sense of what opera cinema could be, of the fascinating artistic directions it could take, and the daring transformations of an historical art form it could produce. And if Jen's comments are anything to go by, there is no reason formal experimentation and opera evangelism should be mutually exclusive. Moreover, opera cinema reveals the expanded palette of experience available to contemporary audiences. By promoting hybridity and coalescences of 'old' and 'new' media phenomena, digital cultures challenge many existing frameworks for understanding art, culture and audience. We need intellectual models for coping with these new cultural experiences. What would it say about live performance, mediatization and audience if – for example – simulcasting develops into an art form in its own right, and we no longer speak of 'a night at the opera - at the cinema', but instead, 'a night at the opera cinema'?

Notes

1 Richard Schechner, *Public Domain* (Indianapolis, IN: Bobbs-Merill), 34.
2 Claudio E. Benzecry, *The Opera Fanatic: Ethnography of an Obsession* (Chicago: University of Chicago Press, 2011), 18.
3 Alexandra Coghlan, 'Why Arias in the Multiplex Fall Flat', *Independent*, 4 December 2012, accessed 12 May 2018, http://www.independent.co.uk/arts-entertainment/classical/features/why-arias-in-the-multiplex-fall-flat-8376 326.html.
4 Jennifer Barnes, 'Television Opera: A Non-History', in *A Night in at the Opera: Media Representations of Opera*, edited by Jeremy Tambling (London: Arts Council, 1994), 40–3.
5 Daniel Snowman, *The Gilded Stage: A Social History of Opera* (New York: Atlantic Books, 2009), 398–409.
6 John Holmes, 'Opera in Cinemas – Audiences Outside London', English Touring Opera, 2014; Hasan Bakhshi, Juan Mateos-Garcia and David Throsby, 'Beyond Live: Digital Innovation in the Performing Arts' (London: NESTA [National Endowment for Science, Technology and the Arts], research briefing, 2010).
7 Martin Barker, *Live to Your Local Cinema: The Remarkable Rise of Livecasting* (Basingstoke: Palgrave Macmillan, 2013).
8 Fiona Tuck, 'Understanding the Impact of Event Cinema: An Evidence Review', Arts Council England and British Film Institute, January 2016.
9 Robert C. Allen and Douglas Gomery, *Film History: Theory and Practice* (New York: McGraw Hill, 1985); Thomas Elsaesser, 'The New Film History as Media Archaeology', *Cinémas: Journal of Film Studies* 14.2–3 (2004): 75–117.
10 Douglas Gomery, 'Theatre Television: The Missing Link of Technological Change in the U.S. Motion Picture Industry', *Velvet Light Trap* 21 (1985): 120–1.

11 Marcia J. Citron, *Opera on Screen* (New Haven, CT: Yale University Press, 2000), 41–2.
12 Ibid., 47.
13 Ibid., 49.
14 Ibid., 47–9.
15 Bakhshi, Mateos-Garcia and Throsby, 211.
16 Marshall McLuhan, *Understanding Media: The Extensions of Man* (London: Ark Paperbacks, 1964), 7.
17 James Steichen, 'HD Opera: A Love/Hate Story Staging the Backstage at Carmen, Live in HD', *Opera Quarterly* 27.4 (2011): 447; Coghlan.
18 Hans Ulrich Gumbrecht, *Production of Presence: What Meaning Cannot Convey* (California: Stanford University Press, 2004), xiii–iv.
19 James Steichen, 'The Metropolitan Opera Goes Public: Peter Gelb and the Institutional Dramaturgy of the Met: Live in HD', *Music and the Moving Image* 2.2 (Summer 2009): 25.
20 Martin Barker, 'CRASH, Theatre, Audiences, and the Idea of "Liveness"', *Studies in Theatre and Performance* 23.1 (2003): 27–8.
21 Norman Taylor, *Cinematic Perspectives on Digital Culture: Consorting with the Machine* (London: Palgrave Macmillan, 2012), 14.
22 Barker, *Remarkable Rise of Livecasting*, 36.
23 Gitelman, 6.
24 Raymond Williams, *Television: Technology and Cultural Form* (London: Collins, 1974), 22.
25 Martin Barker, 'I Have Seen the Future and It Is Not Here Yet; or, On Being Ambitious for Audience Research', *Communication Review* 9 (2006): 9.
26 Sarah Atkinson, *Beyond the Screen: Emerging Cinema and Engaging Audiences* (London: Bloomsbury, 2014), 1–2.
27 Atkinson, 1.
28 Sarah Atkinson and Helen W. Kennedy, 'Introduction – Inside-the-Scenes: The rise of Experiential Cinema', *Participations* 13.1 (2016): 143.
29 Tom Gunning, 'The Cinema of Attraction[s]: Early Film, Its Spectator and the Avant-Garde', in *Early Cinema: Space, Frame, Narrative*, edited by Thomas Elsaesser (London: British Film Institute, 1990), 52.
30 Barker, 'CRASH', 28.
31 Matthew Reason, 'Theatre Audiences and Perceptions of "Liveness" in Performance', *Participations* 1.2 (2004), accessed 22 January 2022, http://www.participations.org/volume%201/issue%202/1_02_reason_article.htm.
32 Willmar Sauter, 'Introducing the Theatrical Event', in *Theatrical Events: Borders, Dynamics, Frames* (Amsterdam: Rodopi, 2004), 11.
33 Peggy Phelan, *Unmarked: The Politics of Performance* (London: Routledge, 1993), 146.

34 Philip Auslander, *Liveness: Performance in a Mediatized Culture* (London: Routledge, 2008), 9.
35 Atkinson and Kennedy, 142.
36 Barbara Klinger, 'Foreword', in *Live Cinema: Cultures, Economies, Aesthetics*, edited by Sarah Atkinson and Helen Kennedy (London: Bloomsbury, 2017), xv.
37 Marcia J. Citron, *Opera on Screen* (New Haven, CT: Yale University Press, 2000), 41–2.
38 Ibid., 47.
39 Bakhshi, Mateos-Garcia and Throsby, 205–12.
40 Brent Karpf Reidy, Becky Shutt, Deborah Abramson, Antoni Durski and Laura Castle, 'From Live-to-Digital', *AEA Consulting for Arts Council England and Society of London Theatre*, October 2016: 84.
41 Amelia Barikin, Nikos Papastergiadis, Scott McQuire and Audrey Yue, 'Screen Cultures and Public Spaces', *Dissect Journal* 1.1 (2013): 66–83.
42 Kerry Segrave, *Drive-in Theatres: A History from Their Inception in 1933* (Jefferson, NC: McFarland, 1993).
43 Andrew Sinclair, *Arts and Cultures: The History of the 50 Years of the Arts Council of Great Britain* (London: Sinclair-Steveson, 1995), 73–4.
44 Marl Brown, 'BP Sparks Campaigners' Fury with New Arts Sponsorship Deals', *Guardian*, 28 July 2016, accessed 5 June 2018, https://www.theguardian.com/business/2016/jul/28/bp-sponsorship-arts-organisations-british-museum-national-portrait-gallery.
45 Barker, 'CRASH', 34.
46 Paul Rodmell, *Opera in the British Isles, 1875–1918* (Routledge: London, 2013).
47 'Opera on the Square', *Vienna: Now Forever*, accessed 7 June 2018, https://events.wien.info/en/e0v/live-opera-on-the-square/.
48 Bondo Wyszpolski, 'New York Met Opera in Torrance AMC Theaters, 2017–18 Season', *Opera Musica*, 4 October 2017.
49 'Box Office Revenues from Event Cinema Screenings in the United Kingdom (UK) in 2017, By Type (in Million GBP)', *Statista*, accessed 7 June 2018, https://www.statista.com/statistics/589216/cinema-events-box-office-revenues-by-type-uk/.
50 'Opera Cinema: A New Cultural Experience?', Symposium at King's College London, 16 June 2017.
51 Nick Clark, '*The Thick of It* Actor Chris Addison to Star at the Royal Opera House', *Guardian*, 6 January 2016, accessed 17 June 2018, https://www.independent.co.uk/arts-entertainment/theatre-dance/news/the-thick-of-it-actor-chris-addison-to-star-at-the-royal-opera-house-a6799841.html.
52 Barker, *Remarkable Rise of Livecasting*, 13.

53 'Tony Hall, Director General of the BBC, Outlines FutureCommitment to Arts following Culture in Quarantine', *BBC*, last modified 5 June 2020, accessed 2 June 2021, https://www.bbc.co.uk/mediacentre/latestnews/2020/ciq-tony-hall.

54 Jake Nevins, 'Musicals Back in Vogue, and Business, as Genre Lights up Broadway and TV', *Guardian*, 14 September 2017, accessed 7 June 2018, https://www.theguardian.com/stage/2017/sep/14/broadway-theater-musicals-big-business-hamilton.

55 Royal Opera House, 'An Introduction to Opera's Voice Types (The Royal Opera)', YouTube video, 00:05:56, uploaded 4 January 2018, accessed 13 June 2021, https://www.youtube.com/watch?v=hLfvkwTnJVM.

56 Citron, 47.

57 'Climate Change Opera seminar', King's College London, 4 April 2014.

58 Daniel Nelson, 'It's Not the Final Curtain for Climate Opera', 20 November 2013, accessed 7 June 2018, http://oneworld.org/2013/11/20/curtains-for-climate-opera/.

BIBLIOGRAPHY

Websites

'About Us'. Courtyard Arts. Accessed 7 June 2018. https://www.courtyardarts.org.uk/about-us/.

'About Us'. *CW Entertainment*. Accessed 7 June 2018. https://tickets.cwentertainment.co.uk/screenloader.aspx?page=usercontent/documents/aboutus.html&type=include.

'Age and Gender Profile of the UK Cinema Audience | Statistic'. *Statista*. Accessed 12 May 2018. http://www.statista.com/statistics/296240/age-and-gender-of-the-cinema-audience-uk/.

'Arts Council England Analysis of Theatre in England'. Final Report by BOP Consulting & Graham Devlin Associates, 2016. Accessed 12 May 2018. https://www.artscouncil.org.uk/sites/default/files/download-file/Analysis%20of%20Theatre%20in%20England%20-%20Final%20Report.pdf.

'Attending a Performance'. *Royal Opera House*. Accessed 7 June 2018. http://www.roh.org.uk/visit/attending-a-performance.

'Box Office Revenues from Event Cinema Screenings in the United Kingdom (UK) in 2017, by Type (in Million GBP)'. *Statista*. Accessed 7 June 2018. https://www.statista.com/statistics/589216/cinema-events-box-office-revenues-by-type-uk/.

'Climate Change Opera Seminar'. 4 April 2014. King's College London.

'Context for Our Approach to Investment in 2018–22'. *Arts Council England*. Accessed 12 May 2018. https://www.artscouncil.org.uk/national-portfolio-2018-22/our-investment-2018-22-helpful-documents.

'Demographic Profile of Welwyn Hatfield'. *Policy and Communication*, 2016. Accessed 8 October 2016. http://www.welhat.gov.uk/CHttpHandler.ashx?id=9345&p=0.

'ECA to Receive Culture Recovery Fund Support'. *Event Cinema Association*, last updated 2 April 2020. Accessed 13 June 2021. https://eventcinemaassociation.org/news/eca-to-receive-culture-recovery-fund-support/.

'Event Cinema Box Office.' *Event Cinema Association*. Accessed 13 June 2021. https://eventcinemaassociation.org/news/event-cinema-box-office/.

'Exploring the Market for Live to Digital Arts'. *MTM*, March 2015. Accessed 12 May 2018. https://www.yumpu.com/en/document/view/48970189/exploring-the-market-for-live-to-digital-arts-full-report.

'Hatfield's Population'. Hatfield Town Council Website, last updated 29 July 2013. Accessed 8 October 2016. http://www.hatfield-herts.gov.uk/hatfields-population/.

'Impact of COVID-19 on DCMS Sectors: First Report'. Culture and the Creative Industries, last modified 12 July 2020. Accessed 13 June 2021. https://publications.parliament.uk/pa/cm5801/cmselect/cmcumeds/291/29102.htm.
'Inequality'. *OECD*. Accessed 8 June 2017. http://www.oecd.org/social/inequality.htm.
'Live from the Royal Opera House 2017/18 – 12 Blockbuster Titles, One Cinema Season'. *Trafalgar Releasing*. Accessed 7 June 2018. https://www.trafalgar-releasing.com/news/live-from-the-royal-opera-house-201718-12-blockbuster-titles-one-cinema-season/.
'National Theatre'. *Angels in America*. Accessed 12 May 2018. https://www.nationaltheatre.org.uk/about-the-national/key-facts-and-figures.
'National Theatre: Key Facts and Figures'. National Theatre. Accessed 13 June 2021. https://www.nationaltheatre.org.uk/about-the-national/key-facts-and-figures.
'Opera Attendance in England 2005–2016 | Survey'. *Statista*. Accessed 12 May 2018. https://www.statista.com/statistics/556334/adults-opera-attendance-uk-england/.
'Opera Cinema: A New Cultural Experience?' Symposium at King's College London, 16 June 2017.
'Opera in the Multiplex'. *Opera Quarterly* 34.4 (2018).
'Opera on the Square'. Vienna: Now Forever. Accessed 7 June 2018. https://events.wien.info/en/e0v/live-opera-on-the-square/.
'Opera Statistics 2017/18'. *Operabase*. Accessed 12 May 2018. http://operabase.com/top.cgi?lang=en&splash=t.
'Political Polarization, 1994–2017'. *Pew Research Center*. 20 October 2017. Accessed 8 June 2018. http://www.people-press.org/interactives/political-polarization-1994-2017/.
'Population and Demographics'. *Population and Demographics – Facts and Figures*. Accessed 12 May 2018. https://factsandfigures.herefordshire.gov.uk/about-a-topic/population-and-demographics.
'Revenues from Opera Productions Screened in Cinemas in the United Kingdom (UK) from 2013 to 2017 (in Million GBP)'. *Statista*. Accessed 7 June 2018. https://www.statista.com/statistics/604172/event-cinema-opera-screening-revenues-in-the-uk/.
'Richard Booth's Bookshop Cinema'. Richard Booth's Bookshop. Accessed 7 June 2018. https://tickets.boothbooks.co.uk/m-1-cinema.aspx.
'Riyal Opera House Live Cinema Season 2017/18; Broadcast Live to the Memo'. Accessed 12 May 2018. https://www.memoartscentre.co.uk/royal-opera-house-live-cinema-season-201718-broadcast-live-to-the-memo/.
'Royal Opera House Head Rejects "Democratising Art"'. *Financial Times*. 31 March 2014. Accessed 12 May 2018. https://www.ft.com/content/8fc034fe-b8f2-11e3-98c5-00144feabdc0.
'Stratford and New Town Demographics'. Newham, England. Accessed 12 May 2018. http://stratford-and-new-town.localstats.co.uk/census-demographics/england/london/newham/stratford-and-new-town.
'The Annual Report 2015/16'. *Royal Opera House*. Accessed 16 December 2017. https://s3-eu-west-1.amazonaws.com/static.roh.org.uk/about/annual-review/pdfs/annual_review_1516.pdf.

'The History of the Opera Dress Code'. English National Opera. Accessed 10 May 2020. https://eno.org/discover-opera/the-history-of-the-opera-dress-code/.
'The Impact of Covid-19 on Jobs in the Cultural Sector – Part 3'. Centre for Cultural Value, last modified March 2021. Accessed 13 June 2021. https://www.culturehive.co.uk/CVIresources/the-impact-of-covid-19-on-jobs-in-the-cultural-sector-part-3/.
'Tony Hall, Director General of the BBC, Outlines Future Commitment to Arts Following Culture in Quarantine'. *BBC*, last modified 5 June 2020. Accessed 13 June 2021. https://www.bbc.co.uk/mediacentre/latestnews/2020/ciq-tony-hall.
'UK Cinema Attendances Dropped by 75 per cent Last Year'. *Time Out*, 4 February 2021. https://www.timeout.com/london/news/uk-cinema-attendances-dropped-by-75-percent-last-year-020421.
'Watch: Katie Mitchell on Lucia Di Lammermoor "My Focus Is 100% on the Female Characters" – Royal Opera House'. *Royal Opera House*. Accessed 12 May 2018. http://www.roh.org.uk/news/watch-katie-mitchell-on-lucia-di-lammermoor-my-focus-is-100-on-the-female-characters.
'Who We Are'. *Event Cinema Association*. Accessed 6 June 2017. https://www.eventcinemaassociation.org/who-we-are.html.
'William Tell: Nudity and Rape Scene Greeted with Boos at Royal Opera House'. *Guardian*. 30 June 2015. Accessed 12 May 2018. https://www.theguardian.com/music/2015/jun/30/william-tell-nudity-and-scene-greeted-with-boos-at-royal-opera-house.

Books

Abbate, C., and Roger Parker. *A History of Opera: The Last Four Hundred Years*. London: Penguin Group, 2012.
Abel, S. *Opera in the Flesh: Sexuality in Operatic Performance*. Colorado: Westview Press, 1996.
Acland, C. *Screen Traffic: Movies, Multiplexes, and Global Culture*. Durham, NC: Duke University Press, 2003.
Adams, Sam. 'Welcome to Poland! Hereford Residents Alter City Signpost to Show Their Frustration at the Influx of Eastern European Workers'. *Daily Mail Online*. 18 July 2012. Accessed 12 May 2018. http://www.dailymail.co.uk/news/article-2174820/Poland-Hereford-residents-alter-city-signpost-frustration-influx-Eastern-European-workers.html.
Adorno, T., and Thomas Y. Levin. 'Opera and the Long-Playing Record'. *October* 55 (1990): 62–6.
Alasuutari, P. 'Introduction: Three Phases of Reception Studies'. In *Rethinking the Media Audience: The New Agenda*, edited by Pertti Alasuutari, 1–21. London: Sage, 1999.
Allen, R. C., and Douglas Gomery. *Film History: Theory and Practice*. New York: McGraw Hill, 1985.
Allor, M. 'Relocating the Site of the Audience'. *Critical Studies in Mass Communication* 5, no. 3 (1988): 217–33.

Althusser, L. 'Ideology and Ideological State Apparatuses (Notes towards an Investigation)'. *Marxist Internet Archive*. Accessed 12 May 2018. https://www.marxists.org/reference/archive/althusser/1970/ideology.htm.

Ang, I. *Watching Dallas: Soap Opera and the Melodramatic Imagination*. London: Methuen, 1985.

Arnott, S. 'Tony Hall: Taking High Culture to the Mass Market'. *Independent*. 11 August 2010. Accessed 12 May 2018. http://www.independent.co.uk/news/business/analysis-and-features/tony-hall-taking-high-culture-to-the-mass-market-2050088.html.

Arnott, S. 'Taking High Culture to the Mass Market'. *Independent*. 12 August 2010. Accessed 13 June 2021. http://www.independent.co.uk/news/business/analysis-and-features/tony-hall-taking-high-culture-to-the-mass-market-2050 088.html.

Artaud, A. *The Theatre and Its Double*, translated by Victor Corti. London: Alma Classics, 1978.

Arts Council of Great Britain, Annual Report 1949/50 (Charter of Incorporation). 1950. Accessed 12 May 2018. https://www.artscouncil.org.uk/sites/default/files/download-file/The%20Arts%20Council%20of%20Great%20Britain%20-%20 5th%20Annual%20Report%201949-50.pdf.

Ashbrook, W. *Donizetti and His Operas*. London: Cambridge University Press, 1982.

Atkinson, S., and Helen W. Kennedy. 'Introduction – Inside-the-Scenes: The Rise of Experiential Cinema'. *Participations* 13, no. 1 (2016): 139–51.

Atkinson, S., and Helen W. Kennedy. 'Live Cinema Presents … Cultures, Economies, Aesthetics'. In *Live Cinema: Cultures, Economies, Aesthetics*, edited by Sarah Atkinson and Helen W. Kennedy, 1–20. London: Bloomsbury, 2017.

Atkinson, S. *Beyond the Screen: Emerging Cinema and Engaging Audiences*. New York: Bloomsbury, 2016.

Attard, Joseph. 'The Opera Virgins Project: Operatic Event Cinema as New Cultural Experience'. In *Live Cinema Cultures, Economies, Aesthetics*, edited by Sarah Atkinson and Helen Kennedy, 139–51. New York: Bloomsbury, 2017.

Auslander, P. 'Afterword: Is There Life after Liveness?' In *Performance and Technology: Practices of Virtual Embodiment and Interactivity*, edited by Susan Broadhurst and Josephine Machon, 194–8. Basingstoke: Palgrave Macmillan, 2006.

Bailey, J., and Lance Richardson. 'Meaningful Measurement: A Literature Review and Australian and British Case Studies of Arts Organizations conducting Artistic Self-Assessment'. *Cultural Trends* 19, no. 4 (2010): 291–306.

Bakhshi, H., and Andrew Whitby, 'Estimating the Impact of Live Simulcast on Theatre Attendance: An Application to London's National Theatre'. *NESTA* 14, no. 4 (2014): 1–17.

Bakhshi, H., Ian Hargreaves and Juan Mateos-Garcia. 'A Manifesto for the Creative Economy'. *Nesta* (2013). Accessed 17 February 2020. https://www.nesta.org.uk/sites/default/files/a-manifesto-for-the-creative-economy-april13.pdf.

Bakhshi, H., Juan Mateos-Garcia and David Throsby. 'Beyond Live: Digital Innovation in the Performing Arts'. London: NESTA (National Endowment for Science, Technology and the Arts Research briefing), 2010.

Balme, Christopher. 'Surrogate Stages: Theatre, Performance and the Challenge of New Media'. *Performance Research* 13, no. 2 (2008): 80–91.

Barikin, A., Nikos Papastergiadis, Scott McQuire and Audrey Yue. 'Screen Cultures and Public Spaces'. *Dissect Journal* 1, no. 1 (2013): 66–83.
Barker, M. 'CRASH, Theatre, Audiences, and the Idea of "Liveness"'. *Studies in Theatre and Performance* 23, no. 1 (2003): 21–39.
Barker, M. 'Distinct/Distinctive: What Opera Audiences Take to and from Cinema Simulcasts'. Paper presented at Opera and the Media of the Future conference, Sussex, 24 October 2014.
Barker, M. 'I Have Seen the Future and It Is Not Here Yet; or, On Being Ambitious for Audience Research'. *Communication Review* 9 (2006): 123–41.
Barker, M. *Live to Your Local Cinema: The Remarkable Rise of Livecasting*. Basingstoke: Palgrave Macmillan, 2013.
Barnes, J. 'Television Opera: A Non-History'. In *A Night in at the Opera: Media Representations of Opera*, edited by Jeremy Tambling, 25–52. London: John Libbey, 1994.
Barnes, J. *Television Opera: The Fall of Opera Commissioned for Television*. Woodbridge, UK: Boydell Press, 2003.
Barthes, R. 'Leaving a Movie Theatre'. In *The Rustle of Language*, translated by Roland Barthes, 345–9. Toronto: Collins Publishers, 1986.
Baudrillard, J. *Simulacrum and Simulation*. Michigan: University of Michigan Press, 1981.
Bazin, A. *What Is Cinema? Vol. 1*, edited and translated by Hugh Gray. Berkeley: University of California Press, 2005.
Beard, Alex. 'Arts Council England: National Portfolio and Bridge Funding Announced'. *Royal Opera House*, 1 July 2014. Accessed 13 June 2021. http://www.roh.org.uk/news/arts-council-england-national-portfolio-and-bridge-funding-announced.
Bell, C. *Ritual Theory, Ritual Practice*. New York: Oxford University Press, 1992.
Belsey, C. 'Shakespeare and Film: A Question of Perspective'. *Literature/Film Quarterly* 11, no. 3 (1983): 152–8.
Benjamin, W., Michael W. Jennings, Brigid Doherty and Thomas Y. Levin. *The Work of Art in the Age of Its Technological Reproducibility, and Other Writings on Media*. London: Belknap Press of Harvard University Press, 2008.
Bennett, S. *Theatre Audiences: A Theory of Production and Reception*, 2nd edn. London: Routledge, 1997.
Benzecry, C. E. *The Opera Fanatic: Ethnography of an Obsession*. Chicago: University of Chicago Press, 2011.
Bielskis, A. *Towards a Postmodern Understanding of the Political*. New York: Palgrave Macmillan, 2005.
Boddy, W. 'A Century of Electronic Cinema'. *Screen* 49, no. 2 (2008): 142–56.
Bolter, J. David, and Richard Grusin, *Remediation: Understanding New Media*. Cambridge, MA: MIT Press, 1999.
Bolter, J. David, and Richard A. Grusin. 'Remediation'. *Configurations* 4, no. 3 (1996): 311–58.
Bordwell, D., and Kristin Thompson. *Film Art: An Introduction*, 9th ed. London: Routledge, 2010.
Bordwell, D., Janet Staiger and Kristin Thompson. *The Classical Hollywood Cinema: Film Style and Mode of Production to 1960*. London: Routledge, 1985.

Bourdieu, P. *Distinction: A Social Critique of the Judgement of Taste*, translated by Richard Nice. Cambridge, MA: Harvard University Press, 1996.
Brown, L. 'Floyd Mayweather vs Conor McGregor to Be Shown Live at Cinemas for Far Less Money than the PPV Cost'. *Independent*. 27 July 2017. Accessed 7 June 2018. https://www.independent.co.uk/sport/general/boxing/mayweather-mcgregor/floyd-mayweather-vs-conor-mcgregor-live-fight-watch-cinemas-movie-theatres-ppv-cost-a7862816.html.
Bruhn. J. K., and Karl Erik Rosengren. 'Five Traditions in Search of the Audience'. *European Journal of Communication* 5, no. 2 (1990): 207–38.
Brydon, L., and Olu Jenze. 'Pop(-up)ular Culture at the Seaside: The British Pleasure Pier as Screening Space'. In *Live Cinema: Cultures, Economies, Aesthetics*, edited by Sarah Atkinson and Helen W. Kennedy, 43–60. London: Bloomsbury, 2017.
Buch, David. 'Mozart and the Theater auf der Wieden: New Attributions and Perspectives'. *Cambridge Opera Journal* 9, no. 3 (1997): 195–232.
Bunting, N. Catherine, and John Knell. 'Measuring Quality in the Cultural Sector. The Manchester Metrics Pilot: Findings and Lessons Learned'. *Arts Council England*, 2014.
Byrne, D., and Gill Callaghan. *Complexity Theory and the Social Sciences*. New York: Routledge, 2014.
Cassaro, J. P. *Gaetano Donizetti: A Research and Information Guide*. New York: Routledge, 2000.
Chandler, Daniel. 'An Introduction to Genre Theory'. *Visual Memory* (1997). Accessed 13 June 2021. http://visual-memory.co.uk/daniel/Documents/intgenre/.
Chapman, J., M. Glancy and S. Harper. *The New Film History: Sources, Methods, Approaches*. London: Palgrave Macmillan, 2007.
Cherchi Usai, P. 'Origins and Survival'. In *The Oxford History of World Cinema*, edited by Geoffrey Nowell-Smith, 6–12. Oxford: Oxford University Press, 1996.
Cherchi Usai, P. *The Death of Cinema: History, Cultural Memory and the Digital Dark Age*. London: BFI, 2001.
Christiansen, Rupert. 'Mahagonny: The Opera That Hitler Hated'. *Telegraph*. 10 March 2015. Accessed 12 May 2018. https://www.telegraph.co.uk/culture/music/opera/11460804/Mahagonny-the-opera-that-Hitler-hated.html.
Citron, J. Marcia. *Opera on Screen*. New Haven, CT: Yale University Press, 2000.
Citron, J. Marcia. 'Subjectivity in the Opera Films of Jean-Pierre Ponnelle'. In *When Opera Meets Film*, edited by Marcia Citron, 97–135. New York: Cambridge University Press, 2010.
Cochrane, B., and F. Bonner. 'Screening from the Met, the NT, or the House: What Changes with the Live Relay'. *Adaptation* 7, no. 2 (2014): 121–33.
Coghlan, A. 'Why Arias in the Multiplex Fall Flat'. *Independent*. 4 December 2012. Accessed 12 May 2018. http://www.independent.co.uk/arts-entertainment/classical/features/why-arias-in-the-multiplex-fall-flat-8376326.html.
Cookson, R. 'Alternative Content at Cinemas Draws In the Masses'. *Financial Times*. 14 June 2013. Accessed 12 May 2018. http://www.ft.com/cms/s/0/f83bef68-d410-11e2-a464-00144feab7de.html#axzz3jSKoORmD.
Cooper, S. 'Event Cinema on Growth Curve'. *Screen*. 16 October 2013. Accessed 12 May 2018. http://www.screendaily.com/news/event-cinema-on-growth-curve/5062554.article.

Copeland, R. 'The Presence of Mediation'. *TDR (The Drama Review)* 34, no. 4 (1990): 28–44.
Corbett, K. J. 'The Big Picture: Theatrical Moviegoing, Digital Television, and Beyond the Substitution Effect'. *Cinema Journal* 40, no. 2 (2001): 17–34.
Couldry, N. 'Liveness, "Reality," and the Mediated Habitus from Television to the Mobile Phone'. *Communication Review* 7, no. 4 (2004): 353–61.
Couldry, N. *Media Rituals: A Critical Approach*. London: Routledge, 2003.
Coyd, K. 'Decoding the Dress Code: What to Wear to the Opera'. *Telegraph*. 14 June 2015. Accessed 7 June 2018. https://www.telegraph.co.uk/culture/breguet-luxury-watches/what-to-wear-to-the-opera/.
Creeber, G. 'Digital Theory: Theorising New Media'. In *Digital Cultures: Understanding New Media*. Berkshire: Open University Press, 2009.
Crisell, A. *Liveness and Recording in the Media*. London: Palgrave Macmillan, 2012.
Crossick, G., and Patrycja Kaszynska. 'AHRC Cultural Value Project'. *Arts and Humanities Research Council*, 2014.
David, J. B. 'A Night at the Opera Cinema'. Paper delivered at Opera Cinema: A New Cultural Experience? Symposium at King's College London, 16 June 2017.
Davis, C. H. 'Q Methodology in Audience Research: Bridging the Qualitative/Quantitative "Divide"?'. *Participations* 8, no. 2 (2011): 560–93.
Dayan, Daniel, and Elihu Katz. *Media Events: The Live Broadcasting of History*. Cambridge, MA: Harvard University Press, 1992.
Debord, G. *The Society of the Spectacle*. London: Zone Books, 1994.
Dunning, C. S. L. *Russia's First Civil War: The Time of Troubles and the Founding of the Romanov Dynasty*. Pennsylvania: Pennsylvania State University Press, 2001.
Durkheim, E. 'What Is a Social Fact?'. *Rules of Sociological Method* (1982): 50–9.
Ellis, J. *Seeing Things: Television in the Age of Uncertainty*. London: I. B. Tauris, 2002.
Ellis, J. *Visible Fictions: Cinema, Television, Video*. London: Routledge, 1992.
Elsaesser, T. 'Digital Cinema: Convergence or Contradiction?'. In *The Oxford Handbook of Sound and Image in Digital Media*, edited by John Richardson, 13–44. Oxford: Oxford University Press, 2013.
Elsaesser, T. 'The New Film History as Media Archaeology'. *Cinémas: Revue Détudes Cinématographiques* 14, nos 2–3 (2004): 75.
Elsaesser, T. 'The New Film History'. *Sight & Sound* 55, no. 4 (1986): 246–51.
Engels, F. 'Anti-Dühring: Herr Eugen Dühring's Revolution in Science'. Accessed 12 May 2018. https://www.marxists.org/archive/marx/works/1877/anti-duhring/.
Engels. 'Letters: Marx–Engels Correspondence 1890'. *Marxist Internet Archive*. Accessed 12 May 2018. https://www.marxists.org/archive/marx/works/1890/letters/90_09_21.htm.
Erich Deutsch, Otto. *Das Freihaustheater auf der Wieden 1787–1801*. Berlin: Deutscher Verlag, 1937.
Ernst, W. *Digital Memory and the Archive*. Minneapolis: University of Minnesota Press, 2013.
Esse, M. 'Don't Look Now: Opera, Liveness, and the Televisual'. *Opera Quarterly* 26, no. 1 (2010): 81–95.

Fallows, A. 'Royal Opera House Cinema Research'. *Royal Opera House*, 2014.
Feuer, J. 'The Concept of Live Television: Ontology as Ideology'. In *Regarding Television: Critical Approaches – An Anthology*, edited by E. Ann Kaplan, 12–21. Frederick, MD: University Publications of America, 1983.
Fischer-Lichte, E. *Ästhetik des Performativen*. Frankfurt am Main: Suhrkamp Verlag, 2004.
Fischer-Lichte, E. *The Transformative Power of Performance: A New Aesthetics*, translated by Saskya Iris Jain. London: Routledge, 2008.
Forster, M. 'Hegel's Dialectical Method'. In *The Cambridge Companion to Hegel*, edited by Frederick C. Beiser. Cambridge, MA: Cambridge University Press, 1993. Accessed 11 May 2021. https://plato.stanford.edu/entries/hegel-dialectics/.
Foucault, M. 'Nietzsche, Genealogy, History'. In *Aesthetics, Method, and Epistemology: Essential Works of Michel Foucault (1954–1984)*, edited and translated by Martin Lister, Jon Dovey, Seth Giddings, Iain Grant and Kieran Kelly, 369–92. New York: New Press, 1999.
Friedberg, A. *The Virtual Window: From Alberti to Microsoft*. Cambridge, MA: MIT Press, 2006.
Gillespie, M. 'Television, Ethnicity and Cultural Change'. In *The Audience Studies Reader*, edited by Will Brooker and Deborah Jermyn, 315–54. London: Routledge, 2003.
Gitelman, L. *Always Already New: Media, History, and the Data of Culture*. Cambridge, MA: MIT Press, 2008.
Goldmann, Lucien. *The Hidden God: A Study of Tragic Vision in the Pensées of Pascal and the Tragedies of Racine*. New York: Routledge, 2013.
Gomery, D. 'Theatre Television: A History'. *J SMPTE* 98, no. 2 (1989): 120–3.
Gomery, D. 'Theatre Television: The Missing Link of Technological Change in the US Motion Picture Industry'. *Velvet Light Trap* 21 (1985): 54–61.
Gopinath, Gita. 'The Great Lockdown: Worst Economic Downturn since the Great Depression'. *IMFBlogs*, 14 April 2020. Accessed 13 June 2021. https://blogs.imf.org/2020/04/14/the-great-lockdown-worst-economic-downturn-since-the-great-depression/.
Gramsci, Antonio. *Prison Notebooks*, edited by Joe Buttigieg. New York: Columbia University Press, 1992.
Gramsci, A. *Selections from Cultural Writings*, edited and translated by David Forgacs and Geoffrey Nowell-Smith. London: Lawrence and Wishart, 1971.
Grossberg, L. *The Audience and Its Landscapes*. Colorado: Westview Press, 1996.
Gumbrecht, H. U. *The Production of Presence: What Meaning Cannot Convey*. California: Stanford University Press, 2003.
Gunning, T. 'The Cinema of Attraction[s]: Early Film, Its Spectator and the Avant-Garde'. In *Early Cinema: Space, Frame, Narrative*, edited by Thomas Elsaesser, 381–8. London: British Film Institute, 1990.
Hall, S. 'Encoding, Decoding'. In *The Cultural Studies Reader*, edited by Simon During, 90–103. London: Routledge, 2007.
Hall, S. *Representation: Cultural Representations and Signifying Practices (Culture Media and Identities Series)*. London: Sage Publications, 1997.
Hall, S. 'The Local and the Global: Globalization and Ethnicity'. In *Dangerous Liaisons: Gender, Nation, and Postcolonial Perspectives*, edited by Anne

McClintock, Aamir Mufti and Ella Shohan, 173–87. Minneapolis: University of Minnesota Press, 1997.

Hansen, M. 'Early Cinema, Late Cinema: Permutations of the Public Sphere'. *Screen* 34, no. 3 (1993): 197–210.

Harvie, J. 'Funding, Philanthropy, Structural Inequality and Decline in England's Theatre Ecology'. *Cultural Trends* 24, no. 1 (2015): 56–61.

Heath, Stephen, and Gillian Skirrow. 'Television: A World in Action'. *Screen* 18, no. 2 (1977): 7–60.

Hefferman, K. *Ghouls, Gimmicks and Gold: Horror Films and the American Movie Business, 1953–1968*. Durham, NC: Duke University Press, 2004.

Held, D. *Introduction to Critical Theory: Horkheimer to Habermas*. California: University of California Press, 1980.

Heyer, P. 'Live from the Met: Digital Broadcast Cinema, Medium Theory, and Opera for the Masses'. *Canadian Journal of Communication* 33 (2008): 591–604.

Hills, M. *Fan Cultures*. London: Routledge, 2002.

Hobson, D. *Soap Opera*. London: Wiley, 2003.

Hoggart, R. 'Contemporary Cultural Studies: An Approach to the Study of Literature and Society'. Paper presented at American Association for Higher Education Conference, Chicago, 20 March 1978.

Holder, J., Niko Kommenda and Jonathan Watts. 'The Three-Degree World: The Cities that Will Be Drowned by Global Warming'. *Guardian*. 3 November 2017. Accessed 8 June 2018. https://www.theguardian.com/cities/ng-interactive/2017/nov/03/three-degree-world-cities-drowned-global-warming.

Holmes, J. 'Opera in Cinemas – Audiences outside London'. English Touring Opera, 2014.

Huebner, Steven. 'Opera Audiences in Paris 1830–1870'. *Music & Letters* 70, no. 2 (1989): 206–25.

Hutcheon, L. *A Theory of Adaptation*. New York: Routledge, 2014.

Hutcheon, L., and Michael Hutcheon. *Bodily Charm: Living Opera*. Lincoln, NB: University of Nebraska Press, 2000.

Jenkins, H. *Convergence Culture: Where Old and New Media Collide*. New York: New York University Press, 2006.

Jones, M. 'Living Cinema Memories: Restaging the Past at the Pictures'. In *Live Cinema: Cultures, Economies, Aesthetics*, edited by Sarah Atkinson and Helen W. Kennedy, 185–98. London: Bloomsbury, 2017.

Judith, M. *Cinema and Spectatorship*. London: Routledge, 1993.

Karpf Reidy, B., Becky Shutt, Deborah Abramson, Antoni Durski and Laura Castle. 'From Live-to-Digital'. *Arts Council England*. Accessed 12 May 2018. https://www.artscouncil.org.uk/publication/live-digital.

Kember, S. and Joanna Zylinska. *Life after New Media: Mediation as a Vital Process*. Cambridge, MA: MIT Press, 2012.

King, N. 'Film-Viewer Relations before Hollywood'. In *Babel and Babylon: Spectatorship in American Silent Film*, edited by Miriam Hansen, 22–59. Cambridge, MA: Routledge, 1991.

Klinger, B. 'Living Cinema Memories: Restaging the Past at the Pictures'. In *Live Cinema: Cultures, Economies, Aesthetics*, edited by Sarah Atkinson and Helen W. Kennedy, xiii–xvii. London: Bloomsbury, 2017.

Klinger, B. *Beyond the Multiplex: Cinema, New Technologies, and the Home*. Berkeley: University of California Press, 2006.

Kolodin, Irving. *The Metropolitan Opera, 1883–1935*. New York: Oxford University Press, 1936.

Krämer, P. 'The Lure of the Big Picture: Film, Television and Hollywood'. In *Big Picture, Small Screen: The Relations between Film and Television*, edited by John Hill and Martin McLoone, 9–46. Luton: John Libbey Media, 1996.

Lawrence, M. 'Report: Future Proof, Britain in the 2020s'. London: Institute for Public Policy Research, 2016.

Lebrecht, Norman. *Covent Garden, the Untold Story*. Boston: Northeastern University Press, 2001.

Levine, Lawrence. *Highbrow/Lowbrow: The Emergence of Cultural Hierarchy in America*. Cambridge, MA: Harvard University Press, 1988.

Lindenberger, H. *Opera: The Extravagant Art*. New York: Cornell University Press, 1984.

Lister, Martin, Jon Dovey, Seth Giddings, Iain Grant and Kieran Kelly. *New Media: A Critical Introduction*, 2nd edn. London: Routledge, 2009.

Lukacs, Georg. *The Theory of the Novel*. Cambridge, MA: MIT University Press, 1971.

Maddocks, F. 'Lucia Di Lammermoor Review – Flawed but Full of Provocative Thought'. *Guardian*. 10 April 2016. Accessed 12 May 2018. https://www.theguardian.com/music/2016/apr/10/lucia-di-lammermoor-review-royal-opera-katie-mitchell-diana-damrau.

Manovich, L. *The Language of New Media*. Cambridge, MA: MIT Press, 2001.

Marcia J. Citron. 'Operatic Style in Coppola's *Godfather* Trilogy'. In *Opera on Screen*, edited by Marcia Citron, 19–57. New Haven, CT: Yale University Press, 2000.

Marriott, S. *Live Television: Time, Space and the Broadcast Event*. London: Sage, 2007.

Marvin, C. *When Old Technologies Were New: Thinking about Electric Communication in the Late Nineteenth Century*. New York: Oxford University Press USA, 1988.

Marx, K. 'Economic Manuscripts: A Contribution to the Critique of Political Economy 1859'. *Marxist Internet Archive*. Accessed 12 May 2018. https://www.marxists.org/archive/marx/works/1859/critique-pol-economy/.

Marx, K. 'The German Ideology. Part I: Feuerbach. Opposition of the Materialist and Idealist Outlook'. *Marxist Internet Archive*. Accessed 12 May 2018. https://www.marxists.org/archive/marx/works/1845/german-ideology/ch01b.htm.

McConachie, Bruce A. 'New York Operagoing, 1825–50: Creating an Elite Social Ritual'. *American Music* 6, no. 2 (1988): 181–92.

McLuhan, M. *Understanding Media: The Extensions of Man*. London: Ark Paperbacks, 1964.

Meyrowitz, J. 'Medium Theory'. In *Communication Theory Today*, edited by David J. Crowley and David Mitchell, 50–77. Palo Alto, CA: Stanford University Press, 1994.

Molleson, K. 'ENO's Peter Grimes on Screen: A Test of What Opera-in-Cinemas Can Deliver'. *Guardian*. 24 February 2014. Accessed 12 May 2018. https://www.theguardian.com/music/musicblog/2014/feb/24/britten-peter-grimes-eno-opera-in-cinemas.

Morley, D., and Carlotte Brundson. *The Nationwide Audience*. London: Routledge, 1980.

Morris, C. 'Digital Diva: Opera on Video'. *Opera Quarterly* 26, no. 1 (2010): 96–119.

Neelands, Jonathan, Eleonora Belfiore, Catriona Firth, Natalie Hart, Liese Perrin, Susan Brock, Dominic Holdaway and Jane Woddis. 'The 2015 Report by the Warwick Commission on the Future of Cultural Value – Enriching Britain: Culture, Creativity and Growth'. Warwick: University of Warwick (2015).

Nelson, D. 'It's Not the Final Curtain for Climate Opera'. 20 November 2013. Accessed 7 June 2018. http://oneworld.org/2013/11/20/curtains-for-climate-opera/.

Nevins, J. 'Musicals Back in Vogue, and Business, as Genre Lights Up Broadway and TV'. *Guardian*. 14 September 2017. Accessed 7 June 2018. https://www.theguardian.com/stage/2017/sep/14/broadway-theater-musicals-big-business-hamilton.

Nicolis, G. *Introduction to Nonlinear Science*. Cambridge: Cambridge University Press, 1995.

O'Neill, S., Joshua Edelman and John Sloboda. 'Opera and Emotion: The Cultural Value of Attendance for the Highly Engaged'. *Participations* 13.1 (2016): 24–50.

Pate, S. 'Movie Rant: Clapping in a Movie Theater'. *Chicagoist*. 14 February 2012. Accessed April 2018. http://chicagoist.com/2012/02/14/movie_rant_clapping_in_a_movie_thea.php.

Pavis, P. *Performance: Theatre, Dance, and Film*, 4th edn. Michigan: University of Michigan Press, 1996.

Pearson, P. 'Silent Cinema 1895–1929'. In *The Oxford History of World Cinema*, edited by Geoffrey Nowell-Smith, 23–42. Oxford: Oxford University Press, 1996.

Pett, Emma. 'Beyond the Metropolis: Immersive Cinema in a Rural Context'. In *Live Cinema: Cultures, Economies, Aesthetics*, edited by Sarah Atkinson and Helen W. Kennedy, 33–42. London: Bloomsbury, 2017.

Pett, Emma. 'Stay Disconnected: Eventising Star Wars for Transmedia Audiences'. *Participations* 13, no. 1 (2016): 152–69.

Phelan, P. *Unmarked: The Politics of Performance*. London: Routledge, 1993.

Popper, Karl. *The Myth of the Framework: In Defence of Science and Rationality*. New York: Routledge, 1994.

Poster, M. *Critical Essays on Michel Foucault. Critical Essays on World Literature*. New York: G. K. Hall, 1999.

Prince, S. 'True Lies: Perceptual Realism, Digital Images, and Film Theory'. *Film Quarterly* 49, no. 3 (1996): 27–37.

Radbourne, J., Hilary Glow and Katya Johnson. 'Hidden Stories: Listening to the Audience at the Live Performance'. *Double Dialogues*. Accessed 12 May 2018. http://www.doubledialogues.com/article/hidden-stories-listening-to-the-audience-at-the-live-performance/.
Rahim, Sameer. 'The Opera Novice'. *Telegraph*. 26 January 2012. Accessed 12 May 2018. http://www.telegraph.co.uk/culture/music/opera/9036780/The-opera-novice.html.
Raynor, Henry. *A Social History of Music: From the Middle Ages to Beethoven*. New York: Schocken Books, 1972.
Reason, M. 'Theatre Audiences and Perceptions of "Liveness" in Performance'. *Participations* 1, no. 2 (2004). Accessed 22 January 2022. https://ray.yorksj.ac.uk/id/eprint/912/1/1_02_reason_article.htm.
Rodmell, P. *Opera in the British Isles, 1875–1918*. Routledge: London, 2013.
Royal Opera House. 'An Introduction to Opera's Voice Types (The Royal Opera)'. YouTube video, 00:05:56, uploaded 4 January 2018. Accessed 13 June 2021. https://www.youtube.com/watch?v=hLfvkwTnJVM.
Sauter, W. 'Introducing the Theatrical Event'. In *Theatrical Events: Borders Dynamics Frames*, edited by Vicky Ann. Cremona, Peter Eversmann, Hans Van Maanen, Willmar Sauter and John Tulloch, 1–14. Amsterdam: IFTR, 2004.
Schechner, Richard. *Public Domain: Essays on the Theater*. New York: Avon Books, 1970.
Schrøder, K., Kristen Drotner, Stephen Kline and Catherine Murray. *Researching Audiences*. New York: Oxford University Press, 2006.
Schroeder, David. *Cinema's Illusions, Opera's Allure: The Operatic Impulse in Film*. New York: Bloomsbury, 2016.
Sconce, J. *Haunted Media: Electronic Presence from Telegraphy to Television*. Durham, NC: Duke University Press, 2000.
Senici, E. 'Porn Style? Space and Time in Live Opera Videos'. *Opera Quarterly* 26, no. 1 (2010): 63–80.
Service, T. 'Opera in Cinemas: Is It Creating New Audiences?', *Guardian*, 30 May 2014. Accessed 12 May 2018. https://www.theguardian.com/music/tomserviceblog/2014/may/30/opera-in-cinemas-creating-new-audiences.
Silverstone, R. *Television and Everyday Life*. London: Routledge, 1994.
Sinclair, A. *Arts and Cultures: The History of the 50 Years of the Arts Council of Great Britain*. London: Sinclair-Stevenson, 1995.
Smith, D. 'Hidden Faultline: How Trump v Clinton Is Laying Bare America's Class Divide'. *Guardian*. 2 October 2016. Accessed 12 May 2018. https://www.theguardian.com/us-news/2016/oct/02/trump-clinton-election-class-socioeconomic-divide.
Snowman, D. *The Gilded Stage: A Social History of Opera*. New York: Atlantic Books, 2009.
Sola Pool, I. de. *Technologies of Freedom: On Free Speech in an Electronic Age*. Cambridge, MA: Harvard University Press, 1983.
Steichen, J. 'HD Opera: A Love/Hate Story'. *Opera Quarterly* 27, no. 4 (2011): 443–59.
Steichen, J. 'The Metropolitan Opera Goes Public: Peter Gelb and the Institutional Dramaturgy of the Met: Live in HD'. *Music and the Moving Image* 2, no. 2 (2009): 24–30.

Stern, L. 'The Tales of Hoffman: An Instance of Operality'. In *Between Opera and Cinema*, edited by Jeongwon Joe and Rose Theresa, 39–59. New York: Routledge, 2002.

Storey, John. '"Expecting Rain": Opera as Popular Culture?'. In *High-Pop: Making Culture into Popular Entertainment*, edited by Jim Collins, 32–55. London: Wiley-Blackwell, 2002.

Storey, John. 'The Social Life of Opera'. *European Journal of Cultural Studies* 6, no. 1 (2003): 5–55.

Svensson, N. A. 'Reinflating the Bubble: A Balance Sheet of 10 Years of Crisis'. *In Defence of Marxism*. 6 March 2018. Accessed 8 June 2018. https://www.marxist.com/reinflating-the-bubble-a-balance-sheet-of-10-years-of-crisis.htm.

Tambling, J. 'Introduction: Opera in the Distraction Culture'. In *A Night in at the Opera: Media Representations of Opera*, edited by Jeremy Tambling, 1–24. London: John Libbey, 1994.

Tambling, J. *A Night in at the Opera: Media Representations of Opera*. London: John Libbey, 1994.

Taruskin, R. *Musorgsky: Eight Essays and an Epilogue*. Princeton, NJ: Princeton University Press, 1993.

Taylor, N. *Cinematic Perspectives on Digital Culture: Consorting with the Machine*. London: Palgrave Macmillan, 2012.

Taylor, R. *Kurt Weill: Composer in a Divided World*. Boston, MA: Northeastern University Press, 1991.

Theresa, R. 'From Méphistophélès to Méliès: Spectacle and Narrative in Opera and Early Film'. In *Between Opera and Cinema*, edited by Jeongwon Joe and Rose Theresa, 1–18. New York: Routledge, 2002.

Thornhill, Ottilie. 'Watch: Katie Mitchell on Lucia di Lammermoor "My Focus Is 100% on the Female Characters"'. *Royal Opera House Website*, 11 March 2016. Accessed 8 October 2016. http://www.roh.org.uk/news/watch-katie-mitchell-on-lucia-di-lammermoor-my-focus-is-100-on-the-female-characters.

Trueman, M. 'English National Opera Chief Attacks Live Cinema Broadcasts'. *Guardian*. 10 May 2012. Accessed 12 May 2018. https://www.theguardian.com/music/2012/may/10/eno-director-hits-live-broadcasts.

Tryon, T. *Reinventing Cinema: Movies in the Age of Media Convergence*. New Brunswick: Rutgers University Press, 2009.

Tuck, F. 'Understanding the Impact of Event Cinema: An Evidence Review'. *Arts Council England and British Film Institute*, 2016. Accessed 15 May 2018. https://www.artscouncil.org.uk/participating-and-attending/understanding-impact-event-cinema.

Turnbull, O. *Bringing Down the House: The Crisis in Britain's Regional Theatres*. Bristol: Intellect Books, 2008.

Upton, G., and Felix Borowski. *The Standard Opera Guide*. New York: Blue Ribbon Books, 1928.

Velde, François R. 'Economic History of Opera'. *Federal Reserve Bank of Chicago*, 2015.

Verosub, K. L., and J. Lippman. 'Global Impacts of the 1600 Eruption of Peru's Huaynaputina Volcano'. *Eos, Transactions American Geophysical Union* 89, no. 15 (2008): 50–62.

Vladica, F. 'Value Propositions of Opera and Theater Live in Cinema'. Papers presented at World Media Economics & Management Conference. Thessaloniki, Greece, 23–7 May 2012.
Wakin, D. J. 'Metropolitan Opera to Reduce Ticket Prices Next Season'. *New York Times*, 26 February 2013. Accessed 12 May 2018. https://www.nytimes.com/2013/02/27/arts/music/metropolitan-opera-to-reduce-ticket-prices-next-season.html.
Walken, Daniel J. 'The Met Will Lower Ticket Prices'. *New York Times*, 26 February 2013. Accessed 13 June 2021. https://www.nytimes.com/2013/02/27/arts/music/metropolitan-opera-to-reduce-ticket-prices-next-season.html.
Weed, M. 'Sport Fans and Travel – Is "Being There" Always Important?'. *Journal of Sport and Tourism* 15, no. 2 (2010): 103–9.
Weinstock, G. *Donizetti and the World of Opera in Italy, Paris and Vienna in the First Half of the Nineteenth Century*. New York: Random House, 1963.
White, D. 'British Expanded Cinema and the "Live Culture" 1969–79'. *Visual Culture in Britain* 11, no. 1 (2010): 93–108.
Willett, J. *Brecht on Theatre: The Development of an Aesthetic*. London: Methuen, 1964.
Williams, R. 'The British Left'. *New Left Review* 30 (1965): 18–26.
Williams, R. *Television: Technology and Cultural Form*, 2nd edn. London: Collins, 1989.
Wise, K. 'Opera in Cinemas'. *English Touring Opera and Guildhall School of Music & Drama*, 2014. Accessed 12 May 2018. http://www.creativeworkslondon.org.uk/wp-content/uploads/2014/05/ETO-Working-paper-May-2014.pdf.
Wocke, B. 'Eating with Your Eyes: Edible Cinema and Participatory Synaesthesia'. In *Live Cinema: Cultures, Economies, Aesthetics*, edited by Sarah Atkinson and Helen W. Kennedy, 231–42. London: Bloomsbury, 2017.
Wyszpolski, B. 'New York Met Opera in Torrance AMC Theaters, 2017–18 Season'. *Opera Music*, 4 October 2017.
Wyver, J. 'The Early Imaginary of Event Cinema, 1878–1953'. Paper presented at Live Theatre Broadcast Symposium at University of York. York, 25 June 2015.
Zelochow, Bernard. 'The Opera: The Meeting of Popular and Elite Culture in the Nineteenth Century'. *History of European Ideas* 16, nos 1–3 (1993): 261–6.

Media texts cited

Albery, T. *Der Fliegende Holländer*. Composed by Richard Wagner, 1843. London, Royal Opera House, 2015. Opera.
Angerer, P. *Passkontrolle*. USA: ORF, 1959. Television opera.
Berg, A. *Lulu*. Premiered Zurich: Zurich Opera. 2 June 1937. Opera.
Berg, A. *Wozzeck*. Premiered Berlin: Berlin State Opera. 14 December 1925. Opera.
Bergman, I. *The Magic Flute*. Stockholm: Sveriges Radio, 1975. Film.
Boyd, Don. *Aria*. California: Miramax. 1985. Film.
Browning, K. *Live from the Lincoln Centre*. 'The Ballad of Baby Doe'. USA: PBS, 21 April 1978. Composed by Douglas Moore, 1956. Live television relay.

Browning, K. *NBC Television Opera Theatre*. 'Amahl and the Night Visitors'. New York City: NBC, 24 December 1951. Composed by Gian Carlo Menotti, 1951. Directed by Kirk Browning. Television opera.

Browning, K. *NBC Television Opera Theatre*. 'Billy Budd'. NBC, 18 October 1952. Composed by Benjamin Britten, 1951. Television opera.

Browning, K. *NBC Television Opera Theatre*. 'Griffelkin'. NBC, 6 November 1955. Composed by Lukas Foss, 1955. Television opera.

Browning, K. *NBC Television Opera Theatre*. 'Labyrinth'. New York City: NBC, 3 March 1963. Composed by Gian Carlo Menotti, 1963. Television opera.

Browning, K. *The Metropolitan Opera Presents*. 'La bohème'. Composed by Giacomo Puccini, 1897. USA: CBS, 15 March 1977. Live television relay.

Browning, K. *Turandot*. Composed by Giacomo Puccini, 1926. USA: CBS, 4 April 1987. Live television relay.

Castle, W. *The Tingler*. California: William Castle Productions, 1959. Film.

Chazelle. *La La Land*. Santa Monica, CA: Summit Entertainment. 2016. Film.

Coppola, Francis Ford. *The Godfather*. California: Paramount Pictures. 1972. Film.

Culshaw, J. *Owen Wingrave*. Britain: BBC2, 16 May 1971. Composed by Benjamin Britten, 1971. Television opera.

Czinner, P. *Der Rosenkavalier*. London: The Rank Organisation. 1961. Television film.

DeMille, C. B. *Carmen*. Jesse L. Hollywood, CA: Lasky Feature Play Company. 1915. Film.

Francillon, A. *The Sleeping Beauty*. Composed by Pyotr Ilyich Tchaikovsky, 1890. London: Royal Opera House, 1993. Opera.

Griffiths, D. *NET Opera Theatre*. 'From the House of the Dead'. NET, 2 December 1969. Composed by Leoš Janáček, 1927. Television opera.

Halverson, G. *The Metropolitan Opera HD Live: I Puritani*. 2007. Composed by Vincenzo Bellini, 1835. Directed for stage by Sandro Sequi, 2006. New York: The Metropolitan Opera House. Simulcast.

Halverson, G. *The Metropolitan Opera HD Live: Roméo et Juliet*. 2007. Composed by Charles Gounod, 1867. Directed for stage by Guy Joosten, 2007. New York: The Metropolitan Opera House. Simulcast.

Halverson, G. *The Metropolitan Opera HD Live: The First Emperor*. 2007. Composed by Tan Dun, 2006. Directed for stage by Zhang Yimou, 2006. New York: The Metropolitan Opera House. Simulcast.

Halvorson, G. *The Metropolitan Opera HD Live: Mozart's The Magic Flute*. 2006. Composed by Wolfgang Amadeus Mozart, 1791. Directed for stage by Julie Taymor, 2006. New York: The Metropolitan Opera House. Simulcast.

Haswell, J. *Royal Opera House Live: Boris Godunov*. 2016. Composed by Modest Mussorgsky, 1874. Directed for stage by Richard Jones, 2016. London: The Royal Opera House. Simulcast.

Haswell, J. *Royal Opera House Live: The Rise and Fall of the City of Mahagonny*. 2015. Composed by Kurt Weill, 1930. Directed for stage by John Fulljames, 2015. London: The Royal Opera House. Simulcast.

Haswell, J. *Royal Opera House Live: Werther*. 2016. Composed by Jules Massenet, 1892. Directed for stage by Benoît Jacquot, 2016. London: The Royal Opera House. Simulcast.

Hooper, Tom. *Les Misérables*. London: Working Title Films. 2012. Film.
Humperdinck, E. 'Hänsel und Gretel'. Composed 1923. BNOC. 9 January 1923. Live radio broadcast.
Humperdinck, E. 'Hänsel und Gretel'. Composed 1923. NBC. 25 December 1931. Live radio broadcast.
Jones, R. *Anna Nicole*. Composed by Mark-Anthony Turnage, 2011. London, Royal Opera House, 2014. Opera.
Kershner, Irving. *The Empire Strikes Back*. California: FOX Pictures. 1980.
Large, B. *La Bohéme*. Saale: Monarda Arts. 1988. Film.
Large, B. *The Metropolitan Opera HD Live: Eugene Onegin*. 2007. Composed by Pyotr Ilyich Tchaikovsky, 1835. Directed for stage by Robert Carsen, 2007. New York: The Metropolitan Opera House. Simulcast.
Large, B. *Tosca*. Composed by Giuseppe Giacosa, 1900. USA: Rada Film and Rai, 1 January 1992. Live television relay.
Lidholm, I. *Holländarn*. Sweden: Svergies Radio, 10 December 1967. Television opera.
Lough, R. *Royal Opera House Live: Don Giovanni*. 2008. Composed by Wolfgang Amadeus Mozart, 1787. Directed for stage by Francesca Zambello, 2008. London: The Royal Opera House. Simulcast.
Méliès, G. *Faust and Marguerite*. Paris: Star Film. 1904. Film.
Méliès, G. *Faust aux enfers*. Paris: Star Film. 1903. Film.
Michieletto, D. *William Tell*. Composed by Gioachino Rossini, 1829. London: Royal Opera House, 29 June 2015. Opera.
Mitchell, K. *Written on Skin*. Composed by George Benjamin, 2012. London: Royal Opera House, 13 January 2013. Opera.
Morahan, A. *Peter Grimes*. 2014. Composed by Benjamin Britten, 1945. Directed for stage by David Alden, 2014. London: English National Opera. Simulcast.
Ophüls, M. *Letter from an Unknown Woman*. California: Rampart Productions. 1948. Film.
Ophüls, Max. *Letter from an Unknown Woman*. New York: Universal-International. 1948. Film.
Patterson, G. *Cave*. Composed by Tansy Davies, 2018. London, Royal Opera House, 2018. Opera.
Porter, E. S. *Parsifal*. New York: Edison Manufacturing Company. 1904. Film.
Puccini, E. 'La bohème'. Composed, 1897. BNOC, 17 January 1923. Live radio broadcast.
Puccini, E. 'Madama Butterfly.' Composed, 1904. NBC, 23 December 1931. Live radio broadcast.
Royal Opera House. 'An Introduction to Opera's Voice Types (The Royal Opera)'. YouTube video, 00:05:56, uploaded 4 January 2018. https://www.youtube.com/watch?v=hLfvkwTnJVM.
Stroyeva, V. *Boris Godunov*. Moscow: Mosfilm. 1956. Film.
Stroyeva, V. *Khovanschchina*. Moscow: Mosfilm. 1959. Film.
Sweete, B. W. *The Metropolitan Opera HD Live: Tristan and Isolde*. 2008. Composed by Richard Wanger, 1865. Directed for stage by Robert Lepage, 2008. New York: The Metropolitan Opera House. Simulcast.
Tikhomirov, R. *Eugene Onegin*. Soviet Union. 1959. Film.

Williams, M. *Royal Opera House Live: Lucia di Lammermoor*. 2016. Composed by Gaetano Donizetti, 1835. Directed for stage by Katie Mitchell, 2016. London: The Royal Opera House. Simulcast.
Winslow, H. H. *Manon Lescaut*. Winslow, AZ: Playgoers Film Company. 1914. Film.
Wood, Sam. *Night at the Opera*. California: Metro-Goldwyn-Mayer. 1935. Film.
Zeffirelli, F. *La Traviata*. Rome: RAI Radiotelevisione Italiana. 1982. Film.

INDEX

2012 London Olympics, 24, 119

Abbate, Carolyn, 4, 76
Abel, Sam, 4, 102
Abramson, Deborah, 70
accessibility, 8, 69, 84, 103, 119–22, 136–7, 146–9, 165, 173–4, 181
Acland, Charles, 115
Adler, Peter, 56
Alasuutari, Pertti, 32–3
Allen, Thomas, 120
Allor, Martin, 32
Altman, Robert, 61
American Broadcasting Company (ABC), 53–6
Ang, Ien, 32, 123
applause, 34, 84, 92, 104, 110, 117, 122, 146–7, 156, 172
Argentina, 108–10
art form, 5, 15–36, 48–73, 86–122, 131–81, 187–202
Artaud, Antonin, 15, 22
Arts Alliance Media, 64–5, 115
Arts and Humanities Research Council (AHRC), 119
Arts Council England, 9, 67–73, 91–120, 194–5
arts funding, 10–14, 21–32, 47–72, 107–21, 141–5, 155–8, 188, 194–200
Atkinson, Sarah, 2, 5, 18, 97, 125, 192
Atlee, Clement, 52
Audience Research
  focus groups, 132–7, 143–56, 160–79, 190, 200

  protocols, 12–13, 84, 112–17, 122, 144–6, 167, 177, 178, 180, 190–2, 199
  testimonies, 100, 132–3, 143, 169, 170, 177
  viewing register, 12–13, 28, 30, 34, 84, 91–2, 112, 116, 117, 122, 134, 159, 161, 168, 176–7, 188, 190–3, 196
Auslander, Phillip, 26–7, 89–90, 93, 162, 193
Australia, 90, 200
Aylsworth, Merlyn H., 50

Bahkshi, Hasan, 67, 68
Bailey, Jackie, 68, 79
Baird, John Logie, 51, 52
ballet, 3, 65–6, 121, 164, 196
Balme, Christopher, 23, 94, 96
Barker, Martin, 2–9, 27–37, 63, 84, 88, 90–3, 104, 111–16, 137, 149, 161, 167–9, 176–8, 187, 190–5
Barthes, Roland, 23, 76, 113
Bayreuth Festival Theatre, 59
Bazin, André, 15, 124
Bell, Catherine, 12
Benjamin, Walter, 56–7, 103
Benzecry, Claudio E., 35–6, 94, 108–10, 121, 168, 172
Bergman, Ingmar, 55, 61
Beveridge, William, 52
Blair, Tony, 66
Boddy, William, 18
Bolter, Jay David, 16–17, 84, 97, 99
Bourdieu, Pierre, 111–12, 145
Brecht, Berthold, 22, 135

British Broadcasting Company (BBC), 49, 51–2, 56, 81, 85, 99, 120, 198
British Musician's Union, 56
Brown, Gordon, 66
Buñuel, Luis, 89
Byrne, David, 29

Callaghan, Gillian, 29
Canada, 63
Cannes Festival, 62
cannibalization, 9–10, 70
capitalism, 16, 27, 32–3, 55, 68, 88, 94, 101–2, 194
Caruso, Enrico, 4, 49, 57, 60, 62
Castle, Laura, 70
Cavell, Stanley, 59
CBS, 53
Cherchi, Paolo, 14
Cinema Exhibitors' Association, 8
Cinemascope, 54
Cineworld, 138
Cirque du Soleil, 133
Citron, Marcia, 4, 55–62
collective experience, 98, 156
Cooper, Sarah, 39, 65
Couldry, Nick, 24–5, 33
Covid-19 pandemic, 9, 48, 63–4, 68, 71–2, 122, 197–8, 200
cultural capital, 101, 145, 157
cultural ecology, 9, 66–7, 99, 120–1
cultural experience, 2–3, 12, 20, 27, 48, 55, 71, 81–4, 88, 90–5, 102, 109–13, 119, 132–4, 144, 151–8, 161–78, 180–1, 188–9, 190–9, 202
Cultural Studies, 33, 134
cultural value, 67, 91, 104, 119, 144–5, 156–7, 191–9
Czinner, Paul, 61

Davis, Charles H., 134
Dayan, Daniel, 24, 32
DeMille, Cecil B., 61
democratization, 10, 48, 66–9, 84, 88, 108, 119–20, 157, 163, 180, 200

demography, 9, 115, 138, 153, 163, 182, 183
dialectical materialism, 15, 29, 30
digital media, 1–3, 9–37, 51–4, 62–73, 82–123, 131, 139, 151, 180, 189–202
Dominion Theatre, 51
Drotner, Kristen, 30
Durkheim, Émile, 24
Durski, Antoni, 38, 70
DVD, 34, 104, 154

economics, 9, 48, 67, 71
Edelman, Joshua, 104, 126, 169, 176, 180
Edison, Thomas, 48, 50
Electrophone, 48–9
elitism, 5, 11, 19, 21, 26, 35, 55, 58, 62, 68, 69–71, 84, 93, 99, 103–11, 120, 137, 141–63, 170–81, 191–99
Ellis, John, 17, 18
Engels, Friedrich, 15, 21, 29
Ernst, Wolfgang, 83
Esse, Melina, 102
Evans, David, 110
event cinema, 2–11, 17–20, 30–7, 51–55, 62–6, 71–2, 91–7, 115, 118, 138–9, 187–8, 194, 196
  Digital Broadcast Cinema, 2
  HD broadcast, 5, 100
  livecasting, 2–7, 44–5, 73, 126–8, 136–8
  NT Live, 64–5, 197
  simulcasting, 2–11, 16–18, 20–6, 34–7, 51–73, 81–122, 135–202
Eversmann, William, 144

Facebook, 3, 102, 133, 199
Festival of Britain, 52, 122, 195
Feuer, Jane, 17
Figuier, Louis, 48
film composers
  Hermann, Bernard, 59
  Rosza, Miklos, 59
  Steiner, Max, 59
films
  Aria, 61
  Damnation du Docteur Faust, 60

INDEX

Faust aux enfers, 60
La La Land, 61
Les Misérables, 61
Letter from an Unknown Woman, 61
Rocky Horror Picture Show, 97
Star Wars: A New Hope, 11, 27, 59
Star Wars: The Empire Strikes Back, 60
The Godfather, 60
The Tingler, 97
First World War 49
Fischer-Lichte, Erika, 90, 162
Fleabag, 64
Forest, de Lee, 36, 49, 57, 71
France, 1, 23
Friedberg, Ann, 99

Gaumont-British Picture Corporation, 51, 52
genre, 4, 20, 139, 178
Gesamtkunstwerk, 59
Gillespie, Marie, 97
Gitelman, Lisa, 12, 18, 84, 113–17, 158, 167, 177, 191
Glaser, Barney, 28
Glyndebourne, 195
Godard, Jean-Luc, 61
Goldmann, Lucien, 15, 29
Gomery, Douglas, 51–3, 73
Gramsci, Antonio, 32
Great Depression, 50
Grossberg, Lawrence, 32
Grusin, Richard, 16–17, 84, 97
Guardian, 133
Gumbrecht, Ulrich, 93, 161, 189

Hall, Stuart, 32, 98, 116, 125
Heraclitus, 29
Heyer, Paul, 5, 49
historical materialism, 21
historiography, 14, 24, 97, 188
Hobson, Dorothy, 32
Holmes, John, 9, 22
hypermediacy, 17, 82, 89, 96–7, 189

immediacy, 17, 28, 82, 90–1, 104–5, 159

immersion, 84, 104, 150, 156, 169, 175–6, 195–6
Independent, 69
institutional dramaturgy, 6, 54, 58, 99–104, 146, 156–8, 190–1

Jacquot, Benoît, 142
Japan, 63
Jenkins, Henry, 18–19, 42, 97
Joe, Jeongwon, 59

Katz, Elihu, 24, 32
Kaufman, Jonas, 83, 138
Kennedy, Helen, 39
Keynesianism, 55, 72
King, Norman, 82, 105, 136, 147, 197
Kline, Stephen, 30
Klinger, Barbara, 12, 93, 114, 194

Last Night of the Proms, 98, 122
Le Télectroscope, 48
Libretto, 86, 140
Lindenberger, Herbert, 76, 102–3
live cinema, 2, 19–21, 54, 63, 97, 143, 164
  Edible Cinema, 119
  Pillow Cinema, 119
  Secret Cinema, 2, 27, 119
live performance, 2–4, 24–7, 49, 55, 82–4, 91–4, 101–4, 118, 151–4, 161–71, 176, 190–5
liveness, 14, 20–8, 33–6, 43–4, 55–6, 83–4, 90–7, 104, 136, 144, 148, 150–4, 161–7, 180, 188–90, 193–8
London, 1, 8–9, 49, 52, 64, 73–9, 98, 109–10, 119–20, 133–8, 141, 147–9, 153–7, 173–5, 197, 201
Los Angeles Times, 64

Major, John, 66
Marriott, Stephanie, 24, 95
Marx Brothers, 61
Marx, Karl, 15, 21, 61
Marxism, 20–1, 29, 98
McConachie, Bruce, 106
McLuhan, Marshall, 13, 192

INDEX

media convergence, 19, 54, 83, 95–7, 108, 112, 131, 188–9
media studies, 13, 18, 22–4, 188
media theory, 25, 193
medium, 2–22, 30–5, 48–9, 54, 59, 60, 66, 81–7, 91–103, 113–22, 131, 144–6, 150–3, 169–78, 187–99
medium theory, 14
Melba, Nellie, 49
Meyrowitz, Joshua, 14, 15
More2Screen, 114–15
Morley, David, 32
Morris, Christopher, 25, 39
multi-mediality, 95–7, 152, 199
Murray, Catherine, 30

National Broadcasting Company (NBC), 50–6
National Endowment for Science, Technology and the Arts (NESTA), 10, 129
National Grand Opera Company, 50
National Lottery, 69, 142
National Theatre, 9, 64–5, 85, 121, 133, 196–8
NBC Opera, 56
NET Opera Company, 57
networked experience, 1, 24, 64, 92, 120
New Film History, 47
New Media, 18–19, 82, 99–101, 108, 116, 119, 120, 131, 148, 167, 188, 191, 193–4, 199
New York, 2, 23, 36, 48–9, 53, 106, 133
New York Evening Post, 106
Newsweek, 63
Norway, 63

O'Neill, Sinéad, 104, 169
Odeon, 52, 139, 141, 158, 159, 175–6
online streaming, 195
ontology, 13, 18, 22, 25, 55, 62, 69, 83, 89, 90, 94, 96, 102, 108, 112, 131, 132, 162, 168, 187, 192–4
opera cinema

double-direction, 36, 82–90, 146, 152–9, 163–77, 189–99
insight films, 83, 95–7, 152, 177, 179
Live from the Met, 2, 5, 10, 34, 50–1, 57, 63, 95, 114, 133, 160, 178
Live from the Royal Opera House, 1, 77
opera cinema directors
Browning, Kirk, 58
Morahan, Andy, 81, 89
Sweete, Barbara Willis, 5
Warner, Keith, 85
Opera composers
Adès, Thomas, 89
Bellini, Vincenzo, 63
Berg, Alban, 60
Britten, Benjamin, 56–7
Donizetti, Gaetano, 100, 140
Dove, Jonathan, 201
Dun, Tan, 63
Foss, Lukas, 56
Gluck, Christoph Willibald, 198
Janacek, Leos, 57
Massenet, Jules, 142
Menotti, Gian, 56
Moore, Douglas, 57
Mozart, Wolfgang Amadeus, 115, 135
Mussorgsky, Modest, 139–40, 159
Rossini, Gioachino Antonio, 63, 198
Tchaikovsky, Pyotr Illych, 63, 139, 178
Verdi, Giuseppe, 4, 115, 198
Wagner, Richard, 59, 100, 105, 110, 115, 135
opera directors
Fulljames, John, 135, 197
Holten, Kasper, 110
Katie Mitchell, 1, 89, 138, 140, 197
Zeffirelli, Franco, 58, 61
opera houses
Bayreuth Festival Theatre, 59, 105
Colón Opera House, Buenos Aires, 109
English National Opera, 10, 81, 85, 135

INDEX

English Touring Opera (ETO), 10, 22, 40, 70, 150, 163
Grand Opéra, Paris, 49
La Scala, Milan, 64
Metropolitan Opera, New York City, 2, 6, 36, 49, 50, 58, 62, 64, 71, 87, 100, 106, 133
   Cross, Milton, 50
   Gatti-Casazza, Giulio, 49
Paris Opera, 108
Royal Opera House, Covent Garden, London, 1, 7–10, 13, 15, 22–5, 36, 49, 52, 56, 64–72, 81–99, 103–21, 135–59, 164–83, 189–200
   Gelb, Peter, 50, 63, 88, 101–3, 119, 176–9, 199
   Hall, Tony, 69, 120, 198
   Moser, Charles, 69
   Southgate, Colin, 69
   Stirling, Angus, 69
San Francisco Opera, 64
Opera Quarterly, 25, 62, 101
operas
Amahl and the Night Visitors, 56
Andrea Chénier, 138
Anna Nicole, 197
Billy Budd, 56
Boris Godunov, 37, 61, 96, 139–43, 159, 166, 168, 175, 179
Carmen, 39, 56, 61, 115
Cave, 197
Der Fliegende Holländer, 110
Der Rosenkavalier, 61
Don Carlo, 102
Don Giovanni, 15, 64, 87
Don Pasquale, 133
Eugene Onegin, 61, 63, 139
Faust, 49, 60
From the House of the Dead, 57
Griffelkin, 56
Guillaume Tell, 140
Hänsel und Gretel, 49, 50
I Puritani, 63
Il trovatore, 4
Khovanshchina, 61
La Bohéme, 49, 57, 61
La Traviata, 61
Labyrinth, 56
Lucia di Lamermoor, 1, 37, 89, 96, 138, 140–3, 155–65, 175–9
Lulu, 60
Madama Butterfly, 50, 201
Manon Lescaut, 60
Otello, 56
Owen Wingrave, 57
Parsifal, 60
Peter Grimes, 81, 85, 89
Ring Cycle, 85
Roméo et Juliet, 63
Salome, 56
The Ballad of Baby Doe, 57
The Barber of Seville, 63
The Exterminating Angel, 89, 202
The First Emperor, 63
The Magic Flute, 55, 61, 63, 92, 105, 107
The Rise and Fall of the City of Mahagonny, 37, 92, 95, 135, 146–52, 159, 168–75
The Threepenny Opera, 135
Tosca, 49, 58, 65
Tristan and Isolde, 5
Turandot, 58, 62, 71, 100
Werther, 37, 142–3, 175
Wozeck, 60
Written on Skin, 138, 197
Opera Television Theatre, 56
overflow, 97

Paramount, 52–4
Parker, Roger, 4
Pavis, Patrice, 22
Pearson, Roberta, 16
performance studies, 23
Petrillo Ban, 55
Phelan, Peggy, 25–7, 43, 90–4, 101, 118, 166, 193
plays
Crash, 27, 111, 161, 170
Hamlet, 64
Mary Poppins, 133
Written on Skin, 138, 197
Ponnelle, Jean-Pierre, 57
Popper, Karl, 29
positivism, 30, 94

Postmaster General, 52
post-structuralism, 23, 32
Prince, Stephen, 91
Proust, Marcel, 48

radio, 2, 19, 24, 34, 36, 47–57, 62, 68, 71, 87, 95–6, 109, 157, 192
Reagan, Ronald, 21
realism, 91, 150
Reason, Matthew, 27–8, 180, 193
remediation, 3, 16–17, 20, 25, 36, 50, 61, 65, 82–7, 92, 99, 100, 103–4, 112, 114, 118, 131, 151, 154, 156, 162, 169, 171, 189, 190, 193, 195
Renaissance, 16, 21, 97
Revue du Cinéma, 62
Richardson, Lance, 68,
ritual, 2, 11–13, 18, 23–4, 28, 84, 114, 117, 164, 177
Royal Shakespeare Company (RSC), 9, 64, 85, 196–7
Russell, Ken, 61
Russia, 1, 61, 64, 139

Sagall, Solomon, 52
Sauter, Wilmar, 118
Schrøder, Kim, 30
Sconce, Jeffrey, 24
Score, 57, 86, 138
Second World War 9, 47, 52, 55, 60
semiotics, 23
Shutt, Becky, 70
Silverstone, Roger, 12
Sloboda, John, 104, 169, 176, 180
Snowman, Daniel, 12, 59, 125–9
social media, 83, 95–102, 136, 141, 155
social science
 Aberystwyth School, 27, 33
 complexity, 29
 Encoding–decoding, 32–3
 Ethnography, 32, 35, 108–9, 134, 197
 Frankfurt School, 32–3, 88
 inductive research, 11, 35, 133, 168
 Q Methodology, 34, 132–7, 143, 147, 160, 168, 177, 179, 190

 Factors, 136–7
 P set, 132
 PQMethod, 133
 Q sample, 133
 Q sorts, 132–3, 143
Qualitative research, 11, 13, 30–5, 44, 89, 111, 132–6, 167–8, 173, 177, 179, 187
Quantitative research, 30–1, 35, 132, 168
Sodero, Cesare, 50
Soviet Union, 32, 61
Steichen, James, 3–6, 100–2, 158, 175, 189, 190
Stephenson, William, 132
Storey, John, 69, 105–6, 108, 110
Strauss, Anselm, 28, 44
structuralism, 23
surtitles, 122, 146, 187

Tambling, Jeremy, 58, 162
Taylor, Norman, 18, 108, 191
Telegraph, 83
Telegraphy, 47, 48
television, 2–4, 11–19, 23–8, 32–6, 47–58, 61–3, 68–77, 82, 86–91, 94–103, 110, 120, 152, 156–7, 169–71, 178, 187–9, 192–4, 200–202
 Relays, 47, 51, 56–8, 62, 65, 71, 89, 156, 194
Terfel, Bryn, 83, 96, 139, 166, 179
Tetrazzini, Luisa, 49
Thatcher, Margaret, 21, 66, 67, 70, 119–20
The Nutcracker, 115
The Opera Virgins Project, 36–7, 131, 134, 144, 153, 168, 180, 190
 Awed Initiates, 168, 170–8
 Campus West, 138–9, 141, 175
 Courtyard Cinema, Hereford, 116, 142, 175
 Curious Traditionalists, 177–9
 Hatfield, 92, 115, 138–9, 143, 159, 163–5, 175
 Hatfield Odeon, 92, 115, 138, 159, 163–4
 Hay-on-Wye, 138

Hereford Odeon, 138, 143, 158–9, 175
Hereford, 116, 138–9, 141–3, 156, 158–9, 175
Immersed Inductees, 175–7
New Purists, 168–79
Opera Cinema Sceptics, 179–80
Opera Cinephiles, 168–79
Richard Booth's Bookshop Cinema, 138–9, 142
Welwyn Garden Cinema, 138–9, 175
The Rank Company, 52
theatre studies, 23
theatre television, 30, 42, 51–5, 62–5, 71
  RCA Corporation, 53–4
  Scophony, 52–3
  Swiss Eidophor, 53
theatrical event, 18, 23, 26, 118
Throsby, David, 67
Tommasini, Andrew, 105
Tryon, Chuck, 114
Tuck, Fiona, 100
Tulloch, John, 35
Twitter, 98, 133, 154–5

United Kingdom, 1–10, 21–3, 30–3, 48–56, 61–72, 79, 95–100, 105–7, 119–22, 134–41, 150, 157, 195–8
United States, 1–3, 21–3, 30, 49, 52–7, 60–4, 105–7, 117, 196
Unitel, 57

Variety, 63
Vaudeville, 16, 17, 47, 54, 107
Verismo, 59–60, 135, 138, 140
virtuality, 1, 6, 54, 58, 66, 83, 89, 97–101, 117–18, 146, 157, 178, 180, 189, 190–3, 198
Vladica, Florin, 34–5, 133, 160, 181–4

Warner Brothers, 54
Washington Post, 61–4, 178
Weed, Mike, 28
Weill, Kurt, 135
White, Duncan, 91
Williams, Raymond, 13–14, 59, 97, 152, 192
Wise, Karen, 10, 70, 91, 96, 163
Wolff, Janet, 106

YouTube, 3, 72, 96, 102, 199

www.ingramcontent.com/pod-product-compliance
Lightning Source LLC
Chambersburg PA
CBHW062143300426
44115CB00012BA/2019